Praise for Vann

Murder Simply Brewed

"Chapman's latest is a mix of mystery and romance with vivid characters, a realistic setting, and themes of loss, trust, and love. The puzzle pieces are revealed slowly so readers can piece the clues together themselves up until the shocking conclusion."

—ROMANTIC TIMES, FOUR-STAR REVIEW

"Vannetta Chapman keeps the action suspenseful . . . as her Amish and English characters work together to solve the mystery. Out of even such dreadful circumstances come moments of grace: between Amber and her Amish employee Hannah and between Amber and Tate, who had each given up on love."

—BOOKPAGE.COM

"Vannetta Chapman has crafted a tightly woven tale in the best tradition of the cozy mystery. . . . Chapman's light touch and thoughtful representation of the Amish culture make Murder Simply Brewed a delightful read for an evening by a warm fire, a cup of tea in hand."

—KELLY IRVIN, AUTHOR OF THE BLISS CREEK AMISH SERIES

"Murder Simply Brewed combines all the coziness of an Amish home with the twists and turns of a great suspense. With a little romance thrown in, you can't go wrong! Vannetta Chapman has crafted a charming story that shows things aren't always as they first appear."

—BETH SHRIVER, BESTSELLING AUTHOR OF THE TOUCH OF GRACE TRILOGY

"Vannetta Chapman's Murder Simply Brewed is a heartwarming whodunit that is sure to satisfy fans of both Amish romance and cozy mystery."

—AMANDA FLOWER, AUTHOR OF A PLAIN DISAPPEARANCE

"A wonderful story of first love, second love, and a murder that pulls them all together in a page-turning way. *Murder Simply Brewed* is a must-read for all Amish fans!"

—RUTH REID, BESTSELLING AUTHOR OF THE HEAVEN ON EARTH SERIES

"Vannetta Chapman has poured us a steaming cup of adventure, mystery, and romance in this enthralling 'can't put it down' yarn. An intriguing blend of piquant Amish, robust *Englisch*, and 'dark roast' characters makes for some tasty hours of reading enjoyment. Top it all off with the whipped cream of one of this genre's most talented writers and you have yourself a book that is a delightful 'espresso' for the mind and heart."

—PATRICK E. CRAIG, AUTHOR OF *A QUILT FOR JENNA*
AND THE APPLE CREEK DREAMS SERIES

MURDER
Tightly Knit

MURDER
Tightly Knit

AN AMISH VILLAGE MYSTERY
BOOK 2

VANNETTA CHAPMAN

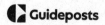

Guideposts

Published by Guideposts a Church Corporation
100 Reserve Road, Suite E200
Danbury, CT 06810
Guideposts.org

This Guideposts edition is published by special arrangement with Zondervan.

All Scripture quotations, unless otherwise indicated, are taken from The Holy Bible, *New International Version®*, *NIV®*. Copyright © 1973, 1978, 1984 by Biblica, Inc.™ Used by permission. All rights reserved worldwide. www.zondervan.com

Any Internet addresses (websites, blogs, etc.) and telephone numbers in this book are offered as a resource. They are not intended in any way to be or imply an endorsement by Guideposts and Zondervan, nor does Guideposts and Zondervan vouch for the content of these sites and numbers for the life of this book.

Art direction: Kristen Vasgaard
Interior design: James A. Phinney

Printed in the United States of America

10 9 8 7 6 5 4 3 2 1

For my friend,
Dorsey Sparks

Blessed is he whose help is the God of Jacob,
whose hope is in the Lord his God.

—Psalm 146:5

Author's Note

While this novel is set against the real backdrop of Middlebury, Indiana, the characters are fictional. There is no intended resemblance between the characters in this book and any real members of the Amish and Mennonite communities. As with any work of fiction, I've taken license in some areas of research as a means of creating the necessary circumstances for my characters. My research was thorough; however, it would be impossible to be completely accurate in details and descriptions since every community differs. Therefore, any inaccuracies in the Amish and Mennonite lifestyles portrayed in this book are completely due to fictional license.

Glossary

ach—oh

aenti—aunt

boppli—baby

bruder—brother

danki—thank you

dat—father

dawdy haus—grandfather's home

Englisch, Englischer—non-Amish, a person who is not Amish

fraa—wife

freind, freinden—friend, friends

gem gschehne—you're welcome

Gotte—God

Gotte's wille—God's will

grossdaddi—grandfather

gudemariye—good morning

gut—good

in lieb—in love

kaffi—coffee

kapp—prayer covering

kinner—children

Loblied—praise song

mamm—mom

naerfich—nervous

narrisch—crazy

nein—no

onkel—uncle

Ordnung—set of rules for Amish living

rumspringa—running around; time before an Amish young
person officially joins the church; provides a bridge between
childhood and adulthood

schweschder, schweschdern—sister, sisters

Was iss letz?—What's wrong?

wunderbaar—wonderful

ya—yes

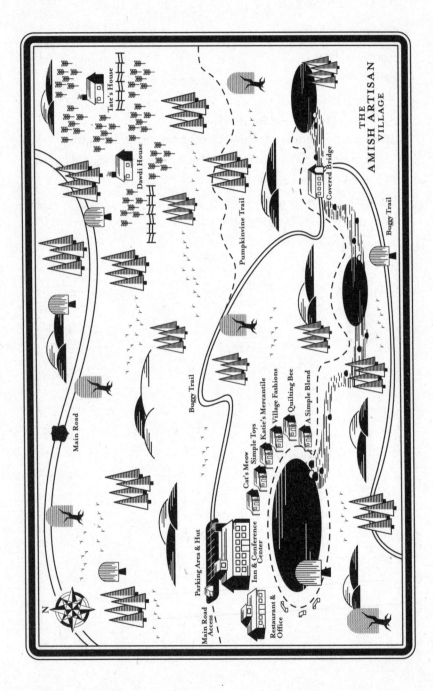

Prologue

Middlebury, Indiana
October 2

On the day he died, Owen Esch left home thirty minutes before sunrise.

The morning was cool and crisp, bringing with it a hint of autumn. As he crept quietly toward his neighbor's deer stand, the eastern sky came alive with color. Ribbons of pink, blue, and yellow peeked through the scattered clouds.

He spent over an hour in the stand, which the neighbor had given him permission to use. He spied three does, a six pointer, and what might have been an eight pointer. The larger buck had lowered his head the moment Owen focused the scope of his rifle on him. Possibly the buck had sensed that he was being watched.

Owen had no plans to harvest a deer that morning. Though his sister and her family could use the meat, he didn't have time to dress a deer before work. No, the purpose of the trip was to watch and see what was in his neighbor's fields to the south of their property. If he'd learned anything in the last few months, it was the importance of being prepared.

Hoping the buck would raise his head and give him a better view, he'd actually stayed longer than he intended. He'd have

1

to hurry or he would be late for work in downtown Middlebury. The furniture shop didn't open until nine, but he still needed to change clothes and clean up, plus grab something for breakfast. He didn't have time to return the way he had come, across his neighbor's place and around the small schoolhouse that separated his sister's farm from her neighbor's. Instead, he took the shortcut by way of the Pumpkinvine Trail.

Pulling out his phone, he checked the time. His sister continually harassed him about getting rid of the small device, but he wasn't ready to do that yet. Just like he wasn't ready to join the church. He would eventually, but eventually wasn't good enough for Naomi.

If she knew his phone had internet capabilities, she'd throw a fit. Fortunately, she wanted nothing to do with it, and he was careful to use it only when he was alone.

Like now. The display told him the time was seven thirty.

Mary would probably be at work. He could speak with her as he walked. Owen had found that a brief conversation with Mary could set his day on the right course. Plus, he needed to talk to her about the night before—about the meeting. And then there was the person he was supposed to meet, here on the trail, in a few minutes. His plan had been to meet him on the way to work, but he'd dawdled. It was close to the time now, and he hadn't even returned home to change clothes yet.

He found the number for The Cat's Meow and pushed Talk. The phone began to ring.

He pressed his cell phone to his right ear and carried his rifle with his left hand. A sound behind and to his right caught his attention—a rustling in the brush. It could have been a bird or small animal.

It could have been a person.

Turning, he glanced behind him, but he didn't stop walking. The trail was empty in both directions, which wasn't too surprising. Employees at the Village would already be at work. Tourists who biked the trail to see the fall foliage wouldn't be out yet. Children generally took the other road to school.

The phone continued to ring, and then he heard the sound again—definitely behind him and on his right. This time when he turned around, he stepped out into the middle of the trail and scanned the path behind him, looking back in the direction he had come.

An Amish man emerged from the brush to the left. At least it looked like a man, and he appeared to be Amish. Owen couldn't be sure because of the distance. He also couldn't make out who it was, but he could see the item the person was holding. Clutched in his left hand was a crossbow.

Where had he been hunting?

The direction the man had stepped from was the same place Owen had come from—his neighbor's farm. As he puzzled over this and raised his hand in greeting, he saw the man lift his crossbow and point it in his direction. Was it a teenager fooling around? The man drew closer, and Owen had the fleeting thought that it was someone he knew. Owen was about to call out to him when he heard the familiar sound of an arrow leaving a bow.

He barely had time to think that there wasn't time to move. Owen understood that an arrow from a crossbow travels between three hundred and four hundred feet per second. That thought flashed through his mind instantly. Before he could react to what he was seeing or to the facts his brain was processing, the arrow smashed into his chest and threw him to the ground.

The pain was instant, searing, and then it was gone.

The next thing Owen was aware of was the canopy of leaves

above him. His rifle lay by his side. His phone had fallen from his hand and skidded across the pavement. He thought he could hear the shop's recording of Mary's voice, but he couldn't speak.

He couldn't call out.

He could only lie there as thoughts and images and sounds swirled through his mind.

Mary in her shop.

The cold wetness of his shirt against his skin.

The buck he'd watched earlier. It was still in the field, still grazing, but now it turned toward him, showing a full rack of eight points. He shouldn't be able to see it here, from the trail, but he could.

His sister's face, worried as she watched out the front door.

The melody of the *Loblied*, rising up and splashing over him—covering him.

Owen knew he was dying.

The bow had pierced his heart.

It no longer hurt, which was a blessing. Owen realized that in a few more minutes he could rest. He was so tired he could no longer continue staring at the canopy of leaves—reds and browns and golds. He was so tired he allowed his eyes to close, to rest.

His final thought was of his parents. He wondered if they'd be waiting when he awoke.

One

The Village
Middlebury, Indiana
Five hours later

annah stood in front of The Cat's Meow, peering through the window and rattling the doorknob.

No answer.

Brushing her *kapp* strings behind her shoulders and then pushing her glasses up on her nose, she squinted, trying to see beyond the Closed for Lunch sign.

No luck.

She could see her own reflection—though the glass made her look wider than she was. Her weight had never been a problem, and she knew it was wrong to be proud of that. As she stared into the glass, she did straighten her *kapp* and pull down her apron. How was it that she became so disheveled at times?

Stepping closer with her nose now nearly on the glass, she couldn't make out much more than the front yarn displays. She thought she saw a light on at the back of the shop. Was Mary in her office eating lunch? If so, she might ignore the knocking, thinking that Hannah was an impatient customer.

Come to think of it, why wasn't the shop open? Their boss, Amber, provided relief for lunch breaks. They were all supposed to stay open from eight a.m. until closing time at five p.m., even her *kaffi* shop, which had recently expanded its hours. They were not supposed to close for lunch—or for any other reason, for that matter. They had procedures for every type of emergency. Most of them involved consulting the list of unassigned employees. Someone was always available to fill in.

She peered through the glass again. The Cat's Meow was a cute shop.

The window display reminded Hannah of when she had worked in the quilt store, The Quilting Bee. Half of the display was supplies—knitting needles, pattern books, and yarn filled three handmade baskets. The other half of the window held afghans, sweaters, hats, and scarves made by Mary and other women in their community. Mary had chosen to display fall colors, which was smart. Folks might not finish a new project until winter, but the fall colors would be appealing. The reds, browns, and golds matched the leaves scurrying along the pavement and past the row of Village shops.

The Village was a collection of buildings—an inn with a conference center, a restaurant, a bakery, and six shops were all situated around a small pond. Amber Bowman was the general manager, and Hannah worked in the *kaffi* shop—A Simple Blend. She loved her job.

Last she'd heard, Mary loved hers too.

So where was she?

Hannah needed to buy some yarn. She'd decided to knit a blue-and-gray buggy blanket for Jesse for Christmas. She didn't blush anymore when she thought about the fact that she was being courted by Jesse Miller. She didn't blush, but her heart rate did kick up a notch. Jesse hadn't asked her to marry him—yet. Some mornings she woke wondering if today would be the day, but other mornings she woke hoping it wouldn't be.

Love was so confusing!

In the meantime, they had become the best of friends.

She turned to make her way back toward her shop—her shop because she'd recently been appointed the permanent manager. Amber had offered her the job back in the summer, after the ninety-day trial period was over. Memories from early spring and all that had occurred at the Village threatened to push through Hannah's thoughts and ruin her good mood.

She tamped down the sobering thoughts.

It was a fine fall day. She was not going to spend it hashing over the events of Ethan's death yet again. "Past is past," as her *mamm* was fond of saying. "Best leave it there."

Hannah had stepped no more than three feet away from the yarn shop when she saw Bradley walking toward her. He was easy to see because he was so tall and had red hair. It seemed to her that he didn't fit in among the Amish or the *Englisch*. Bradley took care of maintenance on the computers around the Village. He also helped with the security system. He could work wonders with anything that was plugged in. He was what her *Englisch* friends called a geek.

She didn't want to run into Bradley, not now. For one thing, he would insist on accompanying her to wherever she was going. For another thing, he seemed to have a crush on her.

Hannah darted into the garden area between The Cat's Meow and Village Fashions. Colorful mums circled the trees. Guests rested and ate and talked at the three small patio tables sporting dark-green umbrellas. She smiled and continued through them, coming out in the alleyway that skirted behind the shops.

Glancing right, she saw the coast was clear.

Then she looked left.

Who was the *Englisch* man standing behind The Cat's Meow? Why was he there, leaning his back against the wall with one foot propped against it and the other planted out in front of him? He appeared to be waiting at the back door as if he expected someone to open it. Hannah couldn't see his face, which was in the shadows. She could tell he was of average height, and he wore a ball cap and a denim jacket. There was no doubt he was a man and not a boy. She couldn't have said how she knew, but she was certain.

There was also no doubt he was *Englisch*. The Amish boys sometimes wore *Englisch* clothes, but they never fit exactly right. This man's ball cap was creased on the bill. She could see the tip of it. His denim jacket was faded but a perfect fit, and glancing down, Hannah saw he even wore cowboy boots. Definitely an *Englischer*.

He turned toward her, and for reasons she couldn't fathom she stepped back into the garden area, returned to the front walk, and peeked out. Bradley had already passed The Cat's Meow, so she turned left in the opposite direction.

She'd go back to her shop and talk to Seth.

Seth worked the afternoon shift at A Simple Blend. Though he sometimes still had mishaps, he'd made vast improvements since he'd started filling in for her.

But she wasn't going back to check on him and see how he was doing. There was another reason she wanted to see Seth. He knew more than she did about what was going on at the Village. Hannah had a tendency to keep to herself and focus on her assignment. She went straight to work and then headed home.

If someone didn't come into her shop, she might not see them for weeks.

Not true of Seth Kauffman.

He had an ear for gossip.

❧

Hannah stepped into the *kaffi* shop, braced for disaster.

Seth was wiping down tables.

The aroma of freshly brewed *kaffi* filled the air.

The instrumental hymn music, piped throughout the store, played softly over the speakers.

No spills. No accidents. No disasters.

It made her nervous.

When Seth wasn't in the middle of a calamity, one was usually brewing on the horizon. Not that she was a negative person, merely a practical one. And not that Seth hadn't improved. He had, which was why the accidents were now usually spaced apart by a few days.

"Hannah, why are you back?"

"Can't I stop by before I go home?"

"You can." Seth smiled at her, his brown hair flopping into his eyes. At seventeen he reminded her of her younger brother. Noah was the same age, but he never would have lasted working inside a shop. If Noah wasn't outside, he was restless and moody. Seth, on the other hand, seemed to enjoy the work.

"But you usually don't." Seth finished wiping down the table and headed behind the counter.

"Could we talk for a minute?" Hannah sat on a chair by the front window. No, she usually didn't stop back by the shop after she left. But something about what she'd seen behind The Cat's Meow bothered her.

"I'm not in trouble, am I? Because I've kept the decaf and caffeinated pots straight since—"

"You're not in trouble."

"Oh." Seth approached the table and hovered. His expression was puzzled and worried at the same time.

"You've done fine this week, Seth."

"It's Thursday."

"I know what day it is."

"And we weren't open Monday."

"I know that too. I'm the one who suggested we close so that Preston could repaint the bathroom without bothering any guests." Preston had recently been promoted to assistant manager of maintenance. Hannah also considered him a good friend.

"So technically this is the third day of our workweek."

"You've made it halfway. Let's celebrate that achievement."

Seth's expression didn't change. He didn't seem convinced at all, but he did sit down.

"I wanted to talk to you about Mary."

"Mary?"

"Mary Weaver." Hannah glanced out the window, as if Mary might appear and explain everything herself. "She manages The Cat's Meow."

"*Ya*, I know who she is."

"I was wondering if you'd heard anything about her."

Seth stared at the menu board on the wall of the *kaffi* shop, then down at his hands.

"I'm asking because you hear things more than I do, and I'm worried about her."

"Worried? Why?"

"Her shop was closed when I went by a few minutes ago."

"And?"

"And it's not supposed to be. You know that."

"Is that all?" Seth squinted at her, as if there was more distance between them than the width of the table.

"*Nein*. There also was an *Englisch* man standing outside the back of the shop. He looked as if he was waiting on her."

"I don't want to say anything that would hurt her reputation."

"But you've heard something."

"Maybe."

Hannah waited, but it seemed as if Seth had turned over a new leaf. A month ago he would have spilled at the first opportunity. Perhaps he was maturing. He had joined the church. She could hope that he was taking his commitment to the gospel and the community seriously.

"I'm not asking you to gossip about her, Seth. I want to help her if I can. If something's wrong."

"It's not exactly gossip. I've seen her myself."

"Seen her?"

"With an *Englischer*."

"Did he look middle-aged to you? Average height? Cowboy boots, jeans, and a ball cap?"

"*Ya*. How did you know?"

"That's who was waiting outside her shop. But why?"

Seth shrugged.

"And why was the shop closed?"

"I heard"—Seth hesitated, then pushed on—"I heard that she was having some sort of financial problems."

"Anything else?"

"That she might be dating this *Englischer* guy."

"This guy didn't act like he was waiting to pick her up for a date. I think he would have used the front door. Plus, who dates in the middle of the workday? None of this sounds like Mary."

"I don't think so either. Plus, she's a little old to be sneaking around with some guy. No offense."

"Why would I be offended?" Hannah's voice screeched slightly.

"You're both, you know." Seth's hand came out as if he meant to shoo away a fly. "Over twenty."

Hannah rolled her eyes and prayed for patience in the same breath. Over twenty? Both she and Jesse were twenty-two, not that far removed from Seth's own age of seventeen. He was acting as if they—and Mary—were ancient, as if they were old horses ready to be put out to pasture.

"Anything else?"

"*Nein*. She's not in trouble, is she? Mary was always nice to me when I used to fill in for her. Even after I allowed that alley cat to come in by accident. It started playing with the yarns and had them unrolled all over the shop. By the time I'd pick one up, two more would be wound around the shelves. You should have seen it."

"You're painting a pretty good picture. *Danki*, Seth. You've been very helpful."

Hannah stood to go. She was pushing on the door, about to step out into the sounds and smells of the Village, when Seth called out to her.

"There's one other thing I heard today, Hannah. Something I thought you'd be happy to know."

She paused, expecting him to say that Amber had complimented them or a customer was especially pleased. *"Ya?"*

"It's about Jesse."

"My Jesse?" The words sounded funny, but it was how she thought of him.

"Henry Yoder came in for a sweet roll. We're selling a lot of those rolls. I think we should—"

"Henry who monitors the parking lot?"

"Same one." Seth stuck his hands in his pockets and shifted from right foot to left foot. "You know Henry hears everything because people stop by as they're coming into work. Nathan, who works on the grounds crew with Jesse, has an eleven-to-seven shift today."

Hannah wanted to shake the information out of him, but Seth had his own way of telling a story.

"Seems Nathan had gone into town before work, and on his way here he stopped by the Dairy Queen for some breakfast. As he was leaving, he saw Andrew step into the parking lot. He'd been on the Pumpkinvine Trail, apparently."

"Who?"

"Andrew Miller. Jesse's *bruder*." Seth allowed himself to smile.

Hannah realized he thought he was delivering good news, and maybe he was.

Maybe.

"Here? In Middlebury?"

"*Ya*. Nathan offered to give him a ride, but Andrew said he'd rather walk, and then he turned and headed down the road." Seth gave the table near him one last brush with the dishcloth. "Jesse's *bruder* has come home."

Two

esse Miller sat at his parents' table, wolfing down his lunch. He'd spent the morning mucking out the stalls in the barn and attending to the horses' hooves—both time-consuming tasks when you had eight horses. Six were Belgian draft horses, used to working in the field. The two buggy horses were American Saddlebred.

He'd been caring for the horses since he was sixteen, and it felt good to be working at home, cleaning and standing in the shade of the barn with the horses. It was a perfect fall day.

Nearly perfect.

The problem was that he still had to pull a four-hour shift at the Village. It was his week to work half a day on the upcoming Saturday, so he'd had the morning free.

Free.

Well, not quite. There had been the horses and the stalls.

"I saw Hannah at the grocery store yesterday." His mother pushed the plate with slices of ham and cheese toward him even though he hadn't finished the sandwich in his hands. "She's a sweet girl."

"*Ya*. Soon our Jesse will be asking to marry her, Rebecca. Isn't that right, son?" His father, Ivan, didn't glance up from his own plate of food, but he didn't have to.

Jesse could sense the laughter lurking behind his father's comment. He seemed to be enjoying Jesse's courting Hannah nearly as much as Hannah and Jesse did.

For his parents, life proceeded in an easy, orderly fashion. You found a girl. You courted her. You married her. Next came a home and children, and then grandchildren, and then a *grossdaddi* home. You worked the land Monday through Friday, went to town on Saturday, and worshipped on Sunday.

The circle of life.

Many things had changed for his generation, though, and not for the better that he could see. Land had become more expensive, so much so that many Amish men his age either moved or chose a different profession than farming. There was also the influx of tourists. As an employee of the Village, he knew these people guaranteed his job. But as a man who might be starting a family soon, he wasn't sure it was beneficial to have so many strangers around.

His parents would be happy if he announced that he and Hannah would be married soon, but in his mind things weren't so simple.

So he nodded and continued to chew. Often that would work. The subject would change or one of his sisters would interrupt. Unfortunately, his three younger sisters were at school, and his oldest sister was at work. No one to deflect the questions.

"How about you invite her over to dinner this weekend?"

"I have to work Saturday, *Mamm.*"

"Sunday then. There's no church this week. It would be nice to have her eat with us."

Ivan grunted as if that settled the matter.

Except it didn't. Some days Jesse felt as if he was leading Hannah on. Things around his house were complicated. His parents didn't seem to realize that, or maybe they'd learned to ignore it, but Jesse thought about it most every day.

He stood up from the table and walked to the counter to fetch the pitcher of water. Something, some movement, drew his attention to the window, and that was when he saw the lone figure strolling up their lane.

It was a figure he knew well. Same height—five feet, eleven inches. Same brown hair—grown a bit too long. Jesse couldn't make out his clothes from the distance, but he did notice what looked like a large backpack slung over his shoulders. He couldn't discern his expression yet, but no doubt the dark eyes would be amused, as they usually were.

Yes, he knew the person as well as he knew himself. He should. He'd followed in his footsteps, literally, as he'd grown and matured.

He had no trouble recognizing his brother, though it had been nearly a year since he'd last seen him. His visit to Chicago seemed like a distant memory. He supposed if it had been a lifetime, he'd still know that lanky frame and confident walk.

In some ways, people didn't change. They might gain or lose weight. They might change their haircuts or their clothing. None of that mattered. Something deep inside Jesse would always know Andrew. More than the image of his brother had been emblazoned on his memory. They shared a childhood. They shared their past.

He stood there staring, not knowing what to say, not knowing how to tell his parents. Each time Andrew visited, their hopes were raised that he would stay, and each time Andrew left, their hearts were broken anew.

Rebecca followed his gaze. She stared out the window for a beat and then pulled in a short, quick breath. She covered her mouth with her hand, as if she needed to keep the hope inside, as if she was afraid to let out the shout.

She stood, pushing back her chair with a loud screech against the linoleum floor.

Ivan was the last to peer out the window. By that point Andrew was close enough that Jesse could see the dark pants and blue shirt he wore.

Not exactly *Englisch* clothing.

Not exactly Amish.

As Jesse watched, Ivan shoved his plate aside, paused to squeeze Rebecca's arm and whisper something, and then stood and rushed out the door.

✣

Jesse was still sitting at the table, still watching his brother thirty minutes later. Andrew had finished off two of the sandwiches made with his *mamm's* fresh bread. He groaned when Rebecca reached for the pineapple cake that had been covered and placed on the counter, waiting for Rebecca to deliver it to their next-door neighbor, who was disabled and had difficulty baking.

"I was saving this for Linda, but let me slice you a piece. I can make her something else this afternoon."

"*Mamm*, I'm full already."

"Not too full for your *mamm's* cake. Look at you! Ten pounds lighter than when we saw you . . . what was it, two years ago?" Ivan was watching Andrew as if he might disappear before his eyes, as if he couldn't believe that he'd actually come home.

Rebecca cut a giant slice from the freshly baked cake and plopped it onto Andrew's plate. Then she glanced up and, remembering her husband was there, cut him a piece, slightly smaller.

Finally she seemed to realize that Jesse was still in the kitchen, so she cut a third piece, smaller still.

His mother had been making baked goods for Linda Rainey for at least two years. Every Thursday, without fail, she would make a pie or a cake or fresh caramel cinnamon rolls. Linda had lupus, and her joints were often so swollen as to be misshapen. Jesse and his sisters understood they were never to touch Linda's Treat, as they'd taken to calling it.

Never.

Today was apparently the exception.

"It's *gut* to see you, son. *Gotte* is *gut* indeed. Your *mamm* and I have prayed for *Gotte* to watch over you each day." There were tears in his father's eyes, something Jesse had seen the few times Andrew had visited—and then left.

Andrew's gaze continually drifted to the window, as if he were searching for someone or something. "I know you have, *Dat*. It's probably your prayers that saw me safely here."

"From where?" Rebecca hadn't cut herself a piece of the cake. She was content to gaze at her eldest son.

"Chicago for a while. Same place where Jesse came to see me."

"Last winter." Jesse pushed his plate away, the piece of cake half eaten. It was suddenly too sweet. His stomach had begun to clench up as if it were protesting the amount of food he'd consumed, or perhaps it was the prospect of dealing with Andrew and the reason he was home. Jesse didn't doubt for a minute that there *was* a reason.

"*Ya*. Hard to believe it's been that long." Andrew finished his milk and smiled when his *mamm* popped up to fetch him more.

"So you've been there, in Chicago, for the last year?" Ivan studied him, waiting for an answer.

"*Nein*. I went north to Wisconsin for a few months, then

across the great lake to Michigan, and finally turned south—to Indiana."

"What matters is that you're home now." Rebecca closed her eyes, no doubt offering yet another prayer of thanksgiving.

Silence cloaked the room as they each considered Andrew's journey. There was so much he wasn't saying. Why had he gone to Illinois to begin with? And what was he searching for in Wisconsin and Michigan? Most important, what had brought him home again, and was he staying or passing through?

Jesse's father broke the uncomfortable silence.

"We've changed the crops some—rotated a few things, added others."

"*Ya?* That doesn't sound like you."

"Jesse and I have done a lot of reading on it. Seemed the prudent thing to do, in this economy."

"You've grown, Jesse. My little *bruder* has become a man."

Jesse thought of responding to that, but he was afraid what would come out of his mouth might not be charitable. No need to start a tiff in front of his parents. They'd experienced enough trouble.

"And my older *bruder* hasn't changed much, which reminds me that I need to leave for work."

"Still at the Village?"

"I am."

"Still doing grounds work?"

Was that sarcasm Jesse heard in Andrew's voice?

"Jesse's been promoted to one of the shift managers for the grounds crew." His mother patted his hand. "You go on to work. We'll help Andrew settle back into your room. Everything's exactly as you left it, Andrew. The clothes you didn't take are still hanging on your hook."

Ivan had pushed back his chair and stood. He was nearly to the mudroom when he stopped and did an about-face. "We should have a special dinner on Sunday. One to celebrate Andrew's return."

Andrew ran his hand along his jaw, again glancing out the window. He finally nodded his head in agreement.

The entire scene made Jesse want to scream. He knew *Englisch* teens who had moved away from home. Their families didn't throw a reunion each time they returned. No one acted like the long-lost son was finally found, and no one wept when he left again. It was the way of the world for many people. But his parents didn't see that. Their entire lives were built around their family, and they wouldn't rest easy until the whole flock was once again reunited.

"I could invite your *aentis* and *onkels*." Rebecca had begun washing the dishes. "They'll be so relieved to hear you are home, and they'll be eager to see you."

"The family's grown since you've been gone. It would be *gut* to join together and celebrate this occasion." Ivan fumbled with pulling his hat off the peg.

In that moment, like so many moments over the last year, he seemed older to Jesse. The loss of his older son had aged his father, and the extra work hadn't helped. What had seemed possible with the three of them had become burdensome when they had been reduced to two.

But now the prodigal son had returned.

Jesse was happy about that. He'd always thought his brother belonged at home, and he hadn't seemed that content in Chicago. But why the sudden change of heart? Had he even had a change of heart? Or was he merely passing through on his way to another town and another adventure? Worry whispered through his mind.

Something told him that his parents' relief might be a little premature. Andrew hadn't said he was staying. He also hadn't explained why he'd left the first time, the second time, or the last time. He hadn't apologized for abandoning the family during harvest. Not when Jesse had visited him in Chicago, and not now.

Jesse knew his parents wouldn't push him for those answers. Instead, they would wait, as they had been waiting.

And they would celebrate, though Jesse wasn't sure exactly what they were celebrating.

At least they weren't planning to kill the fattened calf.

Three

Amber Bowman was having a productive day.

Morning rounds on the property had gone well. And she'd had an actual lunch instead of eating at her desk. She'd eaten at the restaurant with Carol Jennings, manager of The Quilting Bee. One of Amber's new goals was to meet with each manager individually on a rotating basis. If she could make three lunches a week, she could go through all the managers each month. At first it had sounded like a lot, but she found herself enjoying those one-on-one times.

Her staff was beginning to resemble a team again, and their efforts were becoming coordinated. The Village was more successful financially than it had ever been. All of which was a welcome relief after the trials of the previous spring.

Indeed, her life had taken several major turns since that dark time. Facing death could do that to you, she supposed.

Elizabeth tapped lightly on her office door and then entered the room. Her office assistant—and friend—was in her early sixties, round and grandmotherly. She wore her gray hair in a practical, short bob, and her hazel eyes were usually smiling behind her half reading glasses. At the moment, those glasses were hanging from a blue-beaded chain.

"Sergeant Avery's here to see you."

"Gordon?" He hadn't stopped by in months. She couldn't remember the last time. He certainly hadn't been in her office since her wedding. She ran a hand through her shoulder-length brown hair. She'd taken to wearing it naturally curly on weekends, but for work she still straightened it.

"He's waiting in the outer office."

"Oh. Okay. Show him in. Thank you, Elizabeth."

Amber closed the files she was working on. She'd been manager of the Village for twenty-three years. They had been relatively quiet years, up until six months ago. She hoped Gordon's visit didn't foreshadow more trouble.

But perhaps he was stopping by for personal reasons.

Or maybe he happened to be in the neighborhood.

Gordon Avery was nearly six feet tall. He trudged into her office, removing his hat as he did so. A sergeant with the Middlebury police force, he was forty-seven years old, only a couple of years older than Amber. He sported black hair, brown eyes, and an unusually fit physique.

They'd dated in the past, but that was before she knew—really knew—Tate.

She walked around the desk and greeted him with a quick hug, though she had to reach up to do so. Her five-foot-four height had always made her feel like a child standing beside him.

"How are you, Amber?"

"Fine. It's good to see you. It's been awhile."

"It has."

Amber motioned to one of the chairs across from her desk and sat in the other so they were side by side but still angled toward each other. It seemed less formal that way, without her sitting behind the desk. Gordon was a friend, after all.

"How's Tate?" Gordon motioned to the framed wedding picture on her desk.

The photo showed Amber and Tate standing in front of the red covered bridge on the Village property. She was wearing her wedding dress—white, long, and beautiful. Tate wore a black tuxedo. Some days it all still seemed like a dream.

"He's doing well. We both are."

"Sorry I missed the wedding. Bad luck that they sent me for training the week you tied the knot."

There was a small grin on his face, and she relaxed, realizing things were all right between them.

"We didn't exactly give a lot of notice. I decided on an August wedding. Honestly, the main reason for that was I wanted an Alaskan cruise honeymoon, which sort of necessitated an August wedding."

"Sounds like you enjoyed yourself."

"Oh, we did. Tate hasn't been much of a traveler, and it was my first two-week vacation since I started here. I wouldn't mind making a habit out of it."

"You should. You work hard." He tapped his fingers against his leg, and Amber realized he was putting the polite talk behind them.

There was another reason he was in her office.

Still, she couldn't help suggesting, "We should get together with you and Cherry sometime. Do some sort of couples date."

"Cherry and I . . ." He waved toward her picture again. "We're not like that."

"Oh." So the rumors that they were serious were false. Apparently Gordon was still available. She probably knew some-one who would be interested. Anyway, she was relieved to know they weren't dating. For some reason, she and Cherry had never hit it off, and she couldn't help thinking that Gordon deserved someone better suited to life in Middlebury.

Gordon cleared his throat and settled his hat on his knees.

"I'm sensing you didn't stop by for social chatter."

"No. There's been an incident."

"Here?" The word came out too loud and harsh. Amber forced her shoulders to relax and asked again, "Here? On the property?"

"No. Actually, the crime scene is on the Pumpkinvine Trail."

"What happened?"

"A man—Owen Esch—was found there this morning."

"Found?"

"Dead."

"Dead?" She stared at him with wide eyes. She had the vague sense that her past troubles were coming back to visit, but that was impossible. "An accident?"

"No, he was murdered." Gordon's gaze flicked up and away.

"What aren't you telling me?"

"It was rather—unusual."

"Any murder in Middlebury is unusual. We have a quiet, peaceful town."

Gordon twisted the department-issued hat around and around in his hands. "He was killed with a bow."

"A bow?" She was repeating everything he said. She shook her head to clear it. "A bow?"

"A hunting bow. A crossbow. I'm sure you've seen them."

"Yes. I believe Tate has one. I've never seen him use it, but I think one of his sons enjoys bow hunting."

"Most people around here have one, which is going to make this investigation a challenge."

"He was murdered? You're sure it wasn't an . . . an accident?"

"He was standing in the middle of the trail and shot through the heart. I don't see how someone could have mistaken him for a deer."

Amber was speechless. She couldn't help throwing a glance over her shoulder to the wall that had been remodeled. The quilt, the friendship quilt, had been mended and once again hung in the middle, but this time the wall was painted a warm yellow. She'd decided not only to repair but to remodel after the explosion, and the Village owners had agreed.

An explosion.

In her office.

Still hard to believe.

She rubbed her hands over her face, though she realized she was removing what little makeup she'd applied that morning. "Why are you here? It wasn't where the trail intersects Village property?"

"No. Actually, it was nearly two miles to the east."

"And?"

"And I'm waiting for forensics."

"To tell you he died from an arrow through the heart?"

Gordon nearly smiled. Though the topic was tragic, Amber knew he'd always enjoyed their conversations, even when they became heated.

"No. Cause of death is undeniable. Forensics will tell us an approximate time, how close the shooter was standing to the victim, any other marks of violence—"

"A bow is pretty violent."

"True, but maybe they had argued or even fought prior to the murder."

"Fingerprints?"

"The crime techs are checking the arrow as well as the surrounding area. It's doubtful they'll find much. I suspect whoever did this was smart enough to use gloves, and both sides of the trail are covered with footprints due to recent rains."

Amber shook her head. She understood that the world was a cruel place, but this was Middlebury. People cared about one another in their little town. Murder was something unheard of, until recently.

"We did find one piece of evidence that might be useful."

"And that's why you're here?"

Gordon nodded once and then leaned forward, arms braced on his knees. "The victim—"

"I assume he was Amish, given his name."

"Correct. He was holding a cell phone."

Something in Amber's stomach seemed to drop, and she knew she didn't want to hear Gordon's next words.

"He had placed a call immediately before he died. He called one of your shops, Amber. His final words might have been to one of your employees."

Four

annah made her way back across the Village, puzzling over what Seth had said and thinking of Jesse's brother. She wasn't paying attention to the people around her, and she nearly bumped into Amber.

Her boss wore a worried expression, and so did the man with her, Sergeant Gordon Avery.

This day was spinning out of control.

"Hello, Hannah. How are you?"

Hannah didn't know how to answer that. *Gut* would have been a lie, but Amber probably didn't want to know her problems. They were friends, but Amber had a lot of responsibilities. The last thing Hannah wanted to do was add to her worries. She'd seemed so happy since her wedding, and things had been so quiet at the Village—peaceful almost.

When Hannah didn't respond, Amber said, "We're on our way to the yarn shop."

"Mary's?" Hannah's heart began to bang against her ribs. Was her friend in trouble? Is that why the shop had been closed?

"Who is Mary?" Gordon asked.

His uniform made Hannah uneasy, though she knew he was a friend to Amber and a good police officer. She'd seen that first-hand last spring.

"Mary Weaver is the manager of the yarn shop, of The Cat's Meow." Amber turned back to Hannah. "You nearly jumped out of your apron when I said Mary's name. Is there something you're aware of that you want to tell us?"

Hannah pushed up her glasses and rubbed her eyes, but she still didn't say anything.

"You know Mary pretty well. Don't you?"

"Ya. We are in the same district. We attend the same church."

"Would you mind coming with us? Gordon needs to talk to her, and she might be more at ease with you there."

"I was headed home, but if I can help . . ."

"Thank you, Hannah." If Amber had noticed the reluctance in her voice, she ignored it.

Together the three of them walked the short distance to the yarn shop, which was now open.

Mary Weaver stood behind the counter. From what Hannah could see and hear, it appeared Mary was arguing with Helen Stinson. Helen was one of the new employees on the Unassigned List. Hannah knew a little about her because she'd filled in one day when Seth had a dental appointment. Helen was short— even shorter than Amber and Hannah—with long, dark hair, which she wore loose down her back. Today she had fingernails painted a sparkly bright green and earrings that dangled and caught the light.

If two people could have looked more different, Hannah didn't know how. Mary had recently turned thirty. She was tall, which helped to hide her weight. Looking closely, one realized she was a bit on the heavy side of plump. She always dressed in subdued colors—today a dark-gray dress with a light-gray apron. Her blond hair was carefully hidden by her *kapp*.

She did not seem happy about Helen's presence in her shop.

"I don't need help. As you can see, there are no customers at the moment, and I'm perfectly capable of taking care of any who arrive."

Mary still hadn't turned toward them, though the bell over the door had clearly announced their arrival. She was busy arguing with Helen, and Gordon was holding back as if he needed to watch and take notes as the scene unfolded in front of him. At that moment a group of older women pushed past them and into the store, talking and jostling and oohing and aahing at the yarn displays.

Mary glanced up at the customers and saw Hannah, Amber, and Gordon. Her face paled, if that were possible, and she plopped down on the stool behind her counter.

"Hello, Mary." Amber stepped forward first. "I'm the one who asked for Helen to come here and help for a few moments. Sergeant Avery and I would like to have a word with you. Perhaps in your office?"

Mary nodded mutely. Her gaze settled on Hannah for a moment, who shrugged her shoulders up and down. She had no idea what was happening. Had Amber found out the store was closed at lunch? Was Mary in trouble for leaving her post?

But that made no sense. Hannah didn't need to be there for that sort of discussion. Sergeant Avery certainly didn't need to be there.

Sergeant Avery was saying, "We need to check the tape first."

He walked around the counter, pulled a plastic glove from his pocket, and hit the Play button on the shop's recorder. All that could be heard was something falling to the ground, followed by two minutes of nature noises.

"I'll need to take this with me," Avery said.

Mary stood, straightened her apron, and led the way down

the hall to the back of the shop. Her office was small and cluttered. Stacks of paper covered the desk, and unopened boxes of supplies crowded the floor.

There were two chairs.

Amber ducked out into the hall and soon returned with a stool.

"I'll stand," Gordon murmured.

Mary sat perched on the desk chair with her back ramrod straight. Amber took the chair opposite her, pulling it up so they were almost knee to knee. Hannah sat on the stool, though it made her feel like a schoolchild to do so.

"I enjoyed our lunch together last week." Amber waited for Mary to nod and then continued, "Have you met Sergeant Avery?"

Mary shook her head, still mute, but at least responding. When she'd first seen them in the store, Hannah had the crazy thought that she might start hollering at them or insist they leave the shop.

Gordon introduced himself, but he didn't offer to shake Mary's hand. Hannah knew he'd worked and lived around the Amish long enough to understand their customs—women generally didn't shake hands with men, especially Amish women with *Englisch* men.

"Mary, the reason we came by, the reason Sergeant Avery is here, is to ask you some questions."

"All right." They were the first words she'd spoken directly to them. Hannah expected her voice to be shaky and timid, but instead Mary's words came out in a blunt, defiant tone.

"I asked Hannah to come because she's your friend, and I thought you might feel more comfortable."

Hannah met Mary's gaze and offered her best comforting smile. Mary nodded slightly but didn't speak. Her arms were crossed, and she was glowering at them as if they had done something terrible.

"When was the last time you spoke with Owen Esch?" Gordon asked.

Owen! What had happened to Owen? A chill passed over Hannah, and she sat on her hands to warm them and still their shaking.

"I'm not sure."

"Last month? Last week? Today?" Gordon's tone remained neutral, but he was watching Mary closely.

"He doesn't come into the shop much. Men don't as a rule."

"I didn't ask when he last came in." Gordon nodded toward the phone on the corner of her desk. "I asked when you last spoke with him."

Mary stared at the phone as if she'd never seen it before. She finally turned back toward Gordon and shrugged.

"Did you speak with him today?"

"*Nein*. Not today."

"You're positive?"

"*Ya*. I would remember."

"Were you here in the shop between seven fifteen and seven forty-five this morning?"

"Maybe."

"And you're sure you didn't talk to Owen?"

"*Nein*. I didn't. Why are you repeating the same questions?"

"Mary, Sergeant Avery is doing his job. I'm afraid we have terrible news . . . about Owen." Amber looked to Gordon, who nodded slightly as if he was giving her the go-ahead.

"What kind of news?"

"Owen was on the Pumpkinvine Trail this morning, and he was killed. Murdered with an arrow from a crossbow."

Hannah wondered if she was dreaming. This couldn't be happening. Except her palms had begun to sweat and her pulse was racing, which didn't usually happen in a dream.

Murdered?

Owen Esch was murdered?

She'd scarcely had time to process what Gordon had said when Mary jumped up, bumping into Hannah and knocking her off the stool, and fled from the room.

From her spot on the floor, Hannah couldn't see much. Gordon had trouble moving around her, since she was splayed on the floor. Finally he hopped to the right and bounded out after Mary, with Amber following close behind. Hannah heard the back door of the shop open and then slam shut—twice. A shiver traveled slowly down the length of her spine.

Mary was in trouble. That much was clear, but how serious was it? And had she killed Owen?

✺

Jesse was making his way across the parking lot when he saw Mary Weaver dash away from the shops at a full run, weaving in and out of cars.

Gordon Avery was in hot pursuit. He caught her before she reached the end of the lot.

Amber Bowman was behind Gordon. When she saw that Mary was caught, she stopped and bent over, her hand pressed to her side.

And behind Amber was Hannah.

His Hannah.

She skidded to a stop a split second before running into their boss.

Jesse shouted and waved at her, then trotted over.

"*Was iss letz?* Why is he taking Mary?"

Amber held up her hand, still trying to catch her breath.

Hannah hopped from foot to foot, trying to explain but managing to confuse him more. "She ran! Why did she run? And Owen. Jesse, Owen's dead. Owen Esch. Murdered. Can you believe it?"

"Slow down. Hannah, take a deep breath. What are you talking about? I saw Owen yesterday afternoon. He's fine."

"It happened this morning," Amber explained. "I need to see if I should go with Mary. Jesse, stay with Hannah until she's calmed down. This has been quite a shocking day."

Yes, it had. And they didn't even know about the return of his brother.

Jesse accompanied Hannah over to a bench at the end of the parking lot. "Take deep breaths. Then you can tell me everything."

"I don't know everything! I don't know anything!"

He rubbed her back in slow, smooth circles like he'd seen women do with babies.

"Mary's probably frightened. I should go and help her."

"Amber is with her. See? Amber's going with her. It looks like she's following in her car. Mary will be fine. Now, tell me again about Owen. Surely this isn't true."

So Hannah told him what she knew, which wasn't much.

When she finished, she appeared calmer.

"Sergeant Avery was only asking her questions? And she ran out of the shop?"

"*Ya.* It doesn't make any sense. She couldn't have killed Owen. Mary might be opinionated, but she's not violent. I don't think she knew Owen better than any of us. He's barely been back a month."

"Perhaps she was frightened. People do strange things when they're scared. Sometimes they do things that don't make any sense."

"I suppose. There's more, though." In a rush of words she told him about Mary's shop being closed, the man waiting out back, and what Seth had said about seeing Mary with the *Englischer*.

"It's not a crime to be with an *Englischer*. An Amish woman and an *Englisch* man can speak. They can even have lunch. Perhaps he was a supplier, and she was ordering yarn from him. There could be any number of reasons." Jesse paused to wave at one of the grounds crew who was leaving for the day. "I need to go and check in. Are you going to be all right?"

"*Ya*. I'm fine. I was headed home before all this began."

Jesse reached out and squeezed her hand. "Mary will need *freinden*, and we'll be there for her. Don't worry." He sounded as if he was trying to convince someone. He sounded that way to his own ears, even, but Hannah didn't seem to notice, and she stood and straightened her dress.

She peeked around him as if to make sure they were alone, then stood on tiptoe and kissed him on the cheek. "*Danki*."

"*Gem gschehne*."

"Stop by after work?"

"I'll try." He'd stepped away from her when he remembered his morning, his brother, and the celebration dinner.

"Hannah." He waited for her to turn. "*Mamm* wants you to come to dinner Sunday. We're celebrating. My *bruder* is home."

Five

mber parked her little red car as Gordon escorted Mary into the Middlebury Police Station. She'd offered to give Mary a ride, but Gordon waved off the suggestion, reminding her, "Mary's not under arrest, but it would be better for her to ride with me. She seems to be a flight risk."

"What are you going to do?"

"I simply need to ask her some questions."

She'd called Elizabeth during the drive and asked her to cancel her afternoon appointments. She had also called Tate, who offered to meet her at the station.

"No. I'm sure this is all a misunderstanding. Hopefully we won't be here long."

"Gordon must have had a good lead to question Mary versus all of your other employees."

"Yes. The number from Mary's shop was on the dead guy's phone. But that doesn't necessarily incriminate her in any way."

"Not like running does."

"I'll admit that looks suspicious. Perhaps she was afraid. Maybe she thought Gordon was accusing her rather than questioning her . . ." Amber's explanation trailed off as she tried to imagine what could have caused Mary to run. She had to know that Gordon would be right behind her.

"Call me if you need anything, and remember—I'll take care of dinner."

"You always take care of dinner. You're spoiling me."

"Guilty as charged."

And that short conversation was all it took to put her day back in balance. Tate always knew what to say or do or not say or not do. She thanked the Lord for him as she walked into the small police station.

Though they'd dealt with a murder in the spring, she'd never actually gone to the police station. She'd of course driven by the building in the more than twenty years she worked in Middlebury, but she'd never had a reason to stop. The two times she'd been pulled over while driving (once for speeding six miles over the limit and once for failing to come to a complete halt at a stop sign, where both directions were deserted), the officers had given her a warning.

It occurred to her she might not be so lucky now that she was no longer dating the boss. Probably she should watch her speed and stops more closely.

The inside of the station didn't look anything like she had imagined. She'd expected cracked, uncomfortable chairs, a yellowed linoleum floor, and stale odors. She was wrong on all counts. The waiting area held black leather seats and a long table stacked with new magazines—she knew they were the most recent editions because she had two of them at home and hadn't had a chance to read them yet. The television in the corner of the waiting room was a flat screen tuned to a twenty-four-hour cable news channel with the volume muted. The floor was covered with an industrial gray carpet, but it was clean and complemented the black chairs nicely. The room smelled of a lemony cleanser, which was accentuated by a plug-in deodorizer near the television.

A kindly-looking older gentleman with white hair and bright-blue eyes sat behind a counter. The name tag on his uniform read "Walter Hopkins."

"I'm here to see Sergeant Avery."

"He's busy right now."

From where she stood, she could see Gordon leading Mary into his office, a small area in the corner of the room. Glass walls separated it from the rest of the desks and officers. No one would hear them, but everyone could see what was happening. That could come in handy when working with a criminal, but Mary was innocent!

Amber understood Walter was there to keep her on the visitor side of the petition, but she briefly considered rushing past him. By the time he caught her she'd be at Gordon's side. It was true that Walter Hopkins was wearing a holstered gun, but he wouldn't use it. Would he? "Actually, I'm here with the woman he brought in."

"Family has to wait over there." Walter gestured toward the black chairs.

"I'm not family exactly. I'm her boss."

"Still need to wait over there."

At that moment Walter's switchboard beeped. He took the call, his eyes locked on her, and then he said, "Yes, sir," and hung up.

"It's your lucky day. Boss says to go on back."

Amber thanked him and hurried to Gordon's office.

Mary had sat down in the chair opposite Gordon's desk. She didn't look as if she planned on being helpful. Her arms were crossed over her chest as before, and this time Amber could see that her hands were balled into tight fists. Instead of looking at Gordon, or at Amber when she walked in, Mary stared at a spot on the far wall—to the top and right of Gordon's fishing pictures.

"Have a seat, Amber. We were about to get started."

Mary flinched at the last word.

Did she think Gordon was going to arrest her, possibly even charge her with this terrible crime?

"Does Mary need a lawyer?" Amber asked.

"Nein." Mary dismissed the idea before they'd even discussed it.

"Actually, she doesn't, though if she'd like to call one, I'll wait to continue." Mary shook her head again, indicating she did not want a lawyer present. "But I want to be clear. I'm questioning her, not charging her with anything—yet. And I'm allowing you in the room, Amber, in the hopes Mary will realize with your help that I'm reasonable and on her side."

Gordon pulled out a small recorder, pushed the Record button, and informed Mary that the conversation was being taped, they were in the early stages of the investigation, and she was not being charged with anything.

Amber sat on the edge of her seat and reached over to touch Mary's arm. "He needs to ask you questions, Mary. Answer as best you can. Answer truthfully. You don't need to be frightened."

"Actually, she does need to be afraid if she plans on not telling the truth. Lying to an officer during a murder investigation is no small thing."

Closing her eyes, Mary murmured, "I would never lie."

"Maybe not outright. But in the legal sense, not telling me everything—it's the same as lying."

"And how would you know if I'm not telling you something?" Mary glared at Gordon as she spoke.

"How would I know? Investigations come together like a quilt, Mary. You're familiar with quilting, aren't you?" He waited for her to nod and then continued, "Block by block we build our case until we're ready to sew it together. When pieces are missing, we know it. And then we go hunting for them. But by that point, we're not so polite about it."

Amber wanted to ask him how he knew so much about quilting, but then she remembered going with him to the county fair. His mother and grandmother had both entered quilts, and they had both won ribbons. He probably sat at their knees as they pieced and basted and quilted.

"I don't quilt," Mary announced unapologetically. "I knit and crochet. Have you ever done either of those? If you're not careful, yarn becomes tangled, stitches get dropped, you increase or decrease at the wrong time, and things can take the wrong shape."

As if she'd said too much, she sat back in the chair and clamped her mouth shut.

"Is that what happened to Owen? Did he forget to be careful?"

Mary didn't answer.

"Did he get tangled up in something?"

Mary didn't answer.

"Maybe he didn't pay attention to what he was doing, and whatever he was caught up in changed into something else, something he didn't expect, something wrong."

Mary didn't answer.

The silence stretched uncomfortably around them. It was so quiet that Amber could hear the tape recorder turning, whirring its little cassette as it recorded nothing of importance.

The entire topic made her nervous. What did quilting and

knitting and dropped stitches have to do with a poor man cut down in the prime of his life?

Amber stood and walked back into the main room. Two officers were working on computers. She saw what she needed in the corner near the bathrooms. She walked over to the water dispenser, poured herself a cup of water, and drank it. Crushing the paper cup in her hand, she tossed it into the wastebasket. Then she poured water into another cup.

When she returned to Gordon's office, it seemed the two were involved in some sort of staring showdown. Amber handed the water to Mary, who drank it in one gulp.

"Maybe we should start with something simpler," Amber suggested. "I know Mary isn't involved in something as terrible as Owen's death. She's an excellent worker, and she's very dependable. If there's something she's not telling you, then there's a very good reason."

Gordon scowled. "There's no good reason to withhold information from me when I'm trying to find a killer."

"Of course you wouldn't understand, but Amish folks value their privacy." Amber didn't let Gordon's tone ruffle her. She'd seen him irritated before. That last murder investigation had been a burr in his side, until she was in danger.

He'd been there for her then.

He was a good cop, but maybe not such a good interrogator when it came to the Amish in general and young Amish ladies in particular.

"Mary would never withhold information that might allow you to catch someone, especially since this person could still be armed and dangerous."

Mary crumpled the paper cup as her eyes widened.

Amber continued the train of thought before Mary had a chance to recover.

"Murder on the Pumpkinvine Trail. Can you believe it?" She tsk-tsked even though it made her sound like an old woman. "When I think of how often I walk down that trail, it gives me the shivers. And, Mary, you come to work down the trail, don't you? If I remember right, you live not too far from the trail."

"*Ya.*"

"And your brothers and sisters use it too. Probably hundreds of people go down that trail every day. I know you want to catch this person as much as I do, as much as Sergeant Avery does."

Mary threw a distrustful glance at Gordon. "I do." The words were nearly a whisper.

"So let's start with Owen." Gordon picked up his pen and began to doodle with it. "How well did you know him? How did you know him?"

"From church and such. Not that well, though, since he is— was—younger."

"Owen's sister, Naomi Graber, told me he had moved away, to Fort Wayne, and that he returned a month ago."

"Less than a month. A little less." Mary's defiance was being replaced by misery as the full realization of what had happened clearly dawned on her. "Owen was a *gut* boy. A *gut* man, I should say. At least he thought he was a man. After all, he had recently turned twenty-five."

"When was his birthday?" Gordon's questions were smoother now, quiet and unobtrusive.

"August fifth." Mary didn't even hesitate.

"Did you talk to him while he was away?"

"Every now and again. Not from home. We have no phone there, not even in the barn. My parents won't abide it."

Amber wondered how awkward that must be. She knew Mary was thirty years old. They'd spoken of her upcoming birthday when they'd shared lunch the week before. How would it feel to still live with your parents? To still be under your parents' rules?

But what other option did Amish women have if they were unmarried?

It was one of the few things about the Amish life that rankled Amber, but perhaps that was because she'd been a single woman for so long. She understood full well both the hardship of being alone and the joy of being independent.

Both were experiences Mary would never know.

Then again, Mary had a strong support network. She would never want for someone to confide in or a place to live or food on the table.

"Owen was in the habit of calling you at the shop?"

Mary didn't answer straightaway.

Gordon added, "We can check the phone records, Mary. It's best if you tell me what you can."

She pressed her fingers against her closed eyelids. Sitting up straighter, she dropped her hands into her lap and stared directly at him. "*Ya*. While he was away, he would call once, maybe twice a month."

"Why?" I asked.

Mary turned to me. She seemed, for a minute, to forget that Gordon was there.

"To check on things. Ask after his *schweschder* and her family. Learn what was happening in Middlebury. *Englischers* think when an Amish man or woman leaves, when they're on their *rumspringa*, that they don't care anymore. This couldn't be further from the truth. They care very much, but there are not many open channels of communication."

"You were a friend to Owen." Gordon sat back and studied her.

She nodded as a single tear slipped down her cheek.

"When was the last time you spoke with him?"

"Two days ago."

"He was already back. He could have stopped by the shop instead of calling."

"*Ya*, and sometimes he did. By this time we'd become *freinden*, and we enjoyed talking to each other. Owen still had the cell phone he purchased while he was away. He would sometimes call me before work."

"Why was he calling when you talked to him two days ago, on Tuesday?"

"He was excited."

"About?"

Mary again closed her eyes and pulled in a deep breath. When she opened them, Amber had the sensation that she'd made a decision, though what it was she couldn't imagine.

"About a group. He'd been trying to get in with this group, and he said things had gone well the night before, when he visited with one of the members. It was important to him for some reason. He was invited to go to the next meeting."

"When was the meeting supposed to be?"

"Last night."

"What was the name of the group, Mary?"

"It didn't have a name. At least he didn't tell me one. He did mention some letters."

Gordon waited, his pen poised above the pad of paper.

"*I-S-G*." Tears splashed down Mary's cheeks. "I don't even

know what that means. Are they the ones who killed Owen? And who are they?"

But Gordon wasn't listening anymore. He turned off the recorder, stood up, walked over to the door, and opened it. Without another word to them, he strode across the floor to where Walter Hopkins continued to monitor anyone coming into the building. Amber and Mary turned in their seats to watch him. He bent down and said something to Walter, which caused him to jerk upright and grab the phone.

Gordon walked resolutely back toward his office. He didn't sit down or even enter the room. Standing in the doorway, he said, "Thank you, Mary. I may stop by the shop or your home if I have any further questions."

Then he turned and was gone.

Six

Though his stomach tumbled and turned over what had happened, he went about his daily chores in a normal fashion, walking in and out of the barn as he did so. Each time he entered the structure, he peered over at the crossbow hanging on the wall. Each time he walked out, he replayed the scene from earlier that morning.

He hadn't wanted to kill the young man and took no joy in the memory. Killing was a sin, and he understood that well.

But people were depending on him. If he didn't care for them, that would be a sin as well. He had worked too hard for too long to see his life shattered.

Nein.

He'd done the right thing. The young man's life had been complete before he followed him, before he raised the bow and took aim.

Hopefully there would be no others.

Killing was not something he cared to do again.

But if he had to, he would.

Seven

esse was grateful for the work he had to do. The grounds crew was working on three large projects simultaneously. As an assistant manager, his job was to make sure things were progressing as they should.

Painting the covered bridge was nearly done. White trim needed to be added to the edging, but the men had finished with the coat of a rich red color on the bulk of the bridge. The project would be completed by the weekend, which had been their goal.

Patching the barn roof wasn't going so well. The workers had come across wood rot, so the boards needed to be replaced before they could continue. Jesse walked back to the grounds crew office and called the wood shop in town. If his schedule permitted, the owner would sometimes come out and help them on projects. He said he couldn't do it before the next week since he was trying to find someone to replace Owen. Jesse made a note on the work order form and left one copy for his boss and another for Amber. Then he instructed the workers to cover the roof with a heavy tarp. Rain wasn't in the forecast, but it was better to be prepared.

The third and last major project was replacing all the summer flowers with fall plants. That was nearly done. The problem was it should have been done before the first of October, but the local nursery had run out of bedding plants. He moved some of the barn workers to helping with the flowers. With the extra hands, they would finish before dark.

As he went to each project site, he lent a hand where he could and made notes of things the manager, Harvey, would need to handle.

The work kept him busy and helped ease his worries, but occasionally thoughts of his brother's return rumbled through his mind, punctuated every few minutes by the awful realization of Owen's death.

By the time he left the Village, the sun was setting and he was exhausted. Physically, that felt like a good thing. Emotionally, it didn't.

The walk home took him directly by Hannah's place. He turned up the path to her home without even thinking. Some days were like that. Some days he needed to see her.

"We can sit inside if you like." Hannah stood on the front porch, as if she had been expecting him.

As usual, she looked beautiful to Jesse. The gas lights from inside the house cast a halo around her hair, which was still covered with her *kapp*. It made him think of angels and God's provision. It reminded him how blessed he was to have Hannah in his life. Surely God had placed the two of them together for a reason.

From where he stood, Jesse could see Hannah's three brothers, little sister, mother, and father all gathered around the kitchen table, working on various tasks. He could hear them from where he stood at the bottom of the porch steps.

"Could we stay out here? If it's not too cold—"

"The porch is fine." Hannah ducked inside and returned with a sweater to ward off the evening's chill.

They sat on the old wooden swing and watched the last of

the sunset's orange, red, and pink colors fade to dark. Bit by bit, Jesse's tension melted away.

"Terrible thing about Owen." He reached over and laced his fingers with hers.

"*Ya. Mamm* and I spoke a little of it as we prepared dinner. She says we have to trust *Gotte's wille*."

"Difficult to do in this instance."

"That's what I said. Who would kill him? And in such a terrible way? I can't imagine it having been an accident. You have to get so close for a bow shot. And why would anyone do such a thing?"

"I don't know."

"Do you think Owen was in some kind of trouble?"

"Maybe, but there's nothing I've heard about."

"His sister told my *mamm* that he was planning to join the church. She said that since he came back he was a different person—more mature and thoughtful. Naomi insisted that he was ready to put his *rumspringa* behind him."

Jesse said the next words before he had time to think them through. "Sometimes the things we think we've left behind pop up in the middle of our road again."

Hannah didn't answer at first.

As silence surrounded them, Jesse realized what he'd said could apply to Owen, or it could apply to him and Andrew.

"I know his childhood was difficult." Hannah pulled away and pressed her back into the corner of the swing.

He could feel her studying him in the darkness.

"Owen never spoke much to me," she continued. "And his sister was out of school by the time we started. She must be thirty-five now."

Jesse had been pushing against the wooden floor of the

porch with his right foot, gently rocking the swing. He stopped it suddenly, his thoughts focused on the last time he'd spoken to Owen.

"What did you remember?"

"Something Owen said last Sunday."

"After church?"

"*Ya.* I was waiting for you to finish up with the dessert table so we could go for a walk."

"You were waiting for me to bring you some of the walnut brownies."

"That too."

"And Owen said?"

Jesse shook his head. "I'm trying to remember. We were talking about crops and how the long-range forecasts are predicting drought for next spring."

"How can anyone predict weather for six months from now?"

"Beats me. Not sure I even believe it."

"So you were talking about farming and weather. There's a huge surprise."

"It's that or fishing."

Jesse snagged Hannah's hand when she reached out to push him. "Owen said that he didn't want to wait to see how bad spring would be."

Hannah scooted across the swing, erasing the space between them.

"He said we should spend our time preparing for it instead."

"Preparing for drought?"

"*Nein.* I had a feeling he was talking about something else. I sort of laughed and said that *Gotte* would send the rain we need. That *Gotte* would provide as he always has."

"And?"

"And he said rain wasn't the only thing we should be worried about."

Jesse again pushed his foot against the floor of the porch, causing the swing to begin rocking once more. Hannah was now sitting so close they were shoulder to shoulder, and her hand was nestled in his. For that moment, he had no doubt at all that he should ask her to marry him. Perhaps he should do it before she went inside. Perhaps that would settle the nervousness in his stomach.

"Tell me about Andrew," Hannah whispered.

So he did. He told her about lunch, about the pineapple cake, about his parents' unmitigated joy, and about his doubts. He told her everything.

When he'd finished, she squeezed his hand. They sat there, listening to the sounds from her siblings floating through the window and watching the dazzling appearance of a million stars.

⁂

By the time Hannah went inside, her father, brothers, and even her little sister, Mattie, were already upstairs. Her mother was alone in the family room, sitting in her rocker and knitting.

"I'm surprised you aren't in bed too."

"It's nice to sit here, in the quiet, and relax a bit."

"So you weren't waiting up for me?" Hannah smiled as she plopped down on the couch.

"*Nein*. You're old enough you don't need that sort of looking after, Hannah."

"Good to hear."

As Eunice continued knitting, Hannah studied her in the light of the single gas lamp. She thought her mother was beautiful. She was short, like Hannah, with blond hair that was turning gray in places. She had beautiful, kind blue eyes—unless her brothers had been up to mischief, and then those eyes could grow quite stern. Eunice was not one to put up with trouble if it could be avoided, and she didn't hesitate to discipline her children if they needed it.

What she did not do was hold a grudge. Once you were punished, all was forgiven. "Forget your mistakes but remember what they taught you" was a favorite saying heard often in their home.

What would her life have been like without her *mamm*, without her *dat* as well?

"You're thinking deep thoughts over there."

"Do you remember when Owen's parents died?"

"*Ya*. You should too. You were five. You attended the funeral."

"I can't remember anything from that age. I'm lucky to remember what I had for lunch yesterday."

"It was a sad affair, as such funerals are."

Hannah waited. Usually her mother only spoke of *Gotte's wille*. Seldom did she dive further into such tragedies, at least not with Hannah.

"Owen was maybe seven or eight. His *schweschder* must have been ten years older. I remember she was beginning to be interested in boys. She worked at the old quilt shop in town, but she quit after the accident. Stayed home and became a mother to Owen. They looked like two little orphans, though they were never completely alone. The community pitched in and helped with whatever needed to be done."

"What of their family? Their parents must have had *schweschders*, *bruders*, and parents."

"Owen's mother had family in Kentucky, but Naomi wouldn't even consider moving, at least not right after the accident, and soon after that she married."

"How did their parents die?"

"Buggy accident, during a storm. Crossing the bridge over near their place. You know the one."

"But it's a small creek!"

"Now it is. That year we'd had terrible rains, and the creek was like a roaring river. They tried to cross it and were swept away."

Hannah watched her mother knit. The yarn she was using had been dyed a soft lavender, so the item was probably for Mattie. Her little sister dearly loved any item in any shade of purple.

"How could that be *Gotte's wille, Mamm*? For two children to lose both of their parents."

"I can't be speaking *Gotte's* mind, since I don't know it." Eunice smiled over her knitting needles. "But I can remind you of his promise—to never leave us or forsake us."

When Hannah didn't respond, she added, "It's a hard thing, to be sure, but this world is a difficult place, Hannah. It's the next life we're to look to. No more buggy accidents or death there."

Hannah remained in the sitting room for another half hour, listening to the quiet sounds of her mother's knitting and staring out the window into the darkness.

Eight

*A*mber woke the next morning refreshed.

The day before had been like a nightmare, like something from her past had come to haunt her. She kept wishing to wake up and have imagined Owen's death and Mary's questioning. She arrived home exhausted and out of sorts. Then she had walked into Tate's arms, and the day fell away from her like an old cloak dropped to the ground.

They'd spoken some about Owen and Mary and the investigation over dinner, but then they'd gone to the back porch with mugs of decaffeinated coffee and a single piece of strawberry-rhubarb pie, which they shared. The back porch looked out over Tate's fields. The warmth of the coffee, the sweetness of the pie, and a view that reminded her of all God had created worked together to calm Amber's nerves. Then Tate scooted closer to her on the swing. When he began rubbing her shoulders, she practically purred. Her cat, Leo, looked on from his perch on the old oak rocker, with his feet tucked underneath him and his eyes blinking his approval.

Amber sighed and snuggled even closer to her husband. "Moving here was a smart move."

"You think so? What about marrying me?"

"Another smart move. I seem to be full of them."

Tate murmured in agreement as he nudged her neck with tiny kisses.

She reached up and ran her hand over his close-cropped hair.

"You know I'll grow it out if you want me to."

"What?"

"Sure. I'll sacrifice the convenience of a closely shaved head for my woman."

"This is your look." She settled back into his arms. "I'm rather used to it."

"Well, you know it works for me."

"Yes. Less shampoo. I remember. Should I shave my head?"

"Shampoo isn't *that* expensive."

The evening had been calm, quiet, and exactly what she needed.

Waking this morning to the smell of coffee wafting from the kitchen, she paused to thank God for her blessings. It was sometimes difficult to believe that she'd found a man she loved, and one who loved her, at her age. Forty-five! Somehow she felt younger than she had in years. Love could do that to you, she supposed.

But would she always feel so cherished?

She'd seen plenty of couples who acted as if they could barely tolerate each other. "Kissing wears out. Cooking doesn't." That was the advice Hannah had given her at the wedding. Hannah had laughed and wrapped her in a hug as she quoted the proverb, but maybe there was something to those sage words. She made a mental note to pick up more pie from the Village bakery. Tate did most of their cooking, but she took care of dessert— if purchasing from the bakery could be called "taking care" of something.

Entering the kitchen, she wasn't surprised to see her husband sitting at the table, having already finished his breakfast.

He wore a tan work shirt, old blue jeans, and scuffed leather work boots. Taller, bigger, and a little older than she, he seemed to her to be in the prime of his life. It was hard to tell if he had any gray in his black hair since he kept it shaved, but his skin had the healthy look of someone who worked outdoors. His warm, brown eyes and quick smile reflected that he'd managed to hold on to an appreciation for life's blessings, despite having lost his first wife to cancer.

The clock's hands had barely crept past six thirty, but Tate was a farmer at heart and still rose early. He'd reduced the size of his crops, leasing half of the place to a local Amish man. He'd also sold most of the animals, leaving only the two donkeys, two mares, and a few cattle to tend.

"Morning." He lowered his newspaper and gave her an approving smile. Yes, he still read a newspaper each day, though she was trying to convert him to the logic of reading online.

"You look beautiful this morning, Mrs. Bowman."

"You say that every morning."

"Because it's true."

She paused to give him a short kiss, then headed for the coffeepot. Pulling her favorite mug from his cabinet—their cabinet—she marveled again that they were able to combine their households so easily. Tate wasn't one to hoard things, though, and there had been plenty of room. The biggest change for him had been the addition of her cat.

Leo stretched and padded across the floor to rub against her legs.

"Does he still go over to the *dawdy haus* every day?" She reached down and scratched between Leo's ears.

"Usually in the afternoon, after his nap. That is one spoiled feline."

"I suppose there's no harm in him visiting the place since it's usually empty. Preston is at work more than he should be."

"It was good of you to offer him the place free of charge."

"I'd like to think we did it out of the goodness of our hearts, but the truth is that it's a real asset to have someone like Preston on the property all night. He says he doesn't mind being on call."

"I'm sure he doesn't. The military probably taught him that."

"It's amazing to see how much he's changed since coming to work for the Village . . ." Amber's thoughts drifted back to Preston when she'd first met him—sleeping in the local park and scrounging for his meals each day. He'd put on a good ten pounds since coming to work at the Village, and he was an excellent employee.

She toasted a piece of cinnamon raisin bread and then joined Tate at the table. "I was thinking about Owen."

He folded the paper and studied her sympathetically. The events of last spring were still too vivid. Amber didn't feel ready to deal with another tragedy, another murder—how could she? But she realized life often didn't give you choices.

"You're not planning on getting involved with this one, are you?"

"No. Of course not."

"Good."

"Except to the degree that Mary is involved. She is one of my employees."

"Her family will take care of her."

"Maybe, but you know how the Amish avoid police matters. I want Mary to know that I'm there to help her in any way I can."

"And?"

"What makes you think there's an *and*?"

"There usually is, dear." Fortunately, he was smiling as he teased her.

Amber bit into her toast and let her mind rake back over the interview in Gordon's office. There was something that was bothering her. Something she had wanted to discuss with Tate. Something Mary had mentioned . . ."ISG. That's it!"

"Say again."

"ISG. That's what I was going to ask you about. Mary said Owen called her fairly often." Amber stared down at her plate. Her toast was gone. She had no recollection of eating it. "Owen was apparently excited because he'd recently met with this group—ISG—and things went well. It was important to him to be a part of ISG, whatever that is. Mary wondered if they had killed him, but I've never even heard of such a group. Do you think Owen made it up?"

"No." Tate stood and fetched the coffeepot, then refilled their mugs. "ISG stands for Indiana Survivalist Group."

"Huh?"

"I'm sure you've heard of them. The group is comprised of folks who expect and prepare for some sort of disaster."

"Doomsday preppers?" Amber's voice screeched like a mockingbird scolding Leo.

"Well, that's television. I'm not sure I'd believe everything you see there, even if it was on the National Geographic Channel."

"There was another show—"

"There have been several."

"And you're saying we have a group of these people here?" Amber sank back against her chair.

"Yeah. They're here, but as I said, don't believe the stereotypes you see on television."

"Have you been to one of their meetings?"

"No. I'm a farmer. If I can't make it when and if things go south, then I suppose no one can."

"So there aren't any farmers in the group?"

"There are." Tate smiled across the table at her. "I have a few friends who have tried to convert me."

"Oh my. Why have I not heard of this?"

"They don't actually advertise in the paper."

Amber turned her coffee cup around in her hands. "That explains Gordon's reaction. As soon as Mary said ISG, Gordon ended the interview."

"It gives him a place to start looking."

"Do you think someone from ISG could have killed Owen?"

Tate shook his head. "As a group, no. Preppers aren't sitting around waiting for a chance to shoot someone. But an individual . . . well, who can say why one person kills another."

Hearing those grim words, Amber stood and began collecting her things for work. She still liked to arrive by seven, and she'd dawdled too long.

Stepping in front of her, Tate put a hand under Amber's chin and lifted her face so that she had to meet his gaze.

"You're rattled."

"A little."

"Don't be. Gordon's a good cop. He'll catch whoever did this. In the meantime, you're not in any danger, and you don't have to be afraid."

"I'm not—"

Her disclaimer was stopped by Tate's kiss. As she settled into his arms, she realized maybe she was frightened. Maybe she was afraid of being caught up in whatever had happened. But that wasn't going to happen this time. She could trust God to care for Mary and to protect her.

The morning passed quickly at work. Amber was surprised when she checked the clock and it was lunchtime. The thought was followed by a knock on her door. Looking up, she saw Pam Coleman, her new assistant manager. Pam was tall—five foot eight, midthirties, black, and extremely competent. She wore her hair in a fashionable bob, and, most important, she had a great sense of humor. The woman was definitely a godsend.

"Think of me as a dinner bell."

"You mean lunch."

"I mean food—fried chicken, preferably. I smelled it as I passed the restaurant. Reminded me of my momma's cooking."

"Your momma fried chicken?"

"I'm from Texas. My momma fried anything that didn't hold still."

Amber grabbed her tablet and her keys. "That does sound pretty good."

"You know it. I hope you wore your stretchy pants."

"I'm only having one piece."

"Uh-huh."

"And no mashed potatoes this time."

"I'm having mashed potatoes and homemade noodles. Why do you think I work here?" Pam flashed a smile, revealing perfectly straight teeth.

"I think you work here because you get to spend time with me."

They both waved at Elizabeth as they passed through the outer office. She was on the phone but covered the mouthpiece and said, "Make her take at least half an hour."

"You two are ganging up on me." Amber felt like a young girl skipping class as they made their way down the stairs.

"I like that part of my job too," Pam said, picking up on their conversation. "Actually, I had heard about you. That's why I came for the interview." Pam looped an arm through Amber's as they made their way down the hall and stepped into the restaurant, which was full of the most exquisite smells. "But you weren't why I decided to stay. I arrived early the day of my interview and stopped in here. I sat right at that table in the corner to look over my notes."

"And?"

"And I was ready to beg for the job after I'd had the country breakfast."

"You've never told me that story."

"I have a lot of stories I've never told you. But today I want to talk to you about Mary Weaver."

Nine

annah needed to speak to Amber. Using the shop phone, she called the main office and learned that she and Pam had just left for lunch in the restaurant. She didn't like interrupting her boss while she was eating, so she switched plans.

As soon as Seth arrived for his shift, she snatched up her purse and headed to the bakery. Her plan was to purchase two of the large sugar cookies and then visit The Cat's Meow.

Mary Weaver had a sweet tooth. After what she'd been through the day before, Hannah doubted she had the stamina to resist the bakery item. Not that she wanted to tempt her friend, but a little sugar could go a long way toward helping someone relax.

When she walked into Mary's shop, several customers were at the counter and a few others were studying the various types of yarn. Two older women were looking through the pattern books.

Mary was busy checking a customer out. From where she stood, Hannah could hear the woman compliment Mary. "Tatting cotton is hard to find. I'm so glad you carry it."

"Several of the women who work here at the Village enjoy tatting as well."

"I was afraid it was becoming a lost art."

"Not yet. The lace they make is beautiful."

Two of the women standing in front of the yarn bins apparently had a question. They kept glancing over to Mary, so Hannah decided to walk over and see if she could help them.

"There are so many types," Hannah heard the younger woman say. She was probably close to Hannah's age, and she was holding an infant in her arms while gazing at the long line of yarn bins. Rail thin with long black hair, she wore jeans and a T-shirt with the word *Nike* stitched on the front. "How do you choose?"

"Sometimes it's difficult," Hannah interjected. "I try to envision what I'm going to make, and that helps narrow my choices. If I'm planning something for my little *schweschder*, I always choose a purple or lavender."

"You have every color we could want, but we have no idea what type to purchase." This from the second woman, who looked like she was probably the first woman's mother. She was also tall and thin, but her black hair was peppered with gray and cut short. The pink T-shirt she wore said "What Happens at Nana's, Stays at Nana's."

"I don't work here," Hannah admitted. "But I think I can help you."

The younger woman turned to her in surprise.

"Do you knit?"

"I do, and I crochet as well."

The older woman looked from her daughter to Hannah. "We've come to the Village before to purchase Amish-made quilts. I didn't realize that Amish women also knit and crochet."

"*Ya*. In fact, all of the finished items in this shop were made by women in our community. Many of them were done by Mary." Hannah nodded toward her friend, who remained at the counter checking out two women who had chosen several pattern books.

"With crocheting and knitting, most of what we make is for our family members. Occasionally you'll find Amish-made items for sale, but I believe it's rare."

The younger woman jostled the baby from the crook of her left arm to the crook of her right. The little boy—he was swaddled in a blue blanket—looked up at Hannah and smiled.

"How old is your *boppli*?"

"Three months. His name is Cooper."

"Pleased to meet you, Cooper." Hannah reached out and touched his soft, tiny hand, then turned her attention back to the yarns. "So yes, as you can see, Mary carries a wide variety of yarns. She should have whatever you need, depending on what you want to spend and what you plan to make."

"We're beginners." The woman with the "Nana" shirt smiled broadly. "This is something we both have wanted to learn for a long time."

"Mary is considering offering lessons here at the shop."

"You can sign up here if you'd like to receive additional information when they begin." Mary had quietly joined them when the other customers left.

Hannah moved back to one of the large plush chairs and sat to wait as Mary explained the difference between the novelty yarns, synthetics, fleece, cotton, and natural fibers.

"Natural, like"—the young mother wrinkled her nose and squinted her eyes as she glanced around—"sheep?"

"We do have lamb's wool, yes. We also have alpaca and camel."

"Camel?"

Hannah nearly laughed at the expression on the women's faces. But then, that was the reaction most people had when they learned about the man with camels who lived not far from the Village. Manasses Hochstetler had been raising camels for nearly five years now. He sold the milk, and his wife spun yarn from their hair.

Hannah's own brother, Dan, had been helping him the past six months. He was apprenticing with Manasses and would soon have enough money saved to purchase his own camel. Hannah couldn't imagine waking to that sight when she walked outside in the morning.

The women bought three different types of yarn in pastel blue, yellow, and green. No doubt they were making something for baby Cooper. They also took a flyer for classes, although they declined to buy any patterns.

"We found several on the internet." Nana looked slightly embarrassed at the confession. "But thank you."

Hannah realized then that the internet could be a problem for her friend. Could the store be in jeopardy of being closed? If so, what would Mary do for work?

It didn't seem that internet shopping would affect her own shop. *Kaffi? Nein.* Though some people might order *kaffi* beans from internet vendors, many people wanted their morning drinks handed to them—made to order and steaming hot, especially when they were traveling. Her customer base was fairly solid. She hadn't thought to consider how computer shopping might affect the other businesses at the Village.

Finally the store was quiet and empty.

Hannah rattled the bakery bag. "Cookies. Interested?"

"*Ya.* Always."

As they sipped from bottles of water and munched on the sugar cookies, Hannah's anxiety lessened. Mary was sitting beside her, snacking, and acting completely natural. Surely she couldn't be involved in any sort of trouble. She couldn't possibly know anything about Owen's murder.

So she asked her how things had gone at the police station, and Mary told her all about Sergeant Avery's questions as well as her answers.

"I didn't know you were so close to Owen."

"*Ya.*" Her answer was simple, unapologetic, and filled with grief.

"Were you *in lieb* with him, Mary?"

She shook her head, even as two tears escaped and slid down her cheeks. "I said I wouldn't cry anymore, but every time I think of him, it's as if my heart is being squeezed inside by a giant fist."

Hannah reached over and clasped her friend's hand.

"I don't understand how it could happen." She swiped at her cheeks with the back of her hand. "Owen was a *gut* man."

"*Mamm* says as long as we live on this earth bad things can happen, but we must trust and not fear."

"*Ya.* My *mamm* said nearly the same. Owen, though, he was like a younger *bruder* to me. When I opened my eyes this morning, for a moment I had forgotten. Then when I remembered, it was like learning the news for the first time."

Hannah wanted to assure her the pain she was feeling would ease after a time, but how did she know? She'd never lost someone she'd been close to. Even all her grandparents were still alive.

They stood and dumped their napkins and water bottles into the bakery sack Hannah had brought.

"So you're the contact person for our boys who have left, huh? You must have quite a phone bill." Hannah hoped the teasing would raise her friend's mood.

"*Nein.* They call me and only rarely reverse the charges."

"Who are we talking about? Who calls you? And where do they call from?"

"Boys and girls, ones on their rumspringa, call me from all

sorts of places—as close as Goshen and as far away as New York or Florida."

"Do you own a cell phone?" Hannah's voice squeaked, but she lowered it and added, "I know many people our age do."

"*Nein*. I don't even have a phone at home. They call here at the shop, which is one of the reasons I come in early. I wouldn't want to use store time for personal matters."

"Does it show up on the shop's bill?"

"I don't know. I've never actually seen the bill, though customers call all the time to check on what I have in stock. If the personal calls are showing up, Pam and Amber have never mentioned it to me. I sometimes stick an extra ten dollars in the cash register drawer to cover the expense. I wouldn't want to do anything dishonest, but I do want to help those who are struggling. It seemed the best way."

"Is this why you've never married?" The question popped from Hannah's mouth before she considered whether it was her place to ask.

Mary shrugged, but then she conceded, "There is someone I care about. He . . . he hasn't been around much the last few years, until lately."

She'd already said Owen was like a brother. Could she mean Andrew? He was the only other boy in their community who had recently returned. In truth, only a few of the boys from their community had left.

Was Mary suggesting she was in love with Jesse's brother?

Hannah tried to think back to how Mary acted around him, but it had been too long since she'd seen the two of them together.

Three more customers walked into the shop, and Mary hurried behind the counter.

Which was too bad. Hannah had more questions. Like what

was Owen calling her about? What was this group he'd joined called ISG? And who was the man who had been waiting outside the back of The Cat's Meow?

Already one of the new customers stood waiting at the counter to check out. She'd walked straight over to the wool yarn and chosen a rust color. Instead of waiting for Mary to finish checking out the elderly woman, Hannah walked outside into the fall sunshine. And that was when she heard the shouting—unmistakably Amber's voice.

※

Amber stared in disbelief at Roland Shaw, the man standing beside Gordon. She couldn't believe she had just shouted at him. She prided herself in remaining calm, cool, and professional. Unfortunately, Roland Shaw was climbing all over her bad side. This was the person Gordon had explained would be involved in the investigation of Owen's death? Roland towered over her. He must have been over six feet, so she had to tilt her head back to glare at him. He had black hair cut perfectly at the collar line, and his build was a wiry sort of muscular. He held his hands behind his back, as if he were hiding something, as if he were a professor trying to reason with a wayward student.

"What exactly are you saying?"

"That you'll be seeing me around the property until this case is solved."

"And what makes you think you'll find answers here?"

"Call it a hunch." The man was arrogant, irritating, and condescending. She'd known him all of two minutes, and already she didn't like him.

Gordon cleared his throat and jingled the change in his

pocket. "Amber, Roland is a federal agent from Indianapolis. He's working in cooperation with our department to find out exactly what happened and to help us apprehend the guilty party."

"Mr. Shaw." Pam's voice was sweet and carried an accent far more Southern than was usual. "What makes you think this is a federal crime?"

"I can't share that information, ma'am."

Shaw smoothed his tie, a basic black against a plaid shirt. He wore black dress slacks and designer leather shoes. He didn't fit in with Amber's staff or her clientele. He would make everyone nervous, like he was making her nervous. Everything about him screamed trouble, in Amber's opinion.

"It's ISG, isn't it?" Amber clutched her tablet to her chest. "That's why you're here. I did a little research myself today. I discovered that any group with the word *survivalist* in its title is considered antigovernment."

"They are antigovernment." Shaw's voice dropped an octave, all pretense of pleasantness now gone. "And I will not be slowed in my investigation by your desire to protect your friends."

"You're the reason I feel a need to protect them. I will not have you lurking around and intimidating my workers or my guests."

"Why don't we move this inside?" Gordon suggested.

But the last thing Amber wanted was to be in close quarters with this man. He reminded her of a hungry hyena.

"Just because they're Amish doesn't mean they're survivalist."

"I fail to see any difference." Shaw ticked off his reasoning on his overly long fingers. "Large bunkers—"

"I think you're referring to cellars, which most homes around here were built with."

"Large supplies of canned goods put back."

"A practice they have followed for generations."

"Collection of arms." He had ticked off three fingers.

"They hunt," Pam murmured, "which isn't a crime last time I checked."

Gordon, for his part, was looking distinctly uncomfortable, but he also wasn't jumping in to argue with Shaw.

"A distrust of the medical community."

Amber was speechless. How did she explain the Amish culture to this man? He obviously had no desire to hear the truth.

"And most telling of all, a disrespect for the US government."

Amber, Pam, and even Gordon stared at him in disbelief.

"I'm merely pointing out the obvious."

"They are Amish." Amber spoke as if she were trying to reason with a toddler. "Do you know anything about the Anabaptist faith?"

"I'm not asking for a history lesson. In fact, I'm not *asking* for anything. As a courtesy, I stopped by to inform you that I will be watching. I'll also question your employees as I deem necessary. If you have a problem with that, maybe there's something you haven't told Sergeant Avery."

Shaw turned and sauntered off—it was the best word for the way the man walked.

Amber and Pam were left staring at Gordon.

"Stay calm, Amber."

"Calm?"

"I don't like this any more than you do." And with that confession, Gordon trudged off after his new sidekick.

"Trouble in paradise. That's what we have," Pam said.

"Tell me something I don't know." As they walked back toward the office, Amber's mind was whirling.

Shaw's presence had unsettled her day.

The fact that the Village had been thrown into the middle of another murder investigation caused her lunch to turn slightly in her stomach.

But the thing that bothered her most, the thing she knew would distract her from her afternoon work, was what Pam had told her about Mary Weaver.

Trouble in paradise, indeed.

Ten

*J*esse's Friday was turning into a disaster. In fact, it was shaping up to be worse than his Thursday had been. The evening before weighed on his mind, followed him through the day, and set his mood to foul.

All four of his sisters, ages nine to sixteen, had been ecstatic to find Andrew home once again. The youngest hadn't been born the first time Andrew left. Of course, Teresa had met Andrew. He'd managed to show up intermittently through the years. He'd managed to disrupt their lives before.

Susan, Ruth, and Roseann waited on Andrew as his mother had, as if he might disappear before their eyes. And Teresa, the youngest, refused to budge from his side.

Jesse had been sent over to Linda Rainey's with the cinnamon flop cake his mother had made that afternoon, to replace the pineapple cake they'd eaten. It was nearly dark when he crossed the pasture to her house, and he wasn't in much of a mood for visiting. Though it wasn't her fault that his life had taken a curve, Jesse felt his impatience grow as he trudged toward the sprawling one-story house next door.

He remembered Linda's husband, an elderly *Englisch* man named Douglas who drove an old Ford truck. He'd died only two years earlier. Linda could have moved to Indianapolis to live with one of her children, but she insisted that she intended to spend her last days on the farm where she'd lived since she married.

As soon as he spied her sitting on her front porch, his irritation melted away. She'd always been a kind woman, even when he and Andrew were boys and constantly cut across her fields because it was a faster route home. Back in those days, before the lupus had crippled her hands, she'd been the one to bake and offer cookies, brownies, and oat bars to the boys. Now his mother was returning the favor. It was what neighbors did.

"Good evening, Linda." He climbed the porch steps and stopped.

Linda sat in one of her two oak rockers, her hands curled around a lap quilt. Jesse knew she'd probably used it all afternoon, though the day had been warm.

"Jesse, it's good to see you. I do enjoy visitors so much." She motioned to the empty rocker. "Sit and tell me what you've brought today."

Still standing, Jesse replied, "Cinnamon flop cake."

"Your *mamm* knows I won't be eating an entire cake myself."

"She thought you could share it with the nurse who visits."

"Yes, that's a good idea. Also, my grandchildren will be here this weekend. It will be nice to have something sweet to offer them."

"Would you like me to take it inside?"

"Yes, I would appreciate that. I've left the dish from last week near the sink drain. It's washed and ready to go back. And perhaps you could bring us both a glass of lemonade. The pitcher is in the refrigerator." He started inside and she called after him, "Place that cake on the kitchen counter for me and set it well back. Though your *mamm* has wrapped it up nicely, Socks might be tempted to knock it off onto the floor."

Socks was an old, gray tomcat with white feet. Linda had adopted him years ago, and occasionally Jesse spied the cat prowling through the high grass or, more often, lying in the sun, dozing. As far as Jesse knew, he'd never done a thing to earn his keep. He definitely wasn't a mouser; a few weeks before Jesse had set traps behind the stove for a mouse Linda had seen. As he'd baited the traps with cheese and peanut butter, Socks had lain there in the middle of the kitchen floor, methodically grooming himself with a purr that rattled like an old-time coffeemaker. The cat was useless.

There was no sign of him in the house.

Jesse had been in Linda's home many times. It looked no different than it ever had, down to the checkerboard sitting on the table by the window. He knew Linda didn't play checkers, but Douglas had. She kept the board there for the grandchildren. If he remembered right, she had three—two girls and a boy.

He walked back out onto the porch, carrying the empty baking pan under his arm and a glass of lemonade in each hand. He gave one to Linda and drank his in a long gulp. The cold, tart sweetness slid down his throat, easing an ache he didn't realize was there. After finishing the drink, he wavered between the rocking chair and the steps.

"Go ahead and sit. You know you want to."

"*Ya.* It's a nice evening for sitting outside, but I should probably be going."

"Because your brother's home?"

Jesse squinted at her in surprise.

"I saw him walking down the lane toward your house. Near lunchtime, wasn't it?"

"*Ya.*" Jesse sat down in the rocker. When he did, he had a clearer view of Linda. She'd been sitting in the darkened corner of the porch since even the fading sunlight irritated her lupus.

Sinking farther back into the rocker, with the light from a living room lamp spilling through the window, he had a good look at her hands. They were swollen as usual, but they were also covered in an angry red rash that extended up her wrists and probably under the long sleeves of her cotton blouse.

Linda was in her late fifties, maybe even sixty now. Her hair was cut in a short, straight fashion and had turned mostly gray. It reminded him of the wool caps Amish boys and even men often wore. She always wore loose-fitting pants and large cotton shirts. Perhaps the baggy clothes irritated her skin less. As he studied her, she reached up, nudged her glasses aside, and rubbed at her right eye.

"The rash is worse today, but there's no need to look so concerned, Jesse. The Lord won't give me more than I can handle with His help."

He nodded. The words were easy enough to believe when quoted at church meeting, but difficult when looking at Linda's hands. How did she bear it? And what of all the idle time she had? He couldn't think of many things he could do without the use of his hands.

As if reading his thoughts, Linda said, "I enjoy sitting here and watching the world, studying all of God's creation. I decided after Douglas's death that I could either spend my remaining years feeling sorry for myself or appreciating God's handiwork. Appreciation is always the better choice. Now, tell me about your brother."

"As you said, he's home."

"To stay?"

"Hasn't said that."

"I know how your mother worries over that boy. It would be good if he was done with his wandering."

Jesse wondered about that. Would it be good? It had been so long—he had a hard time remembering what life was like with Andrew around on a daily basis. Though he'd resented his brother's leaving, he couldn't say he was thrilled about his return. How messed up was that?

"Seems like only yesterday when you two were dashing across the back of our property, hurrying home from school."

"Do you remember the summer your husband kept a bull in that pasture? It's the one time I can remember him being angry, when we climbed the fence and ran. We were convinced that we could outrun the bull. We did too, but not by much."

Linda smiled, the years falling away. "He came home and told me that you boys were going to give him a heart attack. Douglas found a buyer for that bull the next week and put sheep back there instead."

"Which were much easier to run through."

The stars were beginning to make an appearance. Jesse knew he should head back home, but it was peaceful and quiet on the porch. Sitting there, he could forget about the questions swirling through his mind.

"Andrew must have missed his home."

"I'm not sure that's the reason he returned."

"I say that because I saw him earlier today. First he carried that large pack into your barn, and then he made his way past it—to the creek, I imagine. You two boys used to fish there every chance you had."

"Haven't seen a fishing pole in Andrew's hands in years."

"Perhaps he was soaking up the memories rather than pining for fish."

"Maybe so."

When Jesse stood to go, Linda rose from the rocker, walked to his side, and reached up to place a swollen hand on his shoulder. "You've been a good son to your parents, Jesse. I know your mother and dad appreciate all that you've done, all that you've had to do since you've been the only boy around."

Were his concerns so transparent?

Jesse didn't know how to respond, so he thanked her for the lemonade and left.

⚜

The rest of the evening had passed quickly, and he'd gone to bed before Andrew. He wasn't ready to have a private conversation with him. He didn't understand the uneasiness and confusion he was feeling. Was it Andrew's fault? Or his? And what was he going to do about it?

Now today, as he worked at the Village, he still couldn't say what was causing his unease. Andrew had risen early and helped them in the barn. They'd had breakfast together, and then Andrew had walked to town, claiming he needed to meet someone.

Jesse saw him dart into the barn before he left.

No doubt to reclaim something he'd hidden there in his backpack. The pack had never come into their bedroom, and he had never brought it into the kitchen where Andrew had first appeared during lunch. So he must have stored it outside on the porch until he could take it to the barn, as Linda had seen.

What was in the pack?

Who was he meeting in town?

And why had he gone down to the pond the day before? Had he met someone there? Perhaps he had gone there to make some phone calls in private. Jesse had no doubt his brother had a cell phone. His father wouldn't reprimand him about it unless Andrew brought it into the house.

What—exactly—was his brother involved in?

And did it have anything to do with Owen's murder?

Eleven

annah went in search of Jesse and found him helping the work crew. They were still repainting the old, red covered bridge, though they hadn't been able to start on the barn roof repairs yet. He looked up in surprise when she called out to him.

"I thought you were getting off at five." His response was a blank look, so she added, "You said you wanted to go to the library with me. *Dat* allowed me to bring the buggy because he knew I needed to go into town after work. I stayed late so we could go together."

Jesse removed his hat and wiped the sweat off his forehead with the back of his arm. "I suppose I forgot about that."

"Oh." Hannah glanced around and then back at him. "If you'd rather not go—"

"*Nein*. I want to go. Can you give me ten minutes to help put up these supplies?"

"We'll take care of that, Jesse." Preston Johnstone was the new assistant manager of maintenance. Last spring he'd been helpful in catching Ethan Gray's killer. Though he was homeless at the time, Amber had offered him a job. He was one of Hannah's favorite people at the Village—soft-spoken, friendly, and quick to finish his work.

She'd heard that he once served in the military. Folks said his time in the service fighting had caused him problems when he came home. She couldn't imagine such a soft-spoken man carrying a gun, but she supposed it was possible. He did have a no-nonsense resolve about him.

"Thank you, Preston, but there's no need." Jesse stored his hammer and tape measure in his toolbox and motioned toward the maintenance shed. "I've finished measuring, and now I can order those materials for our roof repairs. I have to pick up my lunch bucket, so I'll take these back since we're going there."

Hannah walked beside him, feeling something was wrong but unable to guess what it was.

Jesse stored his toolbox, found the small cooler he used for a lunch bucket, and led the way out to the parking area.

With a start, Hannah realized what was different, why Jesse seemed so distant. He hadn't smiled once and he hadn't touched her. Usually Jesse reached out and put a hand on her arm, guided her by putting a palm under her elbow, or even held her hand. As they walked toward where she'd left Shiloh, a sleek, black, five-year-old gelding, she shot little glances at Jesse.

He harnessed the horse to the buggy in no time, and they set off toward town. The privacy of the buggy might be the only alone time they had, so she decided to ask him what was going on. Better to know than to wonder and worry.

"Would you like to share with me what's bothering you?"

Jesse looked at her in surprise. "What makes you think something's bothering me?"

"You're acting different."

"Different?"

"*Ya.*" Hannah blushed slightly as she spoke the worries in

her heart. "You're keeping a distance between us, and you seem lost in your own thoughts."

"I believe you're imagining things, Hannah Bell."

The pet name eased some of her worries for a moment, but before they'd ridden another mile those concerns rushed back like a persistent storm. They walked into the library, a new, modern building. Hannah loved visiting it. There were plenty of computers, books, and magazines. Clusters of comfortable chairs were positioned here and there. The library even had a snack area with coffee, sodas, vending machines, and small tables.

Hannah headed toward the magazine racks and proceeded to look through the newest editions for drink recipes. Usually Jesse would spend his time perusing the agriculture magazines or occasionally do online research about some sort of farming technique. This evening he did neither. Instead, he sat in one of the armchairs, a closed magazine on his lap, staring off across the room.

Hannah found two recipes she thought her clients would like, copied the ingredients and directions into her notebook, and returned the magazines to the rack. When she touched Jesse on the shoulder, he jumped and his magazine fell to the floor. He picked it up, set it on the table, and they walked outside where Shiloh was patiently waiting.

Normally at this point Jesse would suggest they go for a scoop of ice cream, or maybe have some coffee and pie at the corner deli. Instead, he directed Shiloh toward home, his shoulders hunched and his hat pulled down low, silently brooding as he stared out the front of the buggy.

Brooding was the perfect description of Jesse at the moment.

Hannah didn't want to push by asking again what was bothering him, but she couldn't figure out what could be causing this drastic change in her boyfriend. And Jesse was her boyfriend. A few days ago she'd thought he might be about to ask her to marry him. Now it seemed he didn't even realize she was in the buggy.

When they reached her home, Jesse glanced around in surprise, as if he hadn't been the one to drive them there.

"I'll help with Shiloh," he muttered.

"And I'll run and tell *Mamm* we're taking care of the buggy." She started toward the house, then turned back toward him. "Don't leave. I'm coming right back out."

"Huh?" Jesse had exited the buggy, too, and was holding on to Shiloh's halter. "Oh, *ya*. Okay."

Hannah closed her eyes, praying for patience and courage.

Then she rushed inside and explained to her mother she'd eat a sandwich after Jesse left.

"Take him some of the cookies, Hannah. I was hoping Jesse would come in. I baked these an hour ago and most of them disappeared, but I kept a few away from your siblings."

"And *Dat*."

"*Ya*, he has a sweet tooth too."

Hannah accepted the cloth napkin, wrapped around still-warm oatmeal cookies. She hurried out to the barn.

Jesse stood there brushing Shiloh, something he didn't need to do. Her brother would have taken care of it the next morning. But perhaps Jesse needed the moments with the horse. Perhaps spending some time caring for the gelding calmed the agitated places in his soul. Hannah felt that way when she quilted or crocheted or knitted, when she needed to quiet the noise in her mind.

She waited and watched him for a few moments. Then she walked back out into the main room of the barn, picked up two milking buckets, and brought them into Shiloh's stall. She turned them upside down. Jesse had already placed a cup of oats in

Shiloh's bin. She took the brush from his hand and returned it to the shelf where they kept grooming tools. Then she covered Jesse's hand with hers and pulled him toward the buckets, where she sat down on one of them.

"Let's talk."

"Talk?" Jesse plopped down on the other bucket.

"Yes. Tell me what has you so distracted. You haven't been yourself all evening."

Jesse wiped his hands against his pants, then sat forward—elbows on knees and his gaze directed toward the floor of the stall. "I'm not sure where to start."

"We're *freinden*. Start there."

She expected him to give her a sheepish smile. That's what the Jesse she knew—the Jesse she loved—would have done. Instead, he worked some dirt out from under a fingernail and shrugged.

"Why are you afraid to talk to me?"

"I'm not afraid."

"Then what?"

"I don't know!" He stood and walked to the other side of the stall, then commenced pacing back and forth across the small area. "Everything's off somehow. I don't understand what to make of it all, and I don't know why it's bothering me so much, but it is."

"It's okay to be upset about something."

"Maybe I'm imagining it."

"Doubtful. Your imagination isn't that good."

Instead of laughing, Jesse stared at her. Finally he returned to the bucket and sat down. "You're right. I don't usually see what isn't there. Remember when we had that project in school to write a story about someone you'd never met?"

"It's the only paper I can remember that you failed."

"*Ya.* My focus is usually on the things I see."

"So what have you seen?"

"Owen's death. Actually, I heard of it. I didn't see it. Then Andrew showing up the same day, the same morning."

Hannah's heart thumped against her chest. "You don't think Andrew was involved?"

"How could he be? But he hasn't said why he's back."

"Maybe—"

"He hasn't said how long he's staying."

"If you—"

"And he's sneaking around, which isn't like Andrew. He's always been bold about his rebellion before."

"He's not a child anymore, Jesse. He's a man. Same as you are."

"But what is he involved in? How can I protect my parents when they think he's the prodigal son returned?"

"I doubt your parents need protecting."

"They do, Hannah. You didn't see them after Andrew left the last time."

"I did—"

"*Nein*. You saw the face they presented in public—at church and work-ins. But at home? They were completely different, broken in some way. These trials with Andrew, they've aged my folks. Just when we seem to reach some sort of balance, he returns. It's not fair. I don't want to see them hurt by him again."

Hannah reached over and claimed one of his hands in hers. "It's *gut* to care for your family, but perhaps you're borrowing trouble."

"I don't think so." Jesse told Hannah about his worries. It seemed to her that he left out nothing, describing his temper, which he had to hold constantly in check, his frustration, and the way his family was openly embracing Andrew once more.

"You need to go and talk to him."

"To Andrew?"

"Who else? Yes, Andrew. Your *bruder*. Talk to him about your concerns."

Jesse considered that but didn't answer. Finally he said, "I haven't tried that yet. I'm afraid the more I know, the more I'll need to know. I'm afraid any answers Andrew gives will only result in more questions. Questions that I'm not sure I want the answers to."

They walked outside, underneath the canopy of stars. Hannah stopped and stared up at the thousands of points of light. She had read about how sailors in the old times used the stars to guide their way. It seemed to her that God had placed them there for her as well, for her and Jesse. The beautiful lights in the night sky struck her as a promise that he wouldn't leave them in darkness. He would help them through whatever it was that was happening.

She handed him the napkin with the cookies. "From *Mamm*, for your walk home."

"It's barely half a mile."

"Wouldn't want you losing your strength."

He pulled her to him then, wrapped his arms around her waist, and rested his chin against the top of her head. "You're perfect for me. You realize that, right?"

Her heart tripped, and she almost reached up to kiss him. Instead, she stepped back and smiled. They were able to see each other by the light streaming through the sitting-room window of her home. His expression was one of love. She knew that without a doubt. As she watched Jesse, he reached up, resettled his hat, and stared at her. She thought he was about to say something.

He didn't.

Instead, he stepped away, though he still held her hand as they walked to the front of the house. Would their relationship always be this way? She wanted him to be open and honest with her, but it seemed at times that he held back. Though she was certain he cared for her, she couldn't help worrying sometimes. A man and a woman needed to be truthful with each other—in all things. Maybe they weren't ready for a relationship. Maybe they had rushed things.

But it wasn't the words of love he didn't utter that bothered her the most. It was the words he said before he turned down the lane that broke her heart. "I wish Andrew hadn't come home. I wish he'd left us alone."

Twelve

*A*mber brushed out her hair while sitting in front of the old-fashioned dressing table. An off-white princess style, it had been designed with an oval mirror in the middle and a single drawer in the center. The matching bench she sat on was covered with a pink fabric. The set had belonged to her mom, and her sister had brought it up to Middlebury four years ago—nearly five years ago now that she thought about it.

Some days she still had trouble accepting that her parents were gone. They'd enjoyed a good and productive life. There was no tragedy there. It was more that she wasn't ready to be an orphan, even at the age of forty-five. Her dad had died of a heart attack at the age of seventy-four. Cancer had claimed her mother six months later, though in fact Amber knew her mom had won over that dreadful disease. She'd never given in emotionally or spiritually. Her mom was a mere seventy-one years old when she'd passed from this life to the next. Amber had been stunned at the double loss of both parents so close together. If there was any silver lining, it was that she and her sister had become extremely close.

Madison still lived in Topeka, Kansas, in their parents' home. She visited Middlebury every other year, and Amber tried to get back to Topeka in the alternate years. The last time Madison had been to see her was for their wedding. She'd arrived a week early so they could spend plenty of time together.

Family had always been important to Amber, more so the older she grew. Perhaps that was part of the reason she was having trouble with her emotions this evening. Her mind seemed to be at least two steps behind her heart.

"I think you've reached a hundred brushes, so why don't you come to bed?"

She glanced up and caught Tate studying her, his book lowered, Leo purring on the pillow next to his head.

"It's like sit-ups. A few extra never hurt."

"Yes, but Leo is eager to spend some quality time with you."

"He told you that, did he?"

"Pretty much. Your cat tolerates me, but he adores you."

"And I adore you both right back."

"See what I mean?" Tate scowled at the yellow cat. "We're in competition, you and me. May the best male win."

"Tell me you're not jealous of a cat." Amber pulled back the covers on her side of the bed and slipped in between the sheets. Leo immediately moved to lie on her feet and resumed his purring.

"That would be ridiculous," Tate agreed, though he continued scowling at the cat.

"Still reading that history book?"

"Yes. Indiana sounds like a different place when I read this." He closed the book and tapped the cover. "The way this author describes Elkhart Prairie and Little Elkhart River, well, it sounds like something from a dream."

"Probably a more peaceful time then. I doubt folks killed each other with crossbows."

"I'm not sure. It's always tempting to romanticize the past.

Though things were simpler, it was a harsh time and violence wasn't unheard of."

Amber thought about that a minute, then shrugged. "If you were reading a good novel, you'd be finished already."

"I don't want to be finished. I enjoy reading slowly." He drew out the last word as she snuggled into his arms. When she didn't respond, Tate asked, "Still worried about Mary?"

"Yes. When Pam told me all that has been going on, it made me wonder if I should contact Mary's parents."

"She's how old?"

"Thirty."

"Would you have appreciated someone contacting your parents at that age?"

"Well, no. But—"

"So she closed the store at lunch a few days. Pam spoke to her about it, and I expect it won't happen again."

"What about the mysterious man she was with?" Amber sat up, plumped her pillow, and leaned back against it. "And did I tell you about the envelope of money Pam found in her shop?"

"Not our business."

"I would agree normally. Pam only went into the shop because something tripped the alarm. When she reached under the counter to shut it off, the envelope fell off the shelf and the cash fell out."

"Maybe she was setting back some of her paycheck each week. We can't know."

Amber sighed and crossed her arms. What Tate said made sense, except who put her own name on an envelope full of money? And wouldn't she have kept it at home instead of at work? Most important, why was the name and number for an ob/gyn doctor in Nappanee also on the envelope?

Mary's confession that she had been helping Amish men and women who had left the community explained some of the strange happenings, but not all of them. Something was not right with the entire situation, but Amber couldn't put her finger on the problem.

"I'm worried about her."

"Thirty-year-olds have minds of their own. Not much you can do but let them know you care and offer help, which they usually turn down."

An image of Tate's older son, Collin, popped into Amber's mind. Collin was married with a seven-year-old daughter named Camille. Amber had held high hopes about being a good grandmother, but some days she wondered if Collin would ever give her the chance. "Now I believe you're talking about a certain twenty-eight-year-old."

"It's possible." Tate rolled to his side and ran his fingers up and down her arm.

"When we married, I thought we'd be one happy family. It hasn't quite turned out that way." Amber's heart twisted when she thought of the last few calls from Collin. They'd arranged to have him come visit twice, but both times Collin had changed his mind. Amber wasn't sure how his wife, Brenda, felt about her or how she viewed Tate's remarrying. Amber had spent so little time with the family that she couldn't begin to guess.

"Give him time. He'll come around. Not to mention Alan thinks you're tops."

"Yes, your younger son and I hit it off right away, probably because we're both business majors."

"And you're both Colts fans."

"How can Collin not like the Colts?"

"I believe they broke his heart when he was a teenager. He's been a Bears fan since."

"Who up and changes their team like that?"

"You changed when you moved here."

"Not the same. I've been away from Kansas longer than I lived there. Why would I still feel any loyalty to the Chiefs?"

"Why do you care about football at all? Still strikes me as a miracle that I fell in love with a woman who is beautiful, manages a complex that includes a bakery, and roots for my football team."

She scrunched back down under the covers next to him, and Tate reached over and turned out the light.

"But I want Collin to like me."

"He will, when he gets to know you."

"If he doesn't avoid us forever."

"He said he'd be here for Thanksgiving."

Amber ran her fingers across Tate's cheek. She liked the feel of his whiskers in the evening, though he shaved them smooth and clean each morning. "It's not like I expected or even want to take the place of his mother."

Tate claimed her hand in his and kissed it once. "Collin was especially close to Peggy. He misses her still, but he will come around. Some people need more time than others."

"And Mary?"

"Perhaps she needs more time too. Maybe, given a few more days, she'll talk to you about what's happening and how you can help."

Amber fell asleep praying that was true. Praying for Mary and her safety. Praying for Collin, that the barrier so evident between them would fall. And praying for Tate, thanking the Lord He had seen fit to give her such a good man. Her last thought as she submitted to the pull of a deep sleep was that God's blessings had been abundant, and He would see them through whatever lay ahead.

❦

Jesse woke in the middle of the night and realized someone was moving around his room. He reached for his flashlight and flipped it on. Andrew barely looked up. He was fully dressed and tying his shoes.

"Going somewhere?"

"That would explain putting on my shoes."

"Not to mention that jacket you're wearing."

"That too." Andrew's voice was matter-of-fact, and he no longer wore the smile he'd had plastered on his face since arriving home.

Jesse swung his legs to the floor and sat up, rubbing at his eyes.

"What time is it?"

"Too late for you to be up, baby *bruder*."

"I'm the baby *bruder*? Look who's acting like a child. Aren't you a little old to be sneaking out of the house in the middle of the night?"

"Yes, I suppose I am." Andrew picked up the money he'd dropped onto the nightstand between their twin beds. "So maybe I'm not sneaking."

"Sure looks like it. And where are you going, anyway? You must be into something you shouldn't be or you wouldn't need to creep out at . . ." Jesse shone the light on the small battery-operated clock sitting on the nightstand. "Two a.m."

"Keep your voice down or you're going to wake *Mamm* and *Dat*."

"*I'm* going to wake them?" Jesse fought against the urge to shout at his brother, but his anger was building. He wanted to grab Andrew and shake him. "How about your sneaking around is going to wake them? Not to mention once they realize you're not here to stay you'll break their hearts again."

"Go back to sleep." Andrew stepped out of the room. Jesse could tell he was carefully avoiding the places on the steps that creaked and groaned as he descended the stairs. Apparently some things about home you never forget. The two of them had been avoiding the noisy side of the staircase for years.

Jesse threw on his clothes and shoes and hurried downstairs after him. Andrew was already out of the house and out of sight, but Jesse knew where he'd find him.

He slipped out the back door as stealthily as Andrew had. Crossing the yard, he didn't worry about making noise. The night had turned cool, and he was sure all the windows in the house behind him were closed. No one would hear them now. When he stepped inside the barn, he wasn't surprised to find Andrew had lit a lantern. He did find it curious that his brother was pawing through his backpack in the middle of the night.

"Why not take the whole thing?"

"I might need to get in and out quickly. The less I carry with me, the better." Andrew pulled out his cell phone, a piece of paper, and a pen. He zipped up the backpack and placed it behind the pails their mother used for harvesting vegetables.

"*Mamm* might be done with those, but *Dat* will start cleaning this place up next week. He does it every October. He's going to find your pack."

"I know. I remember the fall cleaning." Andrew's smile turned wolfish. "I appreciate your concern, but I'll take care of it before next week."

"What does that mean?"

When Andrew reached to turn off the gas lantern, Jesse stayed his hand.

"What does that mean . . . before next week?"

Andrew shook his head.

"Does it mean you'll be gone again by next week?"

"I can't talk about that right now."

"You will talk about it, or I'll wake *Dat* and tell him—"

"Tell him what?" Andrew's eyes stared into his. He looked like a different person suddenly, older and tired.

"I don't know. Maybe that you're in some kind of trouble. If you cared about him at all, you would respect him. You wouldn't be sneaking around like this. All you think about is yourself. Isn't that right? You never stop to consider how the things you do affect our parents."

Something crossed over Andrew's features—something akin to regret. "You think you know my mind."

"I do! I've been following in your footsteps since I learned to walk."

"Not something I'd recommend at this point."

"Why? Because you're selfish? Because you are intent on choosing the wrong path?"

"Don't make the mistake of thinking you've got me figured out. There are parts of my life you know nothing about. Parts you couldn't begin to understand—"

"I don't understand any of it. You're like a stranger to me. Nothing you've done makes any sense, so how can I understand you?"

"I suggest you stop trying."

"Why?"

"There are things I can't explain to you right now, and I have to go."

A deep sorrow filled Jesse's heart, one that cut almost as deep as the sorrow he felt the first day he'd awakened to find his brother gone. "Why don't you care about us at all? What kind of person can be so cold to his own family?"

"You have no idea how I feel. Don't think you can see inside me." Andrew left the lantern on. He walked across the barn and stopped with his hand on the barn door. "But there's one thing I can tell you without any doubt. I do care about you. I care about every person in our family."

"But you keep making the same mistakes over and over."

Jesse thought his brother would leave, walk out into the night without another word. "I have made mistakes. I'll own up to that. There are many things I wish I could change. Things I know I should have left alone. But this? *Nein.* This I will fix."

Then he was gone.

Jesse waited a span of about ten seconds, then he doused the light and took off after him. He'd follow Andrew. He'd make him see reason.

He half ran to catch up with his brother, who was moving quickly and was already a good ways from their house. But then he saw the small automobile pull off the blacktop, stop in front of their lane, and wait with its lights turned down to dim.

Andrew never looked back.

He got into the car and it sped away, leaving Jesse with his own regrets.

Thirteen

He didn't know whether it was wise or foolish to leave his home, especially after what had happened. He only knew that he had to go. He left well before nine on Saturday morning and walked as far as St. Joseph Valley Parkway, also known as Highway 20. From there he hitched a ride to the outskirts of South Bend. The day was pleasant, as fall was still gently coming in, and he didn't mind the time he spent walking. On several occasions he had hired a driver for the trip, but today hitching seemed more prudent. He woke convinced he needed to lie low. He woke with the desire to be in South Bend burning deep in his belly.

He'd barely stepped onto Highway 20 when the long-haul trucker carrying taco shells pulled over. He hopped into the truck quickly, knowing that the less he was out in public, the less visible he could make himself, the better.

Both of his bags fit easily at his feet as he slammed the truck door shut, and they roared off west. The larger of the two bags held all his turkey call samples. The smaller one held clothes. Though he wouldn't need the clothes, it was best to keep up the right appearances. After all, this was supposed to be a business trip, and in some ways it was. He did intend to visit a few of the local hunting stores. More important was the meeting he would be attending later that evening.

He exchanged pleasantries with the trucker, who was white-haired with a large belly and muscular arms. The man was a talker, who fortunately was able to maintain both ends of the conversation. All he had to do was nod at the appropriate times. Perhaps the trucker had needed someone to talk to. Maybe as he barreled down the freeways of Indiana, he had felt alone.

Forty minutes later they passed the Welcome to South Bend sign.

"You can let me off here."

"I'm going through town. Be happy to take you farther."

"Thank you, but here is good."

He climbed down from the truck, pulled out his two bags, and waved a hand at the trucker. As he began walking, his mind flitted back over the morning. He'd finished what chores needed to be done, made sure everything was in place in the event of an emergency, and then gone on his two errands.

Had that been a mistake? It seemed necessary, though, to absolve him of his sins—if that was possible. And in the second case, to avoid future problems. Worry crept through his heart, but he pushed it away.

What was done was done.

There was no turning back now.

At least he had tried to make it right.

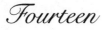

Fourteen

aturday started out calmly enough. Amber and Tate spent most of the day working in the yard. The last of the vegetables had been harvested from their fall garden.

"Next year we could expand it a little."

Tate raised an eyebrow skeptically.

"One more row. So we can have corn and maybe some green beans." She offered her brightest smile.

Amber could practically read her husband's thoughts. They had been married only two months, but that was long enough for her to understand the expression on his face. Tate's opinion was that when you considered the cost of watering the garden, the seed, and the fertilizer if you used any, it was less expensive to purchase the vegetables at the grocer. Not to mention it was much easier given the man-hours they had both spent.

But Amber was swayed by her Amish friends and employees. Hannah, in particular, had explained that it wasn't only what was harvested that made a garden worth the effort. It was also the time spent together tending the plants and appreciating the way God provides.

Tate remained skeptical.

They'd finished with the garden and cleaned off the front and back porches when Gordon Avery drove up in his police cruiser. Amber tensed immediately, worried first that Roland Shaw, aka Creepy Federal Guy, would be with him, and then, when she saw he was alone, that he was bringing more bad news.

"Saw you both outside and thought I'd stop for a minute."

Gordon was in his uniform, so Amber knew he was on duty. At two in the afternoon, his shift wouldn't be over yet. She'd dated him long enough to understand the rotation schedule at the police department. He worked one Saturday a month.

"We were wrapping up with the yard work." Tate stopped at Amber's side, stepping close enough that she could feel steadied by him. Then he reached out and shook Gordon's hand. "How are things going?"

"Not bad, but then again, it could be better. Do you two have time to talk?"

Amber hurried inside and returned with three glasses of sun-brewed tea on a tray. They sat on the front porch—Amber and Tate in the swing, Gordon in the chair facing them. When they'd first married, she'd thought it might be awkward being around Gordon. She had been dating him when Tate stepped into her life. Her relationship with Gordon had been hobbling toward its obvious conclusion, but it had taken falling in love with Tate to see that. She'd been relieved when there were no hard feelings and hopeful that the three could become fast friends. A year ago, she wouldn't have thought that possible, but God could do amazing things.

"I was worried you'd brought Shaw with you." Amber had told Tate all about Roland Shaw, but it was possible that he thought she was exaggerating. Maybe it would have been good if he'd met the man, though she supposed she would spare him that aggravation if at all possible.

"Roland is . . . an interesting guy." Gordon rubbed the condensation from the side of his glass. "And he is one of the reasons I stopped by. It was pretty apparent you two didn't exactly hit it off from the start."

"Not my fault. He thinks all Amish are survivalists. He thinks they're crazy."

Gordon held up his hand to stop her attempt at self-defense. "I'm not saying I agree with his beliefs, but he is on the right side of this. He wants to find Owen's killer as much as we do."

"But he's ignorant and he—"

"I checked him out, Amber. He has a good record. He doesn't prosecute unless he can convict. Roland won't do anything without evidence." He struggled to repress a small smile. "But yeah, he can come across a little strong."

Amber humphed and sat back against the swing.

"Why did this become a federal investigation?" Tate asked.

"Because of the possible connection to the ISG, which was something we had to report to them as soon as Mary mentioned Owen's recent activity with the group. So the feds sent a man over from Indianapolis to work in cooperation with us. Nothing more."

Amber still didn't like it, though it was possible she had the wrong attitude. There probably was a way to change the man's preconceived notions. Maybe they could take him to a work-in or a charity auction, or better yet, an Amish church service.

"The reason I came by today is to show you this."

Amber hadn't noticed that he was carrying his satchel. It was an old, battered, leather thing. He must have retrieved it from the car while she was fetching the glasses of tea.

He opened the clasp and pulled out a sealed evidence bag. Inside was a note.

"One of Naomi Graber's children found this in her mailbox.

Naomi had sent the girl out this morning to put a letter to her aunt in the box. The girl, Lucy, says it wasn't there yesterday, so whoever left it did so last night or early this morning."

Amber had pushed thoughts of Owen's sister from her mind. She didn't know much about the woman, as she rarely came to the Village. She did know that she had an invalid husband, an older man she had married after her and Owen's parents died. Naomi and Jonas quickly had six children, but now raising those children fell squarely on Naomi's shoulders. Hannah had mentioned her in passing, never providing much detail. If Amber remembered correctly, Hannah sometimes took day-old bakery items to her. Amber was more than happy to see the leftovers put to good use. It might seem odd that her own path was now crossing with Naomi's, but that was often the way of things in a small town.

Tate had accepted the note. Amber scooted closer to him on the swing, and together they read it, quickly the first time and then more slowly the second.

Naomi,

> *I regret your bruder is dead.*
> *I don't regret my part in it, only that it had to happen.*
> *We know that when a life ends, it is complete.*
> *I pray that you are able to heal and forgive.*
> *At least Owen was trying to prepare. You should do the same.*

Amber blinked, rubbed her eyes, and read the note a third time. It didn't make any more sense than it had the first or second readings. She glanced up at Tate and then over at Gordon. "This was left in her mailbox?"

"It was, along with five hundred dollars."

"I don't understand." Amber shook her head as she pointed at the evidence bag Tate was still holding. "What does it mean?"

"And why are you showing it to us?" Tate's voice had grown somber. Apparently he was as shocked by the note as she was.

"I was hoping you might recognize the handwriting."

"Why would I?"

"As you can see, he makes his letter *I* in a pretty distinctive way. If the killer is a Village employee, you could have seen it before."

"He's not!"

"You can't know that."

"Why would you even think he would be?"

"There's a connection to the Village through Mary, and we have to follow up on any possible clue." As an afterthought, he added, "I'm asking all of the businesses who hire a large number of Amish. Don't think I'm zeroing in on you."

Amber closed her eyes and sighed heavily. She was too jumpy about all of this. But her emotions were like untrained horses, dashing here and there at the slightest provocation. "If you'll e-mail me a copy, I'll show it to Elizabeth. She handles most of our employment paperwork. Maybe she'll recognize the handwriting."

Gordon nodded.

"Fingerprints on the note?" Tate asked.

"Yeah. Lots of them. But whoever it is must have a clean record. They're not appearing in any of our databases."

"So he hasn't done this before."

"He hasn't been caught before. We also keep a record of fingerprints from unsolved crimes, and his don't match up with anything there."

"You're sure it's a he?" Amber was remembering the last investigation she'd been involved in. It was best not to assume anything.

"Given the violence of the crime and the amount of money—most Amish women don't have that much lying around—yes. I'd bet my pension that it's a man."

"What *about* the money?" Amber felt as if her insides were quivering, but she forced herself to think about this logically. They needed to catch this creep, and Gordon was actually asking for her help, at least in some small way. "It's pretty odd for someone to anonymously leave money with a note. Isn't it?"

"It is odd, though not completely unheard of. Occasionally a murderer experiences remorse and tries to atone for what he's done—not that five hundred dollars is much atonement."

"So you've seen this before?"

"Once or twice, when I worked in Indianapolis."

"What will happen to the money?" Tate asked.

"At the moment it goes in the evidence locker, though eventually it will be returned to Naomi."

"Maybe they were trying to buy her silence." Amber worried a fleck of dirt out from under her thumbnail. "Or trying to frighten her by establishing contact."

"Can't say, but the Amish believe in helping one another through difficult circumstances. It could be as simple as that."

"So you think the killer is Amish?"

"I think he could be. There's enough Amish language in the note to indicate that. Or he could be someone who wants to appear Amish."

"To confuse your investigation." Tate sipped his tea.

Gordon shrugged.

"Sounds like a confession to me." Amber pulled the note back toward her and ran her finger down the lines. "'I regret your *bruder* is dead . . .'"

"The next line is curious." Tate drummed his fingers against the back of the swing. "'I don't regret my part . . .'"

Gordon finished his tea and set the glass on the floor. "Seems to indicate there's more than one person involved, which also would suggest it was premeditated."

"Why do you say that?"

"'My part in it' . . . as if there was more than one part. As for the premeditation, I'm not surprised. People don't usually shoot arrows at one another in a fit of rage."

"So you're looking for two people?"

"Or a group."

"ISG." Tate handed back the evidence bag.

"Could be. Roland is leaning that way, especially given the last line. 'Owen was trying to prepare. You should do the same.'"

"Prepare for what?" Amber asked incredulously.

"Preppers prepare for all sorts of things." Gordon placed the evidence bag back in his satchel. "Economic collapse, famine, plagues, government oppression."

"Hang on, Gordon." Tate sat forward, planting his feet firmly on the floor and stopping the gentle motion of the swing. "I know some of the men in our local group, and they're not the nuts you're making them out to be."

Gordon laced his fingers together and stared down at them, but he remained silent.

"They're folks who are doing some commonsense things, and most of those things are encouraged by FEMA and the Red Cross."

Gordon stood. "I've never had any problem out of them, but

then, I've never been to a meeting. Probably isn't cool to invite the local police sergeant. My attitude until now has been to honor their right to free assembly. But if this was a group effort to kill Owen, I will see them disbanded in our town."

They walked with him back to the police cruiser. "If either of you sees anything, or if you hear anything at the Village, please let me know. Amber, I'll e-mail you a copy of the note. Have Elizabeth look at it first thing Monday." He hesitated, then added, "We can't be sure that whoever did this—whether it's a single person or a group of persons—will stop at one murder. We can't know until we understand who it is and why they chose to kill."

Then Gordon got into the police cruiser and drove away.

Fifteen

*I*t was with conflicting emotions that Jesse joined his family in the sitting room Sunday morning.

The chores were done, breakfast had been consumed, and now it was time for their Bible study. As he listened to his father read from the twelfth chapter of the book of Romans, Jesse stared down at his hands.

He would have been more comfortable if they'd had church service today.

Meeting this way, surrounded only by his family, seemed too personal. His feelings were raw, and he was still uncertain whether his brother's return home was a good thing or a terrible thing. Moreover, his family was so happy, so relieved to have Andrew home, that he was becoming consumed by guilt over his attitude. Was he supposed to just trust his brother? Should he accept him back into their lives with open arms?

His father's voice continued—low, solid, sure. Jesse had heard the scripture many times. Perhaps as a child, he'd even memorized Paul's admonition to present your body as a living sacrifice, "holy and pleasing to God." When he'd heard it before, he'd always thought back over the sins he committed. Those transgressions were minor, he supposed, in most people's eyes, but actions that raked against his heart all the same.

A sharp word to one of his sisters.

Some chore he had completed hurriedly and in a sloppy fashion.

Impatience with his parents.

Bitterness toward his brother—that one always nagged at any sense of peace, unsettling his conscience. He could push it down for a few days, maybe even a week, but he could never forget the troubles his brother's selfishness had caused their family. He realized now, as his father's deep voice read from the German family Bible, that he had never forgiven Andrew.

His oldest sister, Susan, followed along in the Bible she'd received for her birthday. It contained German text on one side, English on the other.

"We have different gifts, according to the grace given to each of us."

Almost against his will, Jesse's gaze drifted up and locked with Andrew's. What was his brother thinking and why had he come home?

Did he have a different gift? Was that why he had left?

He'd never actually asked his brother about his *Englisch* life when he saw him in Chicago. He'd been too busy trying to persuade him to come back to Middlebury, to the farm, to come back home—for good.

"Be joyful in hope, patient in affliction, faithful in prayer."

He had not been faithful in prayer. He'd been too busy working, trying to take on the responsibilities for their household as he saw his parents age. He'd certainly not been joyful or patient. Jesse closed his eyes and bowed his head. He felt a sweet release as he handed his burdens over to the Lord. But he didn't stop there; he petitioned God for His forgiveness and asked for patience that his new resolve to be more Christlike might last beyond their private family service.

His mother led them in singing "Burdens Are Lifted at Calvary." It was an old hymn that Jesse had sung as far back as he could remember. He joined in. His younger sisters—even Teresa—were singing with gusto now. Teresa, in particular, was off-key. Somehow the sound was still sweet, the harmony coming from their relationship with each other rather than the notes.

A faint glimmer of hope sprang up in Jesse's heart. Perhaps everything would work out after all.

Apparently Jesse's mother had invited every family in their district to the celebration luncheon.

The buggies began arriving as Jesse and Andrew created tabletops under the trees. They placed planks of wood across sawhorses to hold the bounty of food—casseroles, shaved ham, cold fried chicken, and all types of sliced sausage and cheese. They created a second table that would normally suffice for a vegetable and dessert area, but today they would need more. Each family seemed to feel they should bring several dishes. Jesse's mouth literally watered as the women placed the food on the makeshift tabletops and stepped away.

He couldn't help but notice the smiles on their faces, the spring in the steps of his friends and family, the lightness in their voices. This was a day of celebration—for all of them.

How many had family members who had left to join the *Englisch* or the Mennonites? It was no longer an event that required shunning, at least not in their district and not if it happened before one had joined the church. Still, such incidents were a tremendous strain on the families involved—emotionally, financially, and of course spiritually.

"Andrew, it's *gut* to see you. Glad to have you home."

His brother was greeted by each person in this fashion, and each time the speaker turned to Jesse, clapped him on the back, and said, "Our Lord is *gut*. *Ya?*"

Jesse tried to find the anger that had consumed him the last few days, but it was gone. Perhaps his time of confession and prayer had worked. Maybe he was tired of fighting the fact that he was glad to see Andrew. He had missed his brother. Possibly the combination of divine intervention and his own exhaustion had pushed him past his own bitterness. He was glad his brother was home. Still worried but glad.

More guests made their way from the parking area near the barn, where Ben, Hannah's older brother, was helping with unharnessing the buggies and pasturing the horses. Every direction he looked, family members were smiling at one another. Jesse realized that this day offered hope to those families who were going through similar situations. They saw Andrew, and in Andrew they recognized their own loved ones.

Perhaps one day they too would be a whole family again.

Few of the boys or girls Jesse knew actually left the church. Sometimes it would take a few years before they settled down. Occasionally someone might spend a year or two working at jobs that might not be offered within the community. Others spent their time away sampling what the *Englisch* had to offer— technology, education, a different life.

Jesse's own *rumspringa* had been exceedingly short. For perhaps six months he had carried a cell phone, texting friends and even watching videos on it. Yes, he'd had the internet, which his father had never known about. At least, he didn't say anything about it if he had known.

But soon the fullness of their lives called him. He would

happen by his shelf in the barn, stop to check the mobile device, and find the phone uncharged. So he would set it aside with the intent of charging it when he went into town. And then he'd forget to carry it with him. One day he picked it up, and the device seemed like a child's toy to him. So he'd thrown it into the trash pile and hadn't thought about it since. Until today. That slight rebellion came back to him with startling clarity as he studied the crowd of folks surrounding his family and offering their blessings.

He had stepped away from their community, from their faith, just as Andrew had.

He simply hadn't stepped as far.

Silence fell over those gathered as Bishop Joseph indicated it was time to bless the food. At that moment, Jesse spied Hannah. His pulse jumped, and he couldn't have stopped the smile spreading across his face. She blushed prettily, glanced at her feet, then closed her eyes in silent prayer.

Joseph pronounced a blessing over Andrew and the entire Miller family. Then he asked them to remember Naomi and confirmed what Jesse had heard several people saying—the funeral would be on Tuesday. Naomi would be accepting visitors to view the body at her home on Monday. Pausing a moment, as if to shift the direction of their thoughts, Joseph once again reminded them of the goodness of the Lord. With outstretched arms, he motioned toward the tables, indicating it was time to eat. Jesse's father held up his hand to stop them and thanked everyone for coming. Then there was an orderly chaos as men and children flooded the tables where the women were serving.

Twenty minutes later, Hannah joined him at the old picnic table under the maple tree. "Lots of people came."

"*Ya*, my *bruder* is quite the celebrity." There was no bitterness in his heart, and he grinned at her as he uttered the words.

"You seem happy today."

"I am." Jesse shoveled a forkful of sliced, maple-glazed ham into his mouth.

"So you talked to Andrew?"

"*Nein.*"

Hannah studied him for a moment, her head cocked and a puzzled expression on her face. Then she shrugged and picked up a piece of fried chicken from her plate. "Maybe it's just as well."

"Maybe so." Jesse glanced back toward the main group. He could barely make out his brother, laughing at something someone had said and then looking toward a table of girls. "Maybe all is well."

And it was possible to believe it that afternoon.

So he spent his time resting, as he had been raised to do on the Sabbath.

Soon he was playing volleyball, Hannah on one side of him, Mary on the other. Mary hadn't wanted to play. He'd heard her offer several excuses to Hannah, but once on the makeshift court, she produced a killer serve.

Andrew was on the other side of the net, with a mixed group of boys and girls. His brother seemed completely at ease, none of the anxiety from their Friday night discussion evident on his face.

Jesse enjoyed more food, another game of volleyball, and then a walk alone with Hannah.

The last of his barriers fell away as he clasped her hand and they walked slowly along the banks of the creek. He thought of asking her then, asking her to be his wife. But something told him the time wasn't right. Soon. At the rate things were going, he would ask her to marry him very soon.

Sixteen

annah needed some time alone with her friend, so she opted to walk home with Mary. They could have ridden in a buggy, but the afternoon had turned warm and sunny. Winter would close in soon enough, and walks down the Pumpkinvine Trail would be less frequent.

She breathed in the scent of falling leaves, final crops that had been harvested, and fall flowers in bloom.

They'd walked along in silence for a few moments when Hannah asked, "How are things at the shop?"

"*Gut.*"

"Any new crochet patterns you're working on?"

"A shoulder bag. I'm using a nice cotton blend that is variegated with a combination of Christmas colors. It's turning out nicely. I purchased a new book of patterns, and my goal is to crochet each of the items, then create a holiday display around them."

"I can't wait to see it. I can crochet, but I'm better at knitting. Maybe you'll convert me."

"The two are very similar, but crocheting is a bit faster."

A comfortable silence once again fell around them as they walked, each lost in her own thoughts.

Mary had seemed to enjoy herself at the luncheon, but once or twice Hannah had caught her staring off into the distance, a disturbed look on her face. If Hannah had been pressed to describe it, she would have said it was a look of fear.

"I suppose you'll go to Owen's funeral on Tuesday."

"Oh, *ya*. If Amber can find someone to take my place at the yarn shop."

"I'm sure she will. If no one else, Seth could do it, and I could stay and work his shift at the *kaffi* shop. You were closer to Owen than I was."

"No offense, but I'm a little afraid to leave Seth alone in my shop."

"He's improving. Honest, he is."

Mary considered that but didn't offer a comment. Instead, she changed the subject. "I'm relieved the police have released Owen's body to Naomi. It's a shame she had to wait."

"Police procedures. That's how the bishop explained it to my *dat* when he asked."

"What difference can their procedures possibly make? Dead is dead."

"*Ya*. I suppose. Though finding whoever did such a terrible thing would be *gut* too. Not that I think he'll do it again."

Mary stopped suddenly in the middle of the trail. She stopped so abruptly that a family with five children, each riding a bike, had to swerve around them.

Her voice quavered slightly, and her next words came out in a bare whisper. "He could. He could do it again."

"Why do you say that, Mary?"

"Because I found . . ." She shook her head but then added, "They should leave it alone. Maybe then he'll go away."

"Who will go away?"

When Mary didn't answer, Hannah reached out and clasped

her arm, squeezing more tightly than she had intended. She moved her hand to Mary's shoulder and repeated, "Who will go away?"

Mary resumed walking but not before Hannah noticed that her hands had begun to shake. She clasped them around her middle and hurried down the trail, as if she needed to make up for lost time.

"Do you know who it is, Mary?"

"How would I know that?"

"Do you know more about Owen than you told the police?"

"I know Owen must have stumbled onto something, and it scared someone. Frightened people do drastic things. We should leave it alone." Her voice was becoming firmer, her tone resolute.

"But whoever did this should pay for what they've done." Hannah walked faster to keep up with Mary.

"He will. *Gotte* will pass judgment."

"Yes, of course, but I don't know about leaving it alone. We can't let a killer run around loose."

She reached out to Mary, intending to slow her down. When she did, she saw the tears sliding down her friend's cheeks.

"What is it? Mary, please talk to me. You can trust me, and maybe it will help."

Mary covered her face with her hands, and Hannah tugged her toward the side of the trail.

"I want things to be . . . to be as they were." Her voice shook, and she pulled in a deep, quivering breath. "I want . . . I want to go back to helping folks, helping to bring about reunions like the one we celebrated today. But I can't with all of this going on. I'm too . . . too . . . scared."

Mary scrubbed her face dry, then stared up at the barren tree limbs that created a dappled canopy over the trail.

Hannah didn't know how to respond to her friend's confession or her fearfulness, so instead she looped her arm through Mary's, and they continued down the trail.

Amber and Tate enjoyed a lovely church service, followed by the congregation's annual fall luncheon. Amber was new to Tate's church, but she wasn't new to Middlebury. She had found fitting in to be easier than she'd expected. Actually, the congregation had welcomed her with open arms. It seemed they were happy to see Tate remarried. Though they were from two different denominations, Amber found the differences in theology and worship minor and not a stumbling block for her at all.

After the luncheon, they headed straight home. Usually they spent Sunday afternoons going for a walk or reading books together out on the back porch—both ideas would have sounded crazy to Amber six months earlier. When she was single, she viewed Sunday afternoon as a time to catch up on the previous week's work. Not anymore. It was her family day, and Tate was her family. The problem was that Tate was packing his bag for a three-day trip with his younger son, Alan.

"You're sure that you're okay with this?" Tate studied her as he zipped his suitcase closed.

"Of course. It's something you do every year, and I don't want you to change your traditions for me."

"You can come. Enjoy the hotel room, maybe visit the spa and pamper yourself a bit."

Amber shook her head even as he pulled her into his arms. "I have work to do this week. Maybe next year I'll plan ahead to take the time off, if Alan doesn't mind my intruding."

"He's the one who suggested you come." Tate lowered his head and kissed her thoroughly. Then he murmured in her ear, "Maybe next year you can golf with us."

"Ha! Stick to whispering sweet nothings. I'm a terrible golfer and you know it. I proved it to you the last time we went out to the course together."

"That was two weeks ago. Things change. You could have improved."

"I haven't improved."

"You didn't hit the ground as often on the back nine."

"I stopped playing on the back nine. At that point I was content to drive the cart."

Tate tilted her face up and kissed her again. "Have I told you lately how much I love you?"

"No, and that's one of my favorite songs. You can sing it to me when you get back."

"Deal."

Hand in hand they walked outside, under the covered awning, and to his truck.

"Call me if you need anything." Tate reached for one more kiss.

It was their first three days apart. Amber was basking in the extra attention, but she knew the reality of his being gone would hit her before he'd made it down the drive. "Sure. You too."

She had been independent from the age of eighteen to forty-four. She was sure she'd have no trouble keeping busy.

Three hours later she was sitting on the porch swing reading, or attempting to read. A part of her mind was wondering if she should go into work for an hour. Old habits die hard, especially when you're left alone on a Sunday afternoon. Then her phone rang, and she dropped her book and grabbed for it. Pam's cheery voice traveled over the line, bringing a smile to Amber's face. Her assistant manager was headed out to the big discount store to purchase supplies.

"I thought you might be bored, with Tate gone and all. Care to ride along?"

"Absolutely."

"Need time to get ready?"

"Nope. I'm good to go. Meet you at the Village?"

"I'll pick you up. Once you were at the Village, I'd never drag you away from your in-box."

As she put up her book and grabbed her sunglasses and purse, Amber wondered how Pam could already know her so well. But she did. She was spot-on with the in-box comment. Amber's thoughts skimmed back over her last assistant manager, Larry. That hadn't turned out so well. She'd certainly traded up.

Waiting on the front porch, she thanked God for Pam—for her work ethic, her fresh insights, and her friendship.

Pam pulled into the driveway, horn honking and hand hanging out the driver's side window, waving. She parked the car and stepped out, revealing an orange outfit that looked like something from an African bazaar. The material was covered with safari animals, and the colors would have looked terrible on Amber. On Pam, they accentuated her dark-brown skin and her shoulder-length hairstyle. She looked saucy.

"Love the outfit, but are you sure you want to wear it to go shopping? You might have trouble wrestling all those supplies into the grocery cart."

"That's why I invited you. Besides, I dress professional all week. Saturday and Sunday I wear whatever makes me smile."

"And today that happens to be elephants and giraffes."

"Exactly. Besides, we had a children's choir from Africa singing at our church today. I wanted to make them feel at home."

No wonder Pam's mood was so chipper. She'd enjoyed a children's choir from Africa. She was wearing a fun and comfortable dress, causing Amber to reconsider her blue jeans, and she wasn't counting the hours until her husband returned.

"I didn't think it would be this hard when Tate left. I'm sort of at loose ends." Amber smoothed out the legs of her blue jeans. They were her most comfortable pair—not too baggy and not too tight. She'd also put on her favorite Indiana Colts T-shirt, which boasted raglan sleeves, bright-blue colors, and a logo that read "We Have Luck."

Yeah, she was wearing happy clothes too.

Maybe the rest of the day would go as well as the beginning. Being with Pam always seemed like an adventure.

First they stopped for drinks at the local burger drive-through. Pam wanted a shake, but settled for a soda. Amber wanted a soda, but settled for an unsweetened tea. Twenty minutes later they were pulling into the parking lot of the giant discount store. As they shopped, they gabbed about their individual church services, their upcoming Thanksgiving plans, and winters in Indiana.

"Being from the South, I'm looking forward to it." Pam consulted her list, then rolled their cart toward office supplies. Most of their general supplies were delivered to the Village, but Pam had taken over the chore of maintaining their office supply stock. At least it had seemed like a chore when Amber had done it alone.

"I've heard that from folks before. The novelty wears off somewhere around the third snowfall."

"Uh-huh. Well, I guess you're used to having four seasons. Where I come from—"

"God bless Texas."

"We had two seasons—hot and hotter. No fall. No spring to speak of. Winters were hot. Summers were hotter."

"No snow?" Amber enjoyed hearing Pam embellish about her hometown of San Antonio.

"Nah. Maybe a little rain. Now and then you could wear a light jacket." Pam glanced across the discount store toward the clothing shelves. "Having winter is going to open up entire new avenues to accessorize. I've bought all sorts of gloves and scarves and hats. I wonder what they have here."

"You might be overpreparing."

"You can never overprepare when it comes to accessories." Pam cocked her head and surveyed Amber's jeans and T-shirt.

"Don't even think about it. My outfit is fine without a scarf or hat." She did love the African dress, though. How would that look on her? In a different color, of course. Were her hips too big to be wrapped in elephants? She had gained a few pounds since marrying.

"Discount store to Amber." Pam nudged Amber with her shoulder. "You left me there for a minute."

"Uh-huh. I'm a little distracted, I guess."

As they walked around the store, her eyes fell on a display of hunting gear—camouflage clothing, hand warmers, even doe urine used to attract bucks. Her mind immediately fell back into the nightmare of the last week, of Owen's death and Naomi's mysterious note.

"Stop that!"

"Stop what?" Amber turned to Pam in surprise.

"Worrying. I can always tell when you're doing it, and you're doing it now. You're thinking about Owen again."

"I suppose." Amber walked up to the display and reached out

to touch a hunting jacket. "Do you think when he went out that morning he had any idea it would be his last day on this earth?"

"No. Fortunately, I don't think any of us have that kind of foreknowledge, and who would want it? Better to enjoy your last few hours."

Amber wasn't so sure. She would want to grab those she loved and hold them close.

As they trundled down the aisles, she tried to banish thoughts of Owen from her mind.

Their cart was nearly full after they had wound through the office supply aisles. Now they were standing in front of an endcap that held first-aid kits for businesses, which apparently came in all shapes and sizes.

Pam ran a French-manicured nail down her list, tapping the sheet when she reached the word *Band-Aids*.

"We need Band-Aids?"

"We need to restock our kits. You know, the ones buried in each shop's supply room?"

"Oh yeah."

"Probably those should be in a more accessible spot. Last week we had a guest with a blister on her heel, and I was called to shuttle over Band-Aids. Carol Jennings had forgotten she had any."

"Not something you use often in a quilt shop."

They both stood staring at the large selection of first-aid kits.

"Who would have guessed there would be so many different kinds and sizes?"

"I thought we were looking for Band-Aids."

"Maybe we should buy new kits. What we have right now are ancient."

"Do you think the new ones are any different from the old ones? I mean, it doesn't seem as if much would have changed in first aid. They all contain Band-Aids, aspirin, antiseptic wipes . . ."

As Amber was listing the things she expected to find in a kit, Pam picked one up and began scanning the list of items enclosed inside it. She stopped and squinted closer at the label. "This one has a blanket."

"A blanket?" Amber shook her head in disbelief. "In that small box?"

"It's a space blanket, whatever that is."

A voice over Amber's shoulder explained, "A space blanket is actually a thin sheet of plastic coated with a metallic agent. It's good for many different types of emergencies."

Seventeen

mber and Pam turned to stare at the woman who had stopped behind them. She appeared to be a few years younger than Amber, had beautiful, curly red hair, and was dressed in a mosaic blue skirt and matching blouse from a high-end store. Amber knew where the outfit was from because she'd drooled over it while paging through their most recent catalog. Ultimately, she'd decided it was too expensive.

"What kind of emergencies?" Pam's voice did nothing to hide her skepticism.

"Weather-related is most common, but there are also power outages, pandemics, and terrorist threats." The woman flashed a genuine smile. "What you're looking at is also called a thermal blanket, and they're a handy thing to have in case of a crisis."

"Oh. Maybe I have seen them before on television." Amber realized her reply sounded somewhat moronic, but she'd actually given very little thought to their first-aid kits.

"Who needs a metal blanket?" Pam asked, setting the kit back on the shelf as if it might contaminate her. "Seems like a quilt or a cotton blanket would be better."

"They're actually not. Space blankets are lighter, can fit into a very small storage area, and are better able to help a person retain their body heat."

Amber and Pam stared at each other.

Pam asked, "Seriously?"

"Yes, ma'am. They prevent or counter hypothermia, and they're waterproof." She reached forward to snag the kit Pam had repositioned on the shelf. Running a perfectly manicured burgundy nail down the list of contents, she mumbled, "This is adequate, but you can purchase these supplies for far less and create your own emergency buckets."

"Do we need emergency buckets?" Pam directed the question to Amber, who shrugged.

After what she'd been through the year before, she probably should have been more focused on the Village's medical supplies, but truthfully she preferred to block those events from her mind. Emergency personnel had arrived in time, and the blood had cleaned up well, erasing all traces of that terrible day. She did still suffer the occasional nightmare. What if Gordon hadn't arrived in time? What if Tate had been hurt more seriously? What if Hannah and Jesse had been in the room during the explosion?

Her dreams always presented unsolvable problems—such as being in a room with no windows or doors. Sometimes she found herself running down a hall that never ended. She'd wake from such nightmares wet with sweat. Tate would wrap his arms around her and whisper into her ear until she fell back asleep. During the day, she tried to push the entire subject from her mind. It hadn't even occurred to her to check the first-aid kits.

Once again she found herself thanking God for Pam. Her assistant manager was proving invaluable, plus she was turning into a good friend.

Staring at the large kits in front of them, she wondered if they would stop her nightmares.

A tall man with a close-cropped beard joined the woman.

"I always know where to find you," he teased his wife—at least Amber assumed they were husband and wife. They both had rings on the appropriate finger, and the woman stepped closer to the man when she glanced up and smiled.

"Guilty."

As if noticing them for the first time, the man held out a hand to Amber and then Pam. "My name's Tom, Tom Rhodes."

"And I'm Sue."

"Hello, Tom and Sue. I'm Pam, and this is my boss, Amber."

Now why did she introduce them that way? Technically the description was correct, but more and more Amber felt they were coworkers.

"We both work at the Village," Amber clarified.

"Sure. I know where you mean," Tom said. "We've eaten there a couple of times. Wonderful restaurant."

"It's what attracted me," Pam murmured.

"We had the chicken pot pie last time," Sue said. "Fresh-baked crust. It was a work of art."

"Thank you. I'll pass your compliments on to our cooks."

"We were buying supplies for our medical kits," Pam explained as she glanced at Amber. "Sue stopped and was explaining some of the contents to us."

"My wife is a nurse, and she teaches emergency preparedness classes for the Red Cross. She often lurks around the medical supply aisle, especially here where they seem to have everything."

"They have it, but their prices are still too high, Tom. We're better off ordering online."

"You use the—what did you call them, emergency buckets—in your classes?" Something was pulsing in Amber's mind, like the low hum of an amplifier. She couldn't quite put her finger on what it was—not exactly a sense of déjà vu, but more like something she'd meant to do and forgotten.

"I do use them, and so does Tom. He teaches an emergency preparedness class at our church." When they named their church, Amber recognized it—she'd seen the large, beautiful structure on the outskirts of town.

The pulsing stopped and the thought Amber had been trying to catch surged forward. "Like preppers? Like the Indiana Survivalist Group?"

Pam adjusted her safari dress. "We need to stay away from that group since they could be tied to Owen Esch's killing."

Sue reached forward and touched Amber's arm. "We read about that in the paper. We're so sorry for your loss."

Instead of correcting the woman, instead of explaining that she hadn't personally known the victim, Amber reached into her purse and pulled out a business card. "I'm Amber Bowman, the general manager at the Village. I wonder if you might have time to meet with me next week. I've had some questions about survivalists and the ISG."

"No problem." Tom pulled out his own business card. "But you might be able to find answers to your questions on our website."

He pointed to a web address on the bottom of the card. "Go to this site and click on Missions, then Classes. You'll find a PowerPoint presentation that explains what we do under Prep to Bless. If you have any questions after you've looked through it, my contact information is at the end of the PowerPoint."

"Thank you. That's very helpful."

"Also, I have Red Cross classes every month. E-mail Tom and he'll forward you my schedule. It never hurts to be prepared."

"We're not members of the local survivalist group," Tom

clarified. "We have our own group at church that has the same function but with a biblical emphasis. We do interact occasionally with the ISG, though, and they're a fine group of folks. I can't imagine them being mixed up in that young man's murder."

Amber nodded, and Pam thanked them for their help.

Both waited until the couple was two aisles away to discuss what they'd heard.

"Church survivalist group? That sounds a little hinky to me." Pam had bypassed the large first-aid kits and dropped three supersize bags of Band-Aids into their cart.

"They didn't look like survivalists, or what I imagined survivalists would look like."

"He didn't have a long beard."

"Exactly."

"She wasn't wearing a prairie dress."

Amber attempted to relax her shoulders. If she wasn't careful, this was all going to give her a giant headache, and that was not how she wanted to spend Sunday evening. "It is interesting that a survivalist happened to pop up while we were shopping."

"I suppose. My momma would say to watch yourself and don't walk too close to trouble."

They were now headed toward the checkout line. "I don't see how it could hurt to look at his website."

"You're not going to find a posted confession from Owen's killer there. Besides, I thought he was Amish. The murderer wouldn't be at Tom and Sue's church if he's Amish."

"Gordon said the murderer could be someone trying to appear Amish. It might help if we could understand survivalists a little better. If we did, maybe we'd figure out where to look for the killer."

"We don't need to look anywhere. Gordon's doing that. Some days I think the Lord sent me here to keep you out of trouble."

"Yes, but—"

"You need to go home and finish that book you were pretending to read when I called you."

How did she know about the book? Not that it was a difficult guess.

Amber stared at the items Pam was stacking on the belt. "No space blankets."

"Nope. I don't want to invite trouble, and space blankets sound like a beacon for trouble. Unless my boss tells me to." She squinted over at Amber. "Then I suppose I'd jog on back to that aisle and pick some up."

"They're cheaper online, remember?"

"Do you believe everything strangers in a store tell you?"

Amber thought of that question later in the evening, when she was scrambling eggs for dinner and thinking how much her life had changed in the last year. As a rule, Amber did not believe everything folks told her. On the other hand, the couple had seemed nice, genuine, and completely counter to what Amber pictured when she thought of survivalists. Wasn't that what Tate had tried to tell her? That preppers were nice folks. But if they were nice, then why . . .Her thoughts swirling, she ate her dinner, listing all her questions on a pad of paper as she savored the eggs, cheese, and bagel. The coffee was decaf, but it still had the psychological effect of rendering her more alert. Twenty minutes later the dishes were rinsed, she'd poured a second cup of java, and she was sitting in front of the computer—her list of questions and Tom's business card beside her.

Eighteen

esse tossed and turned, determined to fall asleep. So far, he'd had no luck at all, which only made his brother's sound sleeping more irritating.

Andrew snored loudly in the bed next to him. Apparently he had no late-night meetings scheduled. He'd offered no explanation for the one on Friday night. In fact, they'd skirted around the subject of Andrew's unexplained appearance and his future plans. Which was fine with Jesse.

Except he couldn't sleep. The more he tossed, the more uncomfortable his bed grew. Finally he threw back the covers and shuffled downstairs. Using his flashlight, he found and uncovered the leftover cinnamon buns and retrieved the pitcher of milk when his oldest sister, Susan, peeked around the corner.

"Have enough of that for two?"

He motioned her into the kitchen.

He hadn't bothered to light any of the lanterns since he didn't want to wake the entire household. Instead, his flashlight sat on the table between them, pointing up to the ceiling, creating a halo of light.

Not one to worry about calories or how much he ate, he finished one cinnamon roll and was reaching for another when an image of Amon Birkey popped into his mind. Amon was a minister in their church, and he also ran a buggy shop. The man was nearly as round as he was tall. If it weren't for his suspenders, he probably couldn't keep his pants on.

Was that what he wanted to look like in a few years?

"Eat it," Susan said. "You work enough that your body burns any calories off before they hit your stomach."

He compromised by cutting it in half and pushing the remaining portion toward Susan. His *mamm's* sweet rolls were big enough to cover a small plate. All that sugar would hit his stomach soon, and he'd sleep like a cat in the sun on a lazy summer afternoon.

Susan picked around the edges of her roll. She wore her nightgown, and her blond hair was braided and pulled over one shoulder. Though she was barely sixteen, Andrew realized that his sister was no longer a child. When had she grown up?

She stood and refilled both of their glasses, then stored the milk pitcher back in the refrigerator. His parents had owned a gas-operated refrigerator—the same one, actually—for as long as Jesse could remember. But at his grandparents' house things had been different.

They'd refused any of the new gas-powered contraptions. He vividly remembered his visits to their home, which was two miles down the road. His grandmother would ask him to fetch more ice, and he'd walk into the storehouse, where the blocks of ice had been cut from the river and then packed in sawdust. He'd marveled that they could remain frozen, even in the summer heat. But the ice house had been built into the side of a hill a few feet behind the main house. The ground's temperature and the sawdust had done the trick. He would fetch the ice, carry it to the kitchen, and place it in the compartment at the back of the ice box.

His grandparents had passed in the last few years, the test of old age finally taking its toll. But they'd lived full and happy lives. There had been no sadness at their funerals, only an ache for the hole left behind in their family and their community.

As he ate his roll, drank the milk, and studied Susan, Jesse realized his grandparents' milk had been every bit as cold as what he was drinking now. He supposed as long as he could have cold milk, he didn't care what type of appliance they had. It was strange to think that if he asked Hannah to marry him, if she said yes, then he would be making those sorts of decisions for their home.

"Heavy thoughts going on over there, *bruder*."

"What do you mean?"

"I can read you as easily as *Mamm* reads a quilt pattern."

"Oh."

"So spill. What's on your mind?"

He and Susan had grown closer over the last few years. Was that one of the blessings from Andrew's absence? He'd never thought of it that way before. Watching his sister in the glow of the flashlight, he realized he could count it as a blessing. What might have been evil, God had used for good. Despite the six-year age difference, they'd pulled together to help out their parents. They'd pulled together to bind the hole in their family caused by Andrew's move.

"Why are you up so late?" Turning the question back on her usually worked. Jesse sat back and rubbed his stomach. He probably should have stopped at the one roll.

Susan shrugged. "Thinking about the luncheon and Andrew being home and Owen's funeral." This last part was a whisper.

"People die, Susan. It's the way of things, and it's not for us to question why."

"People don't die that way, Jesse. So don't get all big *bruder* on me." She smiled at him as she drained the last of the milk from her glass.

Jesse held up his hands, palms out. "I was just saying."

"Uh-huh. I heard that Naomi isn't doing so well."

"Where—"

"Everyone was talking about it. If you weren't so focused on Hannah, you might have noticed." She rubbed her finger around the rim of the glass. "Naomi was counting on Owen's help. She thought he'd returned home for good. Now she's back to raising all those kids alone."

"Her husband is still around. He hasn't died recently, has he?" He gave her a wink to let her know he was joking.

"*Ya*. I hear you. But Jonas is not much help around the house, and he doesn't make any money. His disabilities—" She shook her head, causing her hair to fall forward. "The cancer treatments leave him very weak. Though the docs say he's free of it, his recovery will take some time. And then he's so much older than Naomi. You can stop looking at me that way. I'm only repeating what everyone else is saying."

"Perhaps that is a habit you shouldn't get into."

"Do you practice sounding like *Dat*, or does it come natural?"

"Natural, I think."

"That's not all I heard. I also heard Naomi received a box."

"What kind of box?"

Susan shrugged. "Is there more than one kind? It was a box. Anyway, it had a note in it and money."

When she'd told him what the note said, Jesse sat back and stared at her.

"Does she think it was from the killer?"

"The police do. They took everything—box, money, and note. Said it might have clues or fingerprints on it."

"Huh." Jesse scratched his head. Now he was wishing he'd drunk coffee instead of milk. He felt sluggish from the calories, and his eyes were stinging, a clear sign that he should be in bed. He couldn't seem to wake enough to take in all that Susan was saying.

She crossed her arms and leaned forward onto the table. "So everyone's saying he must be Amish."

"The killer?"

"Who else?"

"That's *narrisch*. Amish aren't violent, Susan. We don't solve our problems that way."

"You have to admit the note sounded Amish. 'When life ends, it is complete.' That's an Amish saying for sure."

"A saying anyone could read in one of the thousands of books lining shelves in the stores in town. Many *Englischers* are fascinated with our lifestyle."

"True, someone could have read it in a book. But what about the rest of the note? Who ever heard of a killer praying for his victim's wife? Sounds like an Amish man with a guilty conscience."

Jesse considered that for a moment but then shook his head. "We're not preppers. The note said something about how she should prepare, right?"

Susan nodded.

"We don't do that. We work hard and trust the rest to *Gotte*."

"We have storerooms," she argued.

"Sure, but it's nothing like what survivalists keep. I . . . um . . . saw one of those television shows once. *Day of Reckoning Preppers* or something like that."

"*Doomsday Preppers*? You watched *Doomsday Preppers* on television?"

"*Ya*. I did have a *rumspringa*."

"For a week or two, that I remember. It was the shortest *rum-springa* I've ever heard of."

"Are you planning something longer?"

Susan's cheeks reddened—he could tell even in the dim light.

"*Nein*, but I wouldn't mind trying a few things before I settle down."

"Like?"

"Clothes. Maybe a phone." Susan tapped her finger against the milk glass. "And you're changing the subject. Don't think I don't notice when you do that, because I do."

Jesse laughed, some of the tension draining from his shoulders. "I thought I was being subtle."

"Like the sound of an ax on firewood."

They stood and carried their plates and glasses to the sink, rinsing them out and leaving them there for washing in the morning.

They were out of the kitchen and starting up the stairs when Jesse reached out and touched her arm. "Did Naomi say anything else? Did anyone see who left the box?"

"*Nein*, but her youngest boy claims he heard hooves and the neigh of a horse outside—even saw the warning triangle on the back of a buggy when he peeked out the upstairs window. The oldest boy was working in the barn at the time and heard nothing. It must have been before five because Naomi was still dressing."

"Someone in a buggy delivered the box?"

"*Ya*, and if that's true then it almost certainly was an Amish person, probably someone from our community. Kind of creepy to think of someone out there, delivering boxes with warnings . . ."

"And money. Don't forget that." Jesse patted her on the back. "Don't worry about it, Susan. No one's lurking in our yard waiting to attack. I don't know why this happened, but it sounds like a personal grudge to me."

As he walked up the stairs and collapsed onto his bed, he found himself thanking God for that buggy. If it was a buggy, then surely Andrew wasn't involved. As he was falling into a deep and restful sleep, he realized that had been one of his worries all along. Not that Andrew was guilty of such a thing—that wasn't even possible. But that he'd somehow become involved with the wrong people, people capable of committing murder.

Now he could stop worrying.

Andrew hadn't driven the buggy since he'd been home. All that time with the *Englisch*, he'd probably forgotten how. And then there was the night Jesse had followed him. A car had picked him up, not a buggy.

Perhaps his brother was involved in something he shouldn't be, but he wasn't involved in the murder of Owen Esch. For that, Jesse was more than grateful.

Nineteen

His guilty conscience bothered him less each day. He woke Monday morning refreshed and feeling more rested than he had since the incident. That was how he thought of it now—an incident that should have been avoided, could have been avoided if people would mind their own business.

The South Bend meeting on Saturday night had confirmed some of his fears and allayed others. The police were looking into local survivalist groups. It seemed they had found out that Owen had attended a meeting. No doubt the boy had blabbed about it to the woman in the shop, Mary. He had glanced down at the phone when the boy dropped it, as he lay dying. The screen had displayed the words Mary, Cat's Meow.

He couldn't know if Owen had talked to her earlier, what he had told her, or if she had shared the information with the police. Since he wasn't yet arrested, he didn't think so. But he couldn't be too careful—not at this point.

He'd taken care of Mary with a note delivered to her before he'd left town. She wouldn't share that with the police. He knew Amish women. They stayed within the lines of the *Ordnung*, even more so than men. No, she wouldn't go to the police. They were sworn to live a life set apart, and that included handling their own problems. If she had any common sense at all, she'd forget anything Owen told her. He was certain the note would convince her to remain quiet.

"Are your eggs all right?"

He looked across the table at Fern. He loved her name. It reminded him of summer days spent down by the creek. He loved everything about her. She was round in the hips, soft, and caring. Certainly God had blessed him the day he'd met her. Certainly he had smiled upon them.

"They're fine. *Danki*."

She stood, kissed him on the cheek, and fetched the coffeepot to pour him another cup.

He vowed then and there, looking around his house in South Bend, that he would do whatever was necessary to protect his home and his family. There was nothing wrong with that. Pacifism was fine, to a point. That point did not include losing what he'd worked for.

The elders might not agree, but then, their lives hadn't been threatened.

And it was his life that was at stake here. He could lose everything, just as if a thief had entered his home in the middle of the night and stolen everything. Was he to stand by and do nothing?

He'd prayed about it, even studied the Scriptures. What he'd found was what he'd already known in his heart—the Old Testament was filled with warriors. Joshua, Samson, Jonathan, Saul, and even David had all battled in the name of the Lord.

He would do no less.

Twenty

annah finished her work at precisely eleven, when she'd hoped to be done. The first few months she'd been manager of A Simple Blend, she'd kept the *kaffi* shop closed on Mondays. About half of the shops did so. Monday was a day for restocking, setting up new displays, and taking care of paperwork.

Seth had been assigned to help her from the very first week, and she'd come to depend on him. It helped that his mishaps were further apart. Though, the week before, he had managed to put one of their flavored syrups into the tiny freezer compartment. When he found it frozen, and someone needed it, he tried microwaving the caramel sauce, which had then exploded, causing quite the mess. To his credit, he had most of it cleaned up by the time she checked in on him.

Yes, work was going well.

The problem was her nagging worries over Mary. Her mother had cautioned her about falling into the habit of fretting over things out of her control. "That will rob the joy from your life faster than many other things." But no matter how Hannah tried to change her focus, Mary kept popping up in her mind.

What did her friend know that she wasn't sharing?

Why was Owen's death affecting her so deeply?

And why was she so frightened?

Hannah was deep in thought, walking toward the Village parking lot, when she nearly bumped into Carol Jennings. Carol had been her boss when Hannah had worked at The Quilting Bee.

"How are you, Hannah?"

"Gut." Hannah realized that was a lie and corrected herself. "Fair."

"I'm glad to hear it. Say, I need more of those quilted lunch bags if you've had time to make any. They fly off my shelves."

"Ya, I've finished a dozen more. I was waiting until you needed them, but I can bring them in tomorrow."

"Excellent." Carol was an older woman. Though she was *Englisch,* she often struck Hannah as being Amish. She was strict in an old-fashioned way, and she wore conservative, simple dresses and no jewelry except her plain gold wedding ring. Her brown hair was cut in a nice fashion just below her jawline, but she didn't bother with dyeing the gray streaks, which accented the brown. Ash gray—was that what Hannah had heard it called? Well, no matter. Carol always looked professional and in control. Perhaps that sort of calmness came when you entered your sixties.

"Is there anything you need, Hannah? Anything I can do? This whole disaster with the young Amish man is awful. It reminds me too much of what happened here in the spring."

"Ya. It is terrible, but today is the viewing and tomorrow the funeral. Perhaps once those are over . . ." Her words trailed off as she realized how foolish she sounded. Putting Owen in the ground would not answer the question of who killed him. It would not make anyone feel safer.

Was that what she was worried about? Their need for protection? Did they need more security around the Village and on the trail? It was hard to believe their little community had come to such a sad possibility. Her confusion must have shown, because Carol lowered her voice and stepped closer.

"Walking through the valley of the shadow of death is always difficult. Psalm 23 has been a comfort to me in the past. Take some time to read it, dear."

Perhaps it was the look of genuine concern, or it could have been the way Carol reached out and touched her arm compassionately. She realized then that Carol was her friend, and they'd been through much together. That was probably what gave her the courage to bring up what was bothering her. "It's Mary I'm worried about right now."

"Mary Weaver?"

"*Ya.*"

"She runs a fine shop. I'm always happy to send customers over to her."

"*Ya*, but . . . something is wrong. Something she won't talk to me about. I don't suppose you've noticed anything unusual."

"Funny that you bring up the subject. We had a breakfast meeting scheduled this morning. We do that once a month to be sure the stock we each carry complements the other's. She missed the meeting but then stopped by later to apologize."

"That's not like her, is it?"

"Heavens, no. Mary is always quite prompt. No one's perfect, though, and there was no harm done. We rescheduled."

"I see. Thank you for taking time to talk with me, Carol. It does help."

"You're so welcome. Remember to bring me those quilted lunch bags."

She would. At first she'd hand sewn the lunch bags together with scraps of fabric left over from her mother's quilting. More recently she'd taken to buying small swatches of fabric Carol rotated into her sales bin. Since she'd begun quilting the bags, they'd sold as fast as the shoofly pie over at the bakery. The bags provided a nice little extra income—money she could use, especially with Christmas less than three months away.

Thoughts of Christmas cheered her a bit. She'd spied the beautiful blue-and-gray variegated yarn at The Cat's Meow. She wanted to knit Jesse that buggy blanket, but she'd need quite a few skeins. Now she'd have the money to do so.

As she hurried home, thoughts of quilting and knitting faded away, and she once again began to worry over Mary.

Why had Mary missed her meeting with Carol?

Had something else happened since yesterday afternoon?

And what should she do about it?

❧

Three hours later Hannah was in the buggy with her *mamm*, *dat*, three brothers, and little Mattie. Since Mattie had been born, and with the boys growing nearly to the size of their father, they didn't fit easily into a single buggy. However, this day it seemed appropriate to all ride together, to squeeze in and draw comfort from each other's presence.

They were all dressed in their sets of black clothes, even Mattie. Her little sister's wild hair did not like to be corralled into a *kapp*, and some golden curls were already escaping. Hannah reached over to tuck them in, and Mattie promptly crawled into her lap.

The boys were acting as if they were headed to a picnic, jostling one another and talking about the fish they'd caught on Saturday. One look from their father settled them down.

"It was quite a *gut* catch," Ben murmured. He was nineteen, and the younger boys looked up to him as if he could do no wrong. To be fair, he rarely did. Ben's life consisted mostly of working and . . . working. Did he even have a girlfriend? Hannah had been so wrapped up in her own problems, she hadn't noticed. At least she hadn't noticed since things had cooled between him and a young girl from Shipshewana.

"Funerals are solemn affairs." Their *mamm* spoke loud enough that they could all hear her over the rattling of the buggy. "Since Naomi only has the one day for viewing, I expect it will be quite crowded."

"Why didn't she take the full three days?" Ben asked. "It's not as if Owen is going anywhere."

"Don't be disrespectful, son." Their *dat* delivered the reprimand softly but firmly.

"*Nein*. I was wondering, is all."

"The police kept the body for so long that Naomi thought it was best to have only the one day. The funeral will be tomorrow, and we'll attend that as well."

When Noah began to protest with, "But I have someone coming to look at my newest litter of pups," Eunice waved away his concerns.

"The buyer will come again if he's interested. We gather together and support one another during such times. Business can wait."

Mattie had been struggling to climb over into the front buggy seat. Eunice helped her over and then wrapped her arms around her youngest child—her surprise daughter.

She'd explained to Hannah that pregnancies sometimes occurred when a woman was going through the change—when she thought her time of birthing was over. It was one of those situations, Eunice had said, when God had other plans.

Hannah sat back against the buggy seat, Ben on her left, Noah and Dan on her right. She'd always thought their family was typically Amish. They spent their days as most Amish families did—farming, quilting, even raising pups. The oddest thing about them had been Dan's fascination with the camels, but it had proven quite profitable for Manasses Hochstetler. Perhaps the two of them would start an entire industry.

As the buggy horse clip-clopped down the lane, Hannah pulled in a deep breath and prayed that they would always remain together, as they were today. Suddenly she didn't mind her brother's mumbled complaints about missing out on a sale or the fact that Mattie still sucked her thumb. Would she ever abandon that practice? Did it matter? Few children sucked their thumbs by the time they began school. So why worry about it today, when Mattie was barely two years old?

Hannah realized how fortunate she was that their family was whole, they were together, and they watched out for one another. She thanked God for that, closing her eyes and allowing the lull of the buggy to calm her nerves.

Perhaps Mary would be fine today.

Perhaps Naomi would be comforted by the outpouring of love from her community.

Perhaps they could put the terrible tragedy of what had happened to Owen behind them.

Within a few moments they were at Naomi's home.

Usually at social gatherings the family would join the others immediately, and their father would stay behind to care for the horse and buggy. He'd catch up with them within a few minutes. But today there looked to be two teams of two men accepting the buggies as they pulled up and walking them down the long line of visitors. They would care for the horses as each family handed over the reins. Hannah looked down the fence rail as she adjusted her *kapp*. The buggies formed a grave, black line.

Hannah, Eunice, Mattie, and the boys waited for their father to give a few instructions regarding the horse. When he'd gathered Mattie up in his arms and moved beside Eunice, they all walked to the house together. Jesse and Andrew stood near the barn, and Hannah had an urge to hurry over and speak with Jesse. But she would have to wait. She knew it wasn't the right time. He did send a pointed look her way and nodded his head once—as if he was thinking the same thing she was. As if he needed to speak with her.

Hannah couldn't remember the last time she'd been to Naomi's, probably when she and Jonas had hosted church service. It could have been the previous winter, but she wasn't sure. At the time, she'd been caught up in so many things—her job at the Village, the two boys who were courting her, and Jesse's friendship. He'd always been there, as if he were patiently waiting for the way to clear, and then suddenly he was more than a friend.

Many Amish houses did look alike, but Naomi's was simpler than most. The garden to the right of the house held a few scraggly vegetable plants, though it was well past harvest. No flowers brightened the rows. The house itself was plain to the point of being almost drab. She supposed with six children and a husband who couldn't work, such things as a trampoline for the children or flowers for the garden were not financially possible.

Their community would help if there was ever a need for money for doctor bills or the rebuilding of a structure. They probably had helped with the burial expense, though that would be minimal. Amish funerals were much like Amish lives—simple.

But the atmosphere permeating Naomi's house was more one

of hopelessness. How did the community help with that? What could they do to bring life back to a place that looked as if it was dying? And now this.

Owen.

Owen's death.

Owen's untimely death.

There was a line of folks waiting at the door. Hannah stood next to Dan. She glanced up and was suddenly aware of how tall he was, taller than she, though he was seven years younger. She noticed what looked like hay on his black coat. Reaching up, she brushed the fabric clean. He glanced down and smiled at her uneasily.

They reached the door, and Hannah took a deep breath.

She stepped inside. Naomi and Jonas were sitting in two straight-back chairs that had been placed near the front of the sitting room. Naomi looked pale and older than her years. How old was she again? Thirty-five? She looked older than Eunice. She looked tired and worn. Her skin was unnaturally pale, and dark circles rimmed her eyes.

Six children, looking to be between the ages of five and fifteen, sat scrunched up on a bench beside them. Boys and girls, all dressed in black. They squirmed on the wooden seat as if hours had already passed—and perhaps they had.

Hannah wondered if they'd grown close to Owen since he'd returned. Would they miss him? He wasn't merely their favorite *onkel*. As far as she knew, he had been their only *onkel*.

Jonas was breathing heavily and sweat beaded his forehead. The room was stuffy, but Hannah thought it was probably a result of his condition rather than the crowd of visitors. Jonas's last round of chemo had been difficult, or so she'd heard. His beard was a spattering of gray and white, and his eyes were a glassy blue.

"We're so sorry for your loss," Eunice said as they moved forward.

"*Danki.*" The word was barely a whisper.

When Hannah reached Naomi, she thought the woman straightened a bit. For a fleeting moment she looked as if she might want to say something more than "*Danki* for coming." But she glanced toward her husband and apparently thought better of it.

Since they had no family in the area, Katie Schmucker, the manager of Katie's Mercantile at the Village, was escorting visitors to view Owen's body. It was set out at the back of the sitting room, which was a long, bare affair. The couch had been pushed into a corner and extra benches brought in, the same benches they sat on during their worship services. Benches lined the kitchen as well, and they were all filled with members from their congregation, all dressed in their black clothes and speaking in low tones.

Hannah followed her parents to the coffin. Somewhere it registered in her mind that Ben had moved forward with her parents, but Noah and Dan were staying back beside her. Mattie was still in her father's arms and seemed oblivious to what was going on around them. They'd all been to plenty of viewings and funerals before, but this one struck Hannah as being unsettling. Perhaps the boys sensed that in some way also.

Katie looked to their *dat* as they stood in front of the hinged wooden coffin. The top portion was open and the bottom half was closed. A sheet covered the body. Hannah's *dat* nodded once, and Katie reached forward to pull back the piece of white linen.

Though Hannah stood behind her parents, she had no trouble

seeing Owen. He looked—in death—much like he had in life. His skin was paler, for sure. The funeral director in town had taken care of the embalming, but again the process was abbreviated— no makeup or fancy hairstyle for the Amish, though Hannah had heard it was often done for *Englischers*. Owen's expression was peaceful, though, as if his last thought in this body had been one of hope.

"Down," Mattie whined, attempting to reach down and touch Owen's clothes. Their *dat* reached for the little girl's hands in time, seconds before she touched Owen. It wouldn't have been proper, though Mattie couldn't have known. Then they were all moving away from the coffin, allowing the next family to step forward.

Hannah found a seat with her family on a bench in the kitchen. She couldn't erase the image of Owen from her mind. It didn't upset her, like she'd thought it might. If anything, it helped to calm her feelings about him. Dressed completely in white, as was their custom, he'd looked at ease, bound for heaven, no doubt leaving all his cares behind.

He hadn't looked frightened or in pain or even worried, so he hadn't been arguing with whoever had done this. And surely his features would have revealed something if he'd been surprised—they would have frozen in some sort of confused expression.

He probably hadn't even realized what had happened, and that was a blessing for sure.

A life cut short, but as the bishop often reminded them, God knows the number of our days before we are born.

Hannah wasn't sure how that figured in regard to murder.

She did feel, deep inside of herself, that the right thing to do for this family would be to find the perpetrator. If that meant working with the *Englisch* police, she would gladly do so. And if it meant pressuring Mary to tell her whatever she knew, then she'd do that as well.

Twenty-One

ary came into the kitchen fifteen minutes later, accompanied by her parents and siblings. Her gaze briefly met Hannah's, and then she quickly stared down at the floor.

Quiet conversations continued, though Hannah couldn't make out what folks were saying. The point, as her mother had reminded her, was to be with Naomi and Jonas and the children during their time of grief.

The point was to share the burden.

Her brothers were behaving moderately well, though Noah appeared to be in danger of falling asleep. He rose even earlier than her *dat* each morning so he could take care of the pups before his regular chores. She wouldn't be surprised if he passed out in the buggy on the way home.

There were a few other women in the kitchen. Fanny Bontrager and Olivia Wagler sat next to each other. Hannah didn't see either of their husbands, but perhaps they were helping with the horses. No cooking was going on. The big meal would be after the funeral tomorrow.

Mattie had hopped down off her father's lap and was making her way down the line of family members. When she reached Hannah, she looked up and patted her arm. "Potty," she insisted.

At two she was still wearing diapers, but she was also using the toilet. They were all trying to encourage the latter, as it would save on a lot of laundry and a little money for the few disposables they bought.

"Potty," she repeated, wiggling from her right foot to her left and then back again.

"Take her," Eunice said. "Best use the outhouse. The one inside has a line."

Hannah clasped Mattie's hand and walked her out through the kitchen door, down the back steps, and across the yard to the outhouse. Some families did have both indoor and outdoor bathrooms, though more and more Amish homes were being built without the outdoor facilities.

There was no line, and Mattie quickly took care of her business. As they exited the outhouse, they both heard a squeal. Walking around to the adjacent pasture, they found an entire group of youngsters all being watched over by the bishop's daughter, Emily.

At fourteen, Emily still had the look of a young girl, all skinny legs and a too-thin body frame, but she also had the maturity of someone older. Perhaps because she was the bishop's daughter, his only daughter among his six boys, she'd grown up rather quickly. Or so it seemed to Hannah. It wasn't uncommon to find her presiding over a large group of youngsters, and today was no exception.

"Mattie can come and play with us," she called out.

Before Hannah could decide if her mother would approve, Mattie was tugging on her hand, pulling her toward the group of children.

"*Dat* says it's better to have them out here, not disturbing the family," Emily explained. Her *kapp* was tipped back on her head, and she reached up to pull it forward. As she did, one of the youngsters picked up a pile of hay and dropped it in her lap. "He's pretending I'm a horse."

Smiling, she motioned toward Mattie. "It will be *gut* for her to play a little."

"Are you sure you want one more?"

"Oh, *ya*. It's not so many, and my *bruder* was helping, but he went inside to fetch some water for the youngsters."

Hannah sat with Emily and the children until John returned. He was ten years old and probably would have fussed about helping with the children any other day. But today all the other boys were still trapped inside the house. He looked relieved to be outside in the fall sunshine.

And who could blame him?

Hannah was in no hurry to return to the heat and solemnity of the kitchen herself.

After promising Emily she'd be back to retrieve Mattie in twenty minutes, Hannah turned and started back toward the house. It was when she was coming back around the corner of the barn that she heard voices. She had no intention of eavesdropping, but thinking that it might be Mary and she might want some company, she stuck her head around where she could see better.

The scene that greeted her eyes caused her to back up, her heart tapping out a skittish rhythm.

She peeked back around, wondering if she'd seen what she thought she'd seen.

Yes.

Mary was there, standing very close to Andrew. Though she was facing in the direction of Hannah, she never looked up, never noticed her at all. She probably wouldn't have noticed one of Manasses Hochstetler's camels if it had stepped out in front of her.

Andrew was holding a piece of paper in his hand, staring down at it and glowering.

Mary was chewing on a thumbnail. If anything, she was paler than she'd been when Hannah had seen her in the house.

"You found this?" Andrew asked.

"*Ya.* Someone slipped it inside the shop door."

Then Andrew said something Hannah couldn't hear. She'd flattened herself against the barn wall, wondering if she should step out and ask what was going on, but she was afraid to interrupt them.

She peeked back around and saw that Andrew had his arm around Mary and was leading her back toward the house. Once they turned around and passed the corner of the barn, they would definitely see her.

What should she do? Step out in the open? Call out to them? Or maybe hide in the barn? Maybe that would be the best thing to do.

She heard their footsteps drawing closer, and then there were other voices. She desperately wanted to peek around and see who was there, but she didn't dare. The voices were male, and their tone was angry. Their sentences were short and choppy.

She couldn't make out exactly what they were saying, but she heard Andrew clearly enough. He made no attempt to lower his voice as the others did.

"Go inside, Mary. I'll take care of this."

"*Nein.* I won't."

"Go inside."

One of the men said something else, and then Mary skittered

across the yard and up the back porch steps, never once looking back where she could have plainly seen Hannah.

Hannah's palms had begun to sweat, though the weather wasn't warm enough to warrant it. Her heart was still racing, and she wondered if she might be about to hyperventilate. Who were the men talking to Andrew? And did they have anything to do with Owen's murder? What was the sheet of paper Andrew and Mary had been reading?

She dared one more glance around the corner.

The two older men had their backs to her. They were definitely Amish, no doubt there for the viewing. She guessed they were older, but she wasn't certain until one reached up and removed his hat, revealing black-and-gray hair. The other struck her as a bit younger, shoulders less slumped, arms more muscular, which she could tell even though he was wearing his jacket.

She knew all the men in their district, but couldn't get a good look to identify these two.

Who were they?

Andrew was facing her, facing the men, actually, and he probably hadn't seen her, he was so engrossed in the conversation—if that was what they were having. It seemed the two men were doing all the talking, and Andrew was merely shaking his head.

Hannah knew she should pull back, knew that eavesdropping was wrong—not that she'd set out to listen in on a private conversation. It had just happened that way. She was torn between going after Mary and heading back to Mattie.

And it was in that moment that Andrew glanced up and saw her.

He didn't blink.

He didn't acknowledge her in any way.

And that, more than anything else, told her that Andrew was in more serious trouble than she had guessed.

❧

Jesse stood staring after the *Englisch* car. A fellow from the neighboring district had arrived and told their bishop, Joseph, that he was needed. One of the older men from their district, who hadn't felt well enough to attend the viewing, had been taken to the *Englisch* hospital in an ambulance, Memorial Hospital in South Bend. From what Jesse heard, the older man would be all right—he was having chest pains again and went as a precaution.

"If anyone asks, I'll be back later this afternoon," Joseph had said as he'd opened the door to the *Englisch* car. Joseph was young for a bishop, in Jesse's opinion. He barely had any gray hair at all. But he'd served well since accepting the position a few years earlier. No taller than Jesse, he was steadily gaining weight—a few pounds a year, but it would add up. His *fraa*, Anna, was an excellent cook.

"What about your buggy?"

"Anna will drive it home." The bishop settled into the car, pulling the seat belt across his lap and then lowering the window so he could turn his attention back to Jesse. "The funeral will be tomorrow as we planned."

When Jesse nodded in understanding, Joseph said something to the driver, and they pulled away, spewing gravel and dirt. It occurred to Jesse—not for the first time—that being a bishop would be a difficult job, especially when your responsibilities as a leader were added to all the everyday chores a father and farmer had.

He was turning back to the row of buggies when he saw Andrew hurrying toward him.

"I need to borrow the buggy you brought."

"What? Why?"

"You can ride home with *Mamm* and *Dat*."

"I'm supposed to stay until late afternoon. They'll be leaving in another hour or so."

"Then get a ride with someone else, or walk."

"You walk!"

Andrew turned on him suddenly. When he did, Jesse saw such a mix of emotions—anger, frustration, and a little fear—that he stepped back.

Scrubbing his hand over his face, Andrew pulled in a deep breath, then stepped closer and lowered his voice. "I'm sorry, Jesse. There is no reason for me to take this out on you."

"Take what out on me?"

"I apologize that I raised my voice, but I need your buggy or I wouldn't have asked."

"You didn't ask."

Andrew looked left, then right, as if to assure himself they were alone. "There's something I have to take care of. If it could wait, then I'd stay."

"I don't know what you're into, but it's about time you told me. Maybe I can help."

Andrew shook his head and stared out across the fields. The silence lengthened between them until finally Jesse shrugged and went to fetch their mare. When he returned, Andrew helped him hitch it to the buggy.

"Don't share with *Mamm* or *Dat* any more about this than they have to know."

"I don't know *anything* about this! What would you expect me to share?"

"Cover for me. All right?"

"What's going on, Andrew? Are you planning to meet with the *Englischers* again? The ones in the car? The ones who came by to pick you up when—"

"I can't talk about it, and it's better if you don't know the details." Andrew hopped up into the buggy and picked up the reins. "And, Jesse . . . if I'm not back by tomorrow, go see Mary. Talk to Mary."

"What? Why?" But Jesse was left talking to the large, reflective caution symbol on the back of the buggy as Andrew pulled away even faster than their bishop had.

Twenty-Two

*A*mber stared impatiently at her phone. She'd left a message for Hannah hours ago. Why hadn't the girl called back? Maybe she should drive over to her home. Or maybe she should try to relax.

Her Amish employees rarely asked for days off. She was fortunate that Owen's viewing was on a Monday and the funeral on Tuesday. Monday wasn't a terribly busy day at the Village, since about half of the shops were closed. Tuesday they could get by with replacement folks.

Except she couldn't wait until Wednesday to talk to Hannah. Something told her this wouldn't keep, that whatever was happening was accelerating.

She'd pulled Leo into her lap and was focused on scratching the feline behind his ears when the phone rang. She dumped him onto the floor and lurched for her cell phone. As she answered it, Leo stretched with his feet placed firmly in front of him and his hind end up in the air. He looked at her reproachfully and stalked off.

"Hello?"

"Amber? This is Hannah."

"Oh. Thank you for calling me back. I wasn't sure you checked the machine every day."

"It was a nice afternoon for a walk and . . ." Hannah hesitated before adding, "I thought maybe Jesse was in town and had called from one of the Village phones to leave me a message."

"We need to talk . . . about everything that's going on, about Owen. Can I come and pick you up?"

"I helped *Mamm* put dinner together already, but we're about to eat, and I should be there to do the dishes afterward. How about in an hour and a half?"

"I'll be there at seven."

"*Gut*, and, Amber—be careful."

Hannah hung up before Amber could ask her what she meant. Be careful? She wasn't the one in danger, but maybe someone was. That was what her heart had been screaming since she'd done her internet research the night before.

She fed Leo. He seemed to forgive her the earlier slight as he crouched down in front of his bowl, purring loudly enough to wake a sleeping giant.

She put together a salad for herself—romaine lettuce, fresh cheddar cheese, tomatoes, and cucumbers, then added a can of tuna to the top. When she sat down in front of it, she took two bites and realized she wasn't hungry.

Scooping the remainder of the tuna into Leo's bowl, she walked to her desk and picked up the file she'd put together the night before. It was possible she should go to Gordon with this, but what did she actually have? Suspicions and nothing more—though the facts were disturbing.

Hannah had helped her solve the mystery of Ethan's killer in the spring. Now they were in the midst of dark waters again. Perhaps, together, they could find their way clear.

Amber parked the car in front of Hannah's home. She wasn't too surprised to see Hannah and Jesse sitting together on the front porch steps. There was a certain look, a certain way of acting around each other, when two people became a couple. She wasn't sure Hannah was even aware of it yet, but she and Jesse were definitely a couple. It was evident in so many little things.

The way Hannah leaned in to talk to him. How Jesse waited until Hannah stood and had moved beside him before he began walking toward Amber's car. The nearly imperceptible way their shoulders practically touched. It was as if they were drawing strength from each other.

"Jesse stopped by after he got home from Owen's viewing. I told him we were meeting—"

"And I asked to come along."

Now that they were closer, Amber could see the lines of tension on Jesse's face. Was he worried about the same things she was?

"Of course. Get in."

"Where are we going?" Hannah turned toward Amber as she buckled her seat belt.

"I think best when I'm eating ice cream."

"The Village?" Hannah turned toward Jesse, who was in the backseat. "What do you think?"

"Dairy Queen?" He stuck his head in between them. "I could use a Blizzard."

"Sounds fattening and exactly right." Amber backed away from the house, turned the small car around in the area in front of their barn, and headed toward the main road.

No one talked as they made their way to town, though Amber had a feeling that, like her, Hannah and Jesse were just waiting for the comfort of ice cream to share more unsettling information.

Amber was also thinking about the sunset, the red, orange, and pink colors, and how it was difficult to distinguish one from the other when they all merged together. Which was rather like the facts and suspicions surrounding Owen's murder. Just when she thought one fact made sense, it merged with a new fact that changed everything right in front of her eyes, much as the colors in the evening sky were changing.

They walked into the fast-food joint and waited in line to order. Hannah glanced at Amber and smiled.

"What?" Amber stared down at her clothes.

"It's just that you're still in your work clothes. Did you even go home before you picked me up?"

"Yes. I went home—a little late, and I really didn't have time to change." She indicated her long-sleeved ivory blouse, black dress pants, and shiny black shoes. "Too dressy for DQ?"

"*Nein*. I was only worried that you hadn't rested at all today."

"I'll go to bed early, *Mom*." Amber looped an arm through Hannah's as they moved to the counter to place their orders.

In less than five minutes they were settled into a booth with no one nearby to overhear them—Jesse and Hannah on one side, sitting as close as two baby birds in a nest. Amber pulled out a pad of paper and a pen.

"I asked you to meet with me because I'm worried. The more I try to figure things out, the more anxious I become."

"*Ya*, same here." Hannah stared out the window at the last of the sunset.

"Make that three, but where's Tate?"

"Out of town. I'll share everything with him when he's home Wednesday, but I hate to ruin his time with his son by talking about this." Amber tapped the pen against the pad. "Still, I couldn't stand it all tumbling around in my head another minute."

Hannah and Jesse nodded in agreement.

"I thought it would help if we write everything down."

"Where's your . . ." Hannah made a motion of typing on the tabletop.

"Tablet? I left it at home. I don't know why, but sometimes when I'm stuck, it helps me to go back to the old way."

"*Ya*. The old ways are *gut*." It was the first smile she'd seen from Jesse that evening, and it eased some of the concern in her heart.

But then he glanced up as a group of Amish teens walked into the room, and his expression changed. Scowling, he stared back down at his hands.

"Someone you don't like in that group?" Hannah asked.

"*Nein*." He tapped his fingers against the table, then admitted, "Reminds me of when we were younger, when times were simple, when there was no murder to worry over."

Amber nodded, then drew two vertical lines on the sheet of paper. She labeled the first column *Suspects*, the second *In Danger*, and the third *Involved*.

Under *Suspects*, she wrote, "Creepy guy behind Mary's shop."

Hannah cocked her head so that she could read what Amber had written. "I understand why you'd suspect the man who was waiting on Mary, but I'm not sure I understand your groups."

"Suspects—that's plain enough. Someone killed Owen, and I think it's about time we figured out who."

"Aren't the police doing that?" Jesse folded his arms and set them on the table.

"They're trying, but Gordon's following the evidence, and I'm not sure there's enough of that to catch anyone. Then there's Shaw . . ." Hannah jotted both names down in her *Involved* column.

"That column I understand." Jesse pointed to the far right

one. "We know Avery and Shaw didn't do it, but they are involved with the investigation."

"Exactly. Roland Shaw rubs me the wrong way, and I think he's focusing on the wrong thing, but he isn't in danger and he's not a suspect."

"Who is in danger?" Hannah asked, her eyes widening.

Amber was about to answer when Jesse stood. "Our Blizzards are ready."

They spent the next few moments gathering spoons and napkins and cups of water. The first spoonful of French silk tasted like happiness in a cup to Amber. "This was a great idea."

"*Ya*, my chocolate chip Blizzard is nearly as good as Hannah's chocolate chip cookies."

"I haven't baked much lately, and *Mamm* usually goes for something healthier—like peanut butter or oatmeal. I haven't made chocolate chip cookies in a while."

"Which is why I'm at Dairy Queen," Jesse explained around a spoonful of Blizzard.

Hannah pushed him with her shoulder as a smile spread across her face. She might want to appear perturbed, but she couldn't hide that I'm-in-love expression.

Amber enjoyed watching the way the two of them interacted, though it did make her miss Tate even more. "What did you get, Hannah?"

"She got double fudge. It's what she always gets."

"Not always." Hannah glanced at them both. "But *ya*, this time it is double fudge."

They were three chocoholics in a booth. Amber took another bite and returned her attention to the list.

"I'm putting Mary under the *In Danger* column."

"*Ya*, she couldn't have done it, but she's acting very strange . . .

and sometimes she seems so afraid." Hannah told them both about the conversation between Andrew and Mary she'd overheard earlier that afternoon.

"You're sure it was my *bruder* she was talking with?"

"I guess I know what Andrew looks like." Hannah scooped another bite of ice cream into her mouth. "*Ya*, it was Andrew and Mary."

"What could they have been looking at? What was on the paper?" Amber circled Mary's name and added a question mark beside it.

"Don't know," Jesse said. "Andrew's acting very odd as well. He left in a hurry before the viewing was over—like there was an emergency."

"Do you know where he went?"

"*Nein*, and he wasn't home when we had dinner, but . . ." Jesse stared out the window. Since darkness had fallen, he was actually staring at their reflections. "He asked me not to speak to our parents, and he told me to go and see Mary if he didn't return by tomorrow."

Amber didn't know what to make of that, but at least they had a solid connection between Andrew and Mary.

"Do you think his emergency had to do with what I saw?" Hannah's brow wrinkled in concentration. "While Andrew was studying the sheet of paper with Mary, two men walked up and started talking to him. Then almost immediately after he saw me and I went to get Mattie, he must have gone to see you."

"What two men?" Amber drew squiggles in the margin of the page while Hannah filled them in on the few details she knew. When she finished, Amber admitted, "It could be related to whatever Mary's dealing with, but we can't be sure."

"I say we put Andrew's name under the *In Danger* column."

Hannah had finished less than half of her ice cream, but she pushed the cup toward Jesse and sat back against the booth.

"No offense, but I have to ask something." Amber hesitated and then pushed forward. "Jesse, is there any chance Andrew killed Owen?"

Twenty-Three

Jesse gawked at Amber. "I can't believe my ears. Did you just ask if my *bruder* is a killer?"

Amber cleared her throat as she drew doodles on the side of her page. Finally she looked up and met Jesse's gaze. "You have to agree there are a lot of coincidences here."

"Like?" Anger pulsed through him, but he vowed not to show it. Suddenly he wished he hadn't finished the Blizzard so quickly. It lay sour in his stomach.

"Like he came home the day Owen died."

"That means nothing."

"How long had he been gone?" Now Amber was looking at him openly, honestly, and it was difficult to hold on to his anger. "Why did he come back when he did? Why did he come back at all? What has he done since he's been here? How close was he to Owen?"

"I can't answer a single one of your questions because I don't know." Jesse punctuated each of the last three words with a fist bump on the table. "*Ya*, I admit it looks bad, but Andrew couldn't do this. It's not in him to behave violently. Arrogant? Sometimes. Impulsive? Maybe. But he would never draw a bow and send an arrow through someone's heart."

"I agree with Jesse." Hannah pointed to the middle column. "Put his name here."

"Do you think Andrew's in danger?"

"It's possible." Jesse sighed as he scrunched down lower into the booth. "I don't know. He's acting strange, even for Andrew, and that's saying a lot."

"And he is connected to Mary somehow, connected to Mary and probably connected to Owen." Hannah clasped her hands together. "He was genuinely concerned for her safety. I could tell that much even from where I was hiding—I mean standing."

"All right. I agree, then. He could be in danger." Amber added his name to the middle column. After a brief hesitation, she added their three names to the far right side—they were definitely involved at this point. "Who else do we have?"

"Seems Naomi should be on there somewhere." Jesse took a big gulp from his cup of water.

"Owen's sister, right?" When they both nodded, Amber asked, "Do you think she was involved in any way? Maybe she knew Owen was in some kind of trouble? Or maybe she suspected that someone might be angry with him? Angry enough to kill him?"

"*Nein.*" Jesse dismissed the idea immediately.

"She has no time for visiting," Hannah explained. "I doubt she knew anything about Owen's comings and goings. She has time for nothing except raising the children and doing the bulk of the work around her place. I explained her husband was ill, *ya?*"

Amber nodded, and Hannah continued, "She'd never hurt her own *bruder*, that I'm sure of. I know she was relieved he had come home. She told me so at church meeting a few weeks ago. But there is the box she received. That confuses me . . ." Hannah hesitated, as if she wasn't sure how to continue.

"Box?" Amber jotted the word at the bottom of the page, drew a square around it, put down her pen, and waited.

Jesse explained about the box Naomi had received with a note and money inside. He added that he had heard the details from his sister, Susan, and then had told Hannah about it just before Amber picked them up.

"You heard it from your sister. Who did she hear about it from?"

"I'm not sure."

"Can you ask your friend at the police department about it?" Jesse no longer felt angry, only exhausted and confused and perhaps desperate. "They have the box, as well as the note and the money."

"I doubt they'll tell me anything. Actually, Gordon shared information about the note and money with Tate and me, but for some reason he didn't mention the box. Could either of you ask Naomi about it?"

"Not at the funeral; that would be . . . terrible timing." Hannah clasped her arms tightly around her waist.

"There's one name we haven't put on this sheet." Amber added the letters *ISG* under *Suspects*.

Hannah sat up straighter, glancing from Amber to Jesse and back again. "I still don't understand exactly who they are. I know Mary said Owen was trying to join—you explained that to me. But why? And who are they exactly?"

"I've been trying to get a handle on that myself," Amber said. "I spent a few hours last night researching. The more I know, the more this worried feeling gnaws at my stomach. But I can't figure out how Owen's murder and ISG could be connected."

"I don't know much about the group." Jesse was glad they

were talking about something other than Andrew. "Maybe I've heard a few of the men in our community mention them."

"Are you saying there are Amish folk in this group?"

"Could be."

Amber played with her earring, turning it round and round, and then she described the couple she'd met at the discount store, when she'd gone there with Pam.

"They're part of this ISG?" Hannah asked.

"I don't think so, but their group is similar in many respects. I was able to find out a little about them from a simple internet search. First I went to their site, but that led me to others. I expected to find a bunch of rabble-rousers. I suppose that's why I was surprised at what I actually found."

Amber pulled a folder out of her large handbag.

They sat there quietly, completely engrossed in the pages they passed from one to another, what represented hours of research. Jesse forgot all about the teens coming in and out of the restaurant. He forgot to be angry that he didn't have such a carefree life that included buggy rides and Monday nights spent with a group of friends. He forgot everything except what he was reading.

All of Amber's pages pointed to the same thing—the Indiana Survivalist Group was growing, and they were under pressure from federal law enforcement to disband.

"I was pretty skeptical about these groups when I first began researching them, but those feelings quickly dissipated. I found nothing to support that fear. I found no indication of trouble at all."

"If I'm reading these correctly, what's more important is what you didn't find. Not a single shred of evidence . . ." Jesse flipped back through the pages. "Not one news report of violence or crimes committed by group members. They appear to be squeaky clean."

"Maybe they haven't been caught yet," Hannah said.

"Possibly." Amber stared out the window. "In mystery stories, large groups of people are usually found out quite easily. I don't think they're involved in this. In my opinion, the single name under our Suspects list, ISG, doesn't appear to be a guilty party at all."

Jesse wanted to argue with her, but he couldn't.

Which left them where they'd started, with no clue as to who had killed Owen Esch.

Twenty-Four

Hannah, Amber, and Jesse walked back out to Dairy Queen's parking lot and stood by Amber's little red car. The coolness of the October evening felt refreshing to Hannah. She suddenly realized what a long day it had been and how much she wanted to crawl into bed and pull the quilt over her head.

"So it's not ISG." Hannah rested her back against the side of the car. "At least it doesn't seem to be."

"No. I don't know what I expected to find, but a group focused on conservation and individual rights doesn't sound like an organization harboring killers."

"Someone killed Owen. He didn't walk into a flying arrow." Jesse pulled his wool cap down over his ears. "And it seems to me that it was someone he knew, or he would have called out, screamed, tried to run, something. He wouldn't have stood there as if he trusted the person."

The word *trust* was echoing through Hannah's mind when hollering erupted from a corner of the parking lot. A pickup truck sat idling behind a horse and buggy.

Hannah hurried over, trying to keep up with Amber.

"What's the problem here?" Amber stood with her hands on her hips and a scowl on her face. Though it was now pitch dark, the parking lot lights revealed that the *Englischers* were boys—three of them who all looked to be in high school still. One was scrawny, one was huge, and the other was still sitting in the truck behind the steering wheel. Hannah couldn't see him well enough to determine his size.

The Amish kids were two couples—Hannah's brother, Noah, one of his friends, and two girls. They had the closed look of caution that Hannah had seen on Amish folk so many times before. The look seemed to say, "If we're very still and very quiet, this situation will go away."

Amber reminded Hannah of a schoolteacher who had walked in on an unacceptable situation in the classroom.

"I asked if there was a problem."

"Yeah. There is. Their stinky horse and decrepit buggy are taking up two parking spaces." The boy who said this had long, unkempt hair, was very thin, and wore a black T-shirt.

"Stop being such a jerk, Cory." This from an *Englisch* girl with short blond hair. She had been walking to her car but had stopped to see what was happening. She was holding the hand of a little girl who stepped closer to hide behind her legs.

"We were trying to teach them some manners." The big guy must have been an athlete. He crossed his arms in front of him, reminding Hannah of the pictures of the Jolly Green Giant in the ads for vegetables she sometimes saw in the magazines from the library. Except this guy wasn't green, and he wasn't taller than buildings. His black hair was cut short—nearly to the scalp. He didn't look fazed at all by the attention they were drawing.

"You want to teach them manners?" Amber's voice sounded to Hannah like the low rumble of an automobile.

"Yeah. I do."

"And who put you in charge of teaching?"

"Hey, lady." The scrawny boy, Cory, had sauntered his way forward until he was standing directly in front of Amber. "You don't want to get involved with their kind of people." He hooked a thumb toward the Amish kids. "They kill each other with a bow and arrow. How messed up is that?" The kid's speech was slurred, so it came out sounding to Hannah like "How smeshed uh is dat?"

Amber pushed Cory aside and stomped over to the driver of the truck. "Are these two here with you?"

When the boy nodded, Amber pointed a finger at him and said, "Then I suggest you take them home."

"Or what?"

Hannah moved to the right but she still couldn't clearly see the driver. She could hear the sneer in his voice.

"Or I call the cops." Amber whipped out her cell phone. The light on it flashed when she pushed a button. "Is that how you want to spend your evening? Visiting with Middlebury's finest?"

The larger of the two boys standing outside the truck had turned his back on Noah and his friends. He had been opening the passenger side door to climb back into the truck. On hearing Amber's questions, he slammed the door shut and crossed back around the front toward her. He towered over Amber as he moved even closer and snarled, "You should probably stay out of this. We wouldn't want a little thing like you to get hurt."

"Cory, leave her alone!" The *Englisch* girl fumbled in her purse and pulled out her phone. Would she call the police?

It was at that point that everything went crazy.

Hannah and Jesse had been slowly making their way toward Noah and his friends. Noah shook his head once and held up a hand as if to stop them. Hannah glanced over at Amber and saw everything that happened next. She had a perfect view of the big guy, who made a move to push Amber, but she was having none of it. Instead, she darted to the right, then raised her foot and brought it down hard on the big guy's toe. He let out a howl as Amber's short, spiky heel pierced his tennis shoe.

He was hopping around on one foot, shouting and pointing, when the driver put the truck in park and hopped out to join the skirmish. He was also an athletic guy, though not as big as the other. His curly brown hair poked out from under a green-and-gold ball cap.

Everyone started shouting, and Hannah winced, waiting for the first punch to fly. Except there was no fight. There were four Amish kids standing next to their buggy, Jesse and Hannah in no-man's land, Amber and the *Englisch* girl holding their phones, and three *Englisch* boys wondering whether the brawl they'd been trying to start was worth it.

At that moment a police siren chirped twice, and a cruiser pulled into the parking lot with its lights flashing, effectively cutting off any escape by the pickup truck.

A uniformed woman stepped out of the cruiser. She looked young to Hannah, maybe in her twenties, and was thin and muscular. Her long red hair was pulled back with a black elastic band. It hung down her back, nearly reaching her belt.

"She's been at the Village before—last spring, I think." Jesse spoke in a whisper.

"*Ya*, her name is a fruit—Cherry. Now I remember. She was helping Sergeant Avery with the investigation."

"Everyone needs to take two paces back from where they're standing." Cherry's tone left no room for argument. She'd obviously scanned the scene and seemed to have come up with her own conclusion of what had happened. She spoke into the radio clipped to her shoulder, which squeaked once and then fell silent. Scowling, she waited for everyone to step back and quiet down before she said anything else.

Cherry walked up to all three boys, closely scrutinizing first the scrawny kid, then the big guy, and finally the driver. "Cory Monroe, Blake Jones, and Sam Hollister. Why am I not surprised that you three are involved in this?"

"Hey, we didn't—"

All three were protesting at once, but Cherry cut them off with a flick of her wrist and the words, "I said to move back."

The Amish kids attempted to back up, but they were already standing with their backs against their buggy. So instead, they took two steps to the right, sliding down the side of the buggy. Noah's face was flushed—a sure sign that he was battling his temper. The other boy with him looked worried, and the two girls were talking quietly to each other.

In the meantime, Cherry had pulled out her flashlight, flipped it on, and shone it into the truck—first the front seat, then the back, and finally the bed. Apparently she found nothing of interest. She surveyed the group and said, "I had a disturbance call."

"From her?" The sports guy pointed an accusing finger at Amber. "She practically broke my toe!"

"You started it, Cory." The *Englisch* girl had picked up the little girl, surely her sister—Hannah could now see the resemblance. She stepped closer to Cherry and said, "I didn't see it all, but I saw enough. If you need a witness I'd be happy to provide a statement."

"Did you call it in, Sandy?" The big guy looked hurt, more hurt than he had been by Amber.

"You're such a jerk." Sandy switched the little girl to her other hip and stomped off to her car.

"The call came from the manager, who is not happy that you're disrupting business. Now what exactly is going on here?"

"We wasn't doing nothing." Cory had trouble with the word *nothing*. It was as if he had a big ol' mouthful of shoofly pie and couldn't make his words come out right. He was still trying to back up and talk to Cherry at the same time. It was no surprise that he tripped over the curb and landed on the ground.

"Have you been drinking, Cory? That is not what your dad is going to want to hear."

"But—"

"Don't move."

Cherry turned back to the large boy, Blake. He was walking in a small circle and limping as if he'd had a table dropped on his foot. Hannah almost wanted to laugh. Amber was half his size. There was no chance her weight could have caused any damage, though the spiky heel probably did cause a bit of pain.

"You ought to arrest her. She stomped that stupid shoe on me for no reason at all—"

Amber touched a button on her phone, and suddenly they were all hearing again the events of the past few minutes. Hannah wasn't close enough to see, but the way Cherry was looking at the screen, she suspected that Amber had recorded the entire thing—audio and visual.

"That's all I need to see. I'm taking all three of you in for fighting."

"But we didn't even throw a punch," the driver argued, pulling off his ball cap and then repositioning it on his head.

"Sam, am I supposed to wait until you hurt someone? Move your truck to an open space, and then you're coming with me. And don't even try driving off. I've already made a note of your license plate. I'd love to add fleeing arrest to the list of charges."

Now Noah stepped forward. "There'll be no charges. It was only a misunderstanding."

Cherry shook her head. "These knuckleheads won't learn unless you—"

"*Nein*. It's not our way." Noah looked up, found Hannah and Jesse, and smiled slightly. "Thank you for coming, but now we'll be going home."

The driver laughed and said something under his breath.

"Amber? Would you like to press charges against this boy?" She pointed at the one Amber had stomped.

"No. I'm hoping he's learned an important lesson—such as minding his own business."

Cherry shook her head, her lips a thin, straight line. Finally she said, "Go on, then."

When Cory attempted to stand, she said, "Not you. I'm taking you in for being under the influence. You are still a minor, Cory."

"Yeah, but—"

"But nothing. Go stand beside my cruiser."

Amber continued to talk to Cherry after the truck had pulled away, but Hannah was no longer paying attention. She and Jesse had closed the gap between them and her brother. By the time she was sure everyone was fine, Cherry had placed Cory in the back of her police vehicle and left the parking lot.

"Are you all good to drive home?" Amber asked.

Noah reached for the hand of the girl closest to him and said, "*Ya*. We wouldn't normally have come in on a weeknight, but most of us are off tomorrow because of the funeral."

"I'm sorry this happened."

"Not your fault. No need to be sorry."

Hannah realized then that her brother was no longer a boy. Sometime when she hadn't been looking, when he'd been raising dogs and working the farm with her father, Noah had crossed over to being an adult.

Jesse and Hannah declined to ride back with Noah. Instead, they followed Amber to her car.

The ride home was quiet, the road swishing by as they drove through the night. By the time they reached Hannah's home, she'd practically forgotten the scene in the parking lot. Her mind was worrying over the list in Amber's purse.

"Thank you both for coming with me." Amber turned off the engine and cut the lights. "I'm not sure what we accomplished, but I do feel a little better. At least random bits of information aren't chasing each other around in my brain."

"We wouldn't want that." Jesse leaned forward and tapped her head with one finger. "Could give you a headache."

"Indeed it could."

"How about if we each take one person on the list?" Hannah squirmed in her seat so that she was facing Jesse and Amber. "Since our Suspects list isn't helpful, and our Involved list only contains our names and the police, let's break up the—"

"*In Danger* list." Amber pulled the pad of paper out of her bag and opened it to the sheet she'd been writing on. She touched a button, and the dome light in the car cast a glow down on the paper.

"The one name I have any association with is Mary." Amber tapped the paper. "I could try to speak with her at work on Wednesday."

"And I'll take Naomi." Hannah knew it was the right thing to do the moment she said it. "I might not be able to talk to her tomorrow, but I can talk to the kids and see how she's doing. I'll tell them to call the phone shack or come down to our house if there's anything that scares them."

"I'll take Andrew." Jesse was once again leaning between the two front seats.

Hannah's heart always beat faster when he was standing or sitting close to her. Was that love? Would her heart constantly trip at a faster rhythm if they were to marry?

Marrying would also mean they would know each other better than they knew any other person. That was happening already. She could tell by his scowl that he was worried, not angry. He was also determined. She'd seen that expression often enough.

Jesse glanced up at her, then over at Amber. "One way or another, my *bruder* is going to talk to me."

Twenty-Five

He was not happy about being back in Middlebury. His plan had been to stay in South Bend until at least Tuesday evening, maybe Wednesday. Then he'd seen the notice in the local paper about Owen's funeral—front-page news because of the sensational way he'd done it. There weren't too many murders with bows and arrows. It wouldn't do for him to miss the funeral. Might arouse suspicion. Theirs was a fairly small community, and everyone was expected to turn out and support the family of the deceased.

He'd caught a ride back home with an old gent in a decrepit-looking pickup truck. Little chance their paths would ever cross again.

Now he sat in his buggy, in a long line of buggies, as they made their way toward Owen's final resting place. A steady downpour obscured most everything around them. The rain was a blessing, though—would help the land and the animals. It would also help to cover any tracks he might have left on his errands.

"Terrible thing about Owen," his wife said. The observation was delivered in a flat tone and with no expression at all. Typical.

"*Ya*, God has numbered each of our days."

The words slipped out before he had a chance to consider them. As silence once again reclaimed the buggy, he realized that perhaps he'd hit on something. God did number each of their days. The psalmist proclaimed as much.

Did he have the power to overrule God? *Nein.* It wasn't possible. So perhaps Owen would have died anyway—hit by a car or seized by a terrible illness.

Perhaps he had no reason to feel at fault.

Glancing toward her, he saw the pinched face and too-thin figure, and guilt flooded his heart, but not because of Owen. There were times he didn't think he could stand up to this responsibility one more day.

The Amish did divorce.

It was rare, but it had been done.

The bishop couldn't disallow what the law provided for—the dissolution of a marriage. However, within their community he would pay the price. He'd be banned from the church and need to leave the area for good. What would become of his farm? Was he willing to go that far?

It might be necessary. He acknowledged the possibility to himself for the first time. It wasn't the solution he would choose, but it might be the only solution if his situation became worse.

Not now, of course. Best to wait for things to settle down.

A sigh escaped his lips as he focused on the road and followed slowly in the long line of buggies to the graveyard. He didn't relish leaving her alone, with no one to provide for her—but then again, the community would provide.

It wasn't the future he'd hoped for, but then, life hadn't turned out according to his wishes. Which was why he'd had to take matters into his own hands.

What was it the *Englisch* said?

Drastic times called for drastic measures.

In his case, that had certainly held true.

Twenty-Six

Rain pelted against the roof and thunder rumbled in the distance. Amber sat in her office, sharing a cup of coffee with Elizabeth.

"So you told Tate all that has happened with Owen's case?"

"Yes." Amber shook her head. "I didn't intend to. I didn't want to worry him, but somehow when we were on the phone the words spilled out of their own accord."

"It's part of being married, the need to share everything with one another."

"I suppose. Fortunately, he took it all in stride, which is Tate's way."

"He wasn't worried about the altercation with the teenagers?"

"Not at all. He knows all three families, and he said their parents would take care of things."

"And what did he think of your list?"

"His exact words were 'Agatha is at it again.'"

"Still teasing you about the books you read."

"He is! But he also understands my concern for Mary."

"She's a kind woman, and she has always been a good employee."

"How could she be tied up in this?" Amber reached for her

cup of fruit. The idea occurred to her that if she'd been eating a cinnamon roll she could probably think better.

"Let's see." Elizabeth removed her glasses and wiped them clean with the hem of her skirt. "We know she became a sort of go-between for Amish teens who left home."

"*Ya.* While they were away, they would call her to receive information about local events within their community. According to Hannah and Jesse, most of those who leave do come back."

"Why Mary?" Elizabeth asked.

"I suspect she stepped into the role because she wasn't courting or married, which I still don't understand. She's a pretty girl in her own way."

"That's exactly what my momma used to say about my homely cousin."

"Still, she would make someone a good wife, and the Amish focus less on appearances."

"Or so we hear. It seems to me that it's more a matter of a girl's opinion of herself. If she feels good about herself, then she has a different posture and attitude."

"True. Mary's attitude is mostly defensive—at least it has been lately."

"That sometimes happens when you don't follow the role that's been carved out for you."

"Marrying young?"

Elizabeth folded her glasses carefully and allowed them to hang from the chain around her neck. This one was made of tiny maroon and gold beads that twinkled each time she moved.

"Since most Amish girls do marry young, perhaps she felt some pressure because she hadn't. For whatever reason, Mary immersed herself in her job here and in helping Amish breakaways." Elizabeth sipped her coffee and stared out at the rain.

"She became close friends with Owen, close enough that he was calling her the morning he was killed."

"Why would he be calling her on the morning he died? What could have been his reasons?"

"To talk about his morning? To share tidbits about someone else? To talk about ISG? Maybe to talk about a girlfriend— get some relationship advice? Who knows? Kids are on those phones all the time. Have you seen the studies about how many texts they send?"

Amber nodded. She received less than a dozen texts a week, and usually those were work-related. Occasionally she'd receive one from her sister. She and Tate rarely texted, probably because her work was so close to home. One or the other could drop in if necessary. But she had seen the numbers on teen texting. "Most teens send an average of sixty texts per day. That was on the news the other night."

"I wonder if Owen sent any texts on that phone of his."

"Good question. I'm sure the police know. They still have the phone. Also, why didn't the killer pick up the phone? He had to know it could provide some evidence."

"Maybe not." Elizabeth tapped her fingernail against the side of her glass. "Older Amish, especially, aren't always aware of the existing technology. He—we can assume it was a he—might not even be aware that the phone call record was available to police."

"That makes sense. A teenager or young adult probably would have nabbed the phone and disposed of it."

"Unless they were too afraid."

"Remember Ethan's killer?" Amber shook her head. "No fear there."

"No touch with reality either."

"True, but my point is, to be able to do something as atrocious as killing someone, the person's emotions must be turned off to some extent."

"Unless it's a crime of passion." Elizabeth stood and collected the remains of their midmorning snack, dumping it all into the trash. "So Hannah and Jesse are helping you on this?"

"They are, though both are at the funeral today. Which reminds me that I need to go and talk to someone."

"Business or a murder lead?"

"Possibly both."

"All right. But be careful."

"Will do, my friend." She said the last word with a smile and then walked around the desk to hug Elizabeth. The woman was a combination of best friend and mother, and Amber thanked the Lord every morning that she walked into their offices and saw her smiling face. "I should be back in half an hour. Be sure to let me know when Pam checks in. I need her to be my sidekick tonight, if she's willing."

"If I've learned one thing about Pam Coleman since she came to work here, it's that she's usually willing."

⁂

Amber stepped into The Cat's Meow, pausing to shake the rain off her umbrella and close it before allowing the door to shut behind her. Immediately her tension level dropped. Who could remain anxious around so much yarn? Every color she could imagine winked at her from the myriad bins that filled the store.

Oh, but she wished she knew how to use some of it. Mary had once offered to teach her, but Amber had never had time to take her up on it. Perhaps she should make time. She couldn't spend all her hours working and chasing murderers. Television rarely appealed to her. If she knew how to knit or crochet, perhaps those evenings when Tate was away, though they were few and far between, wouldn't stretch on interminably.

"Can I help you, Mrs. Bowman?" Helen Stinson stood behind the counter. The girl was so short that folks often mistook her for a young teenager.

Amber guessed she topped out at five foot two. Her long, dark hair slid down her back like a beautiful mane. Indeed, Helen was a very pretty young girl, though her style of dress often drew odd looks from the Amish employees. Today she was wearing blue jeans with a bright pink T-shirt that read "Keep Calm and Carry On."

Amber had considered insisting the staff wear uniforms, but with so many of her employees being Amish it had seemed like a waste of time. Although Helen's choice of clothing was often unusual, there was nothing wrong with the jeans or T-shirts she wore. They were always clean and even—as Amber could see when she stepped closer—pressed. The crease lines were evident on the shoulders of her T-shirt. Amber had never brought up the subject of Helen's appearance, and she was glad she hadn't.

As usual Helen wore a fashionable pair of glasses, this time with bright-red frames. She had several pairs that she switched out regularly. Helen's mother was the optometrist in town, so Helen probably received the glasses at a discounted price. The mom had confessed to Amber that she'd hoped Helen would work for her selling eyeglasses, but Helen had other plans. With her ambition, no doubt she would be vying for Pam's job in a few years—or Amber's.

The girl was all attitude, energy, and goals. Helen set the bottle of water she'd been drinking down on the counter, and Amber noticed her nails were painted a bright-pink color with a dash of shiny silver across each nail. Helen had her own style. That was certain. Would she go to college? Or would she decide experience was more important? Helen was at the point in her life when anything seemed possible, but then, weren't they all? It only took a decision to act and the will to follow it through.

"Actually, you might be able to help me. How's business today?"

"Comes in spurts, as usual, but no problems. Mary trained me well, once she understood I was her replacement whether she liked me or not."

"Now, Helen. I can't imagine Mary disliking anyone."

Helen cocked her head, a gesture that reminded Amber of Leo when he was considering how best to pounce on a mouse. Finally she shook the thought away and shrugged.

"How has Mary been lately?"

"You mean since her arrest?" Helen tapped a long nail against her lips.

"She wasn't arrested, exactly. She was questioned and released."

"Do you mind if I ask, like, why you want to know? I wouldn't want to tattle on anyone."

"Of course not. It's only that I'm worried about her. She missed a meeting and she seems . . . troubled."

"Yeah. That's a good way to put it."

"So you have noticed something?"

Helen plopped down on the stool behind the counter. Amber was a big proponent of stools, as long as her clerks didn't use them while customers were in the store. She actually was for anything that would keep her employees happy without compromising the professionalism of the Village. Happy employees equaled long-time employees, and longtime employees meant less expense spent on training.

"I guess. She seems, you know, distracted. A couple of times she left for lunch and forgot to take her lunch bag with her." Helen rolled her eyes. "Stuff like that."

"Oh." What had Amber expected? That Mary might have left a journal sitting around, detailing her activities?

"Then there's that guy who has been hanging around."

"What guy?"

Helen shrugged. "I don't know his name. He won't come into the shop. He knocks on the back door and then waits until Mary can step away for a moment. Not that she takes too many breaks or anything. That's only happened a few times, but three of them were since that guy's murder. Do you think it's related?"

"I doubt it, but could you describe this person to me?"

Helen stared up at the ceiling, as if that would help her remember. "Average height, wears a ball cap and blue jeans—and boots. He always has on those boots."

Where had she heard that description before? From Hannah! It had to be the same guy.

"You're saying he's *Englisch*?" she asked.

"I guess, but how can you be sure? Amish kids on their *rumspringa* often dress like us. When they dress like us, they look like us—except for the haircut, and I couldn't see that because of the ball cap."

Amber suppressed a smile. "They *are* like us, Helen. They're people. It's only that they live a little differently."

"A little? The no-cars thing I could maybe deal with. Cars are a big expense, and we could all do with a little more walking or public transit. But no makeup? No nail polish? I'd die."

"Hmm." Amber waited a moment, trying to envision an autopsy report stating cause of death as "*lack of beauty supplies.*" "So this person, you don't know his name?"

"Nope. He's never introduced himself. He asks for Mary and that's about all he says."

"How does she act when he comes by?"

"Worried, but then, that's her go-to disposition."

Amber wanted to reprimand the girl, to tell her not to be so judgmental, but then again, her analysis was pretty accurate. Mary was a worrier.

"You've been very helpful. Thank you, and I appreciate your filling in all day today while Mary's out."

"Not a problem."

"By the way, Helen"—Amber had been walking to the front door, but now she turned and studied the girl—"has anyone ever mentioned that you have a very attractive style?"

Helen looked at Amber as if she was clueless to what she was saying.

"The T-shirts, matching nail colors, pressed jeans . . . and choice of glasses. It all blends together nicely, and you make it look as if you effortlessly threw it together. That kind of coordination takes a little work. I'm sure customers feel energized when they come in and are waited on by you."

A blush had started to creep up Helen's cheeks, and a smile was tugging at the corners of her lips. "Uh . . . thanks."

"You're welcome."

As Amber stepped back out into the rain, she made a mental note to compliment the girl more often. A little honest praise was a powerful thing.

Twenty-Seven

Amber wanted answers. She decided to stop by the employee break room. She didn't do that too often, as she wanted it to be a place where employees could rest and not worry about their boss hanging around. But today she was still thinking about a cinnamon roll, and she knew that Georgia often placed the day-old bakery items in the room for employees.

The rain had weakened her resolve to watch her sugar intake. Plus, another cup of hot coffee sounded fabulous. Soon she'd have so much sugar and caffeine in her system, she'd speed through her to-do list like Wonder Woman.

The break room was set up in the back of the inn, next to the maintenance rooms. What had started out as a plain room, twelve by fifteen feet with a single window, had turned into a small haven. Two couches sat against the walls. The flat-screen television positioned on top of the bookcase was on but muted. Some of the girls had sewn curtains for the window, which softened the room considerably. An employee bulletin board was filled with everything from items for sale to birth announcements. A mishmash of lamps, tables, and chairs finished up the room.

Two of the grounds employees sat in a corner playing checkers. Amber had noticed that both Amish and *Englisch* were enjoying the board games they added. It was nice to see young people actually interacting with one another, not mesmerized by some electronic device. But then she noticed Bradley, sitting in a corner chair, long legs spread out in front of him, red hair falling into eyes glued to the screen of his phone.

She had hired him to handle technology. It should not come as a surprise that he was mesmerized by electronic things. She was pretty sure his eyes were dilated as he stared at the screen, his thumbs pushing buttons. Texting or gaming. Amber did not understand the fascination with online gaming.

The three employees offered a hello but didn't seem overly interested in her. Amber sidled up to the treats table to see what was available—buttermilk sugar cookies, snickerdoodles, and two cinnamon rolls. Score!

She plopped one of the rolls onto a napkin and poured herself a cup of coffee. She intended to take it back to her office, but when she turned around, she noticed Preston Johnstone had walked into the room.

"Preston, it's so good to see you."

"Morning." Her assistant manager of maintenance was a soft-spoken man, tall, clean shaven, and extremely conscientious about his work. He was a bright spot in Amber's employee files.

"Do you have a minute to talk? I'd love to hear how you're doing."

"Sure. I stopped in to grab some coffee and check the bulletin board. I'm considering buying a car, if I find the right used one."

"I'll wait over at the table. You do what you need to do, then grab the last of Georgia's cinnamon rolls. They're the perfect snack for a rainy day."

Five minutes later they were settled at a table on the far side of the room. "Any luck on the car?"

"No. I'm not in a hurry, though. I've gone this long without one. In fact, I rather like walking, but it might be nice to be able to drive out of town for the day."

She couldn't help shaking her head as she studied Preston.

"Is my hair sticking up again?" He patted down his hair at the top, but they both knew it was shaved too close to actually stick up. She could hardly tell it was brown, he wore it so short. That was probably a habit left over from his stint in Afghanistan.

"I was thinking that you hardly resemble the man I met six months ago."

"Which is a good thing." He took a giant bite of the sweet roll.

"Now, you didn't look so bad even then."

"Maybe you should have seen the expression on your face when we first met."

"I'd never met a homeless man before. You could cut me some slack."

"I suppose I could, especially since you gave me this job."

"You earned this job, Preston. You started out on a conditional three-month trial, same as everyone else."

"But you didn't allow everyone else to sleep in your barn."

"It was only for a few weeks. Special circumstances call for . . . you know."

"I do." Preston took a sip of his coffee. "But you did let me stay until Norman offered me a room at his place, and I appreciate that."

"What was it like . . . living with an Amish person?" Amber sat forward, her hands clasped around her coffee cup. "I know Norman's a good guy. He makes amazing toys, and his shop here at the Village is one of our most popular. But what was it like living with him?"

"About like you'd imagine." Preston's slow smile lit up his face. "Sort of like living with my grandparents when they had a home back in the woods."

"And now you're living in our *dawdy haus*. I think it's perfect!"

He sat back, glancing around the room before he said, "I owe a lot of folks. Without my friends and this community, I might not have found my way back. I want to thank you for all you've done for me—all you and Tate have done."

"And I would like to thank you for how hard you work. How do you like the *dawdy haus*? I enjoyed it while I was living there."

"Fine. Staying there has been very convenient, especially since I don't have transportation at this point."

Amber wrapped up the rest of her cinnamon roll. "You're helping us out by doing it. Now we have someone on the property all night, which takes a big worry off my shoulders."

"It's rare that I receive a call in the middle of the night."

"Not too many coons loose in the inn?"

"Not this month."

It was remarkable how much Preston had changed. When she'd met him, when she'd been trying to solve Ethan Gray's murder, Preston had looked like a completely different man. He'd sported a beard then and had always worn an old army coat. Preston had been homeless, living wherever he could catch some sleep without being harassed. The evening Tate took Amber to meet him, Preston had been staying near Krider Gardens, under a giant statue of a mushroom.

Amber was only forty-five, and Preston had recently turned thirty. But in many ways, he felt like the son she'd never had. In many ways, she was closer to him than she was to Tate's children. That wasn't something she had expected, but then, life sometimes took unforeseen twists and turns.

"You were a big help to me when we were trying to figure out who killed Ethan."

"Which was the job of the police. I'm still not clear on how you became entangled in that mess." The words sounded like a reprimand, but the look on Preston's face was one of pure concern.

"Well, the police were working the case. I certainly didn't plan to become involved, but since he was my employee, more clues fell into my lap than theirs."

"I hope you're not planning on a future in law enforcement."

She could tell by his tone that he was half teasing, half serious.

"Not at all. I'm happy running the Village, thank you."

"Ah. That's a relief. I was worried you might become involved in this current case, the one with the guy killed by an arrow."

Amber stared down at her hands. "I wouldn't say I'm not involved. I'd say I'm less involved."

"Meaning what?"

"Meaning I'm trying to figure it out, but I'm not having much luck."

"Why?"

"Why what?"

Preston leaned forward and lowered his voice. "Why do you allow yourself to become swept up in something like this? Leave it to the professionals."

"Pooh. You sound like Sergeant Avery."

"And Tate?"

"He might agree with both of you, but if he does, he isn't being too vocal about it. He keeps reminding me to be careful."

"Smart man."

"To tell you the truth, I'm rather stuck. It's one of the reasons I was seeking solace in a giant roll covered in sugar."

"So maybe you should step away. In the military you learn to compartmentalize. If it's not your assigned duty, you don't spend any mental or physical energy on it."

"I imagine in the military that's necessary to survive." Amber fidgeted with the napkin wrapped around the remainder of her roll. She appreciated what Preston was saying. It wasn't often that he shared any of his experiences in the military. She knew he'd had major problems adjusting when he came home and that was why he had been homeless. She didn't know any of the details.

"It's Mary I'm worried about," she confessed.

"Mary Weaver?"

"The same."

"I heard about her being taken in for questioning."

"Have you heard anything else?"

Preston didn't answer immediately. He downed the last swig of coffee, collected his trash and hers, and then gestured toward the door. "Not here," he said, the eyebrows over his brown eyes forming a V of concern.

Amber nodded, picked up her umbrella, and followed him out the back door of the inn and into the weather. The rain was still coming down, so they stood under the eaves of the roof, both of their backs against the building.

"You've heard something?"

"There are always rumors passing from one department to another, one person to another. Hard to know what's true and what's from folks watching too much crime television."

"All right. What did you hear?"

"That it could have been an Amish person, one with a grudge to settle."

"Amish folks don't settle grudges."

"Normally they don't—"

"They forgive and forget."

"Yes, but there's an exception for every stereotype." Preston bent his knee and placed one foot against the wall. She could tell by the way his voice changed that once again he was remembering. "Sometimes threats can come from a place you would never expect. Owen didn't expect it, and that's why he's dead. The world can be a dangerous place—even for the Amish."

"Yes, I know it can be. You're right, of course. But who is saying the killer was Amish? Is it the *Englisch* employees? Because there's some existing animosity between the two groups. Not much, but it flares up occasionally. I saw it myself in town last night."

"Was there a problem?"

"Nothing I couldn't handle, with a little help from the Middlebury PD."

Preston folded his arms and stared out at the rain. "It wasn't *Englisch* employees suggesting the killer was Amish, and before you ask me—I don't know who. I've heard a few things, but the conversations stop when I walk into the room."

"Welcome to management."

"I've also heard that it could be an *Englisch* person, an enemy Owen made while he was away."

"That would have to be some enemy to follow him back to Middlebury, lay in wait for him, and then kill him with a bow and arrow."

"True. Sounds like a lot of planning, but think about it. What better way to cast suspicion upon someone from Owen's community?"

Amber chewed on that possibility for a minute. "One more question and I'll let you go. Someone has been stopping in to see Mary. He always waits at the back of the shop."

"Amish guy. I've run into him a couple of times."

"You're sure he's Amish?"

Preston nodded.

"I'd heard he was *Englisch*. Blue jeans, baseball cap, and—"

"Boots. Yeah, I know. But under that ball cap his hair is still cut in a chili-bowl fashion. And the accent? Definitely German. Want me to keep an eye out for him?"

"Maybe. If you see him on the property again, text me. I might want to ask him a few questions. Preston, what I would like . . ." She reached out and touched his arm. "I'd like for you to keep an eye on Mary and possibly Hannah and Jesse too. I don't want anyone else getting hurt."

Twenty-Eight

he funeral for Owen Esch was a dismal, wet affair.

At least folks had turned out, as they always turned out to help one in need. The outpouring of love was also evident in the large spread of food set up inside Naomi's kitchen. Due to the size of the crowd, even larger than the day before, many of the men were crowded outside on the front porch. Virtually all the children, younger and older, had taken their plates of food to the barn. The rain continued to pour from the sky, as if from a faucet that wouldn't be turned off.

"I believe I'll take some of the desserts out to the children," Hannah said to her mother. "We have plenty, and I'm not sure they had room on their plates when they left."

Eunice smiled in agreement and turned to help one of their elderly members.

Hannah nabbed a plate of brownies and another of sugar cookies. Stuffing them inside a bag her mother had used to bring their dishes, she hurried out into the rain. Her hope was that if she moved quickly enough, she wouldn't be too drenched by the time she reached the barn.

She needn't have worried.

Andrew appeared at her side, holding an umbrella over her and directing her around the puddles, which were quickly turning into small ponds.

When they reached the barn door, Andrew collapsed the umbrella and turned to smile at Hannah.

"Perfect timing. *Danki*."

"*Gem gschehne*." His eyes twinkled as he opened the barn door. When she passed him, he leaned closer and whispered, "Good cover story, bringing sweets."

She nearly dropped the bag. "Cover story?"

"*Ya*. Jesse told me you were trying to get information out of Naomi's *kinner*."

Jesse had told him that?

"Where is Jesse?"

"Grabbing a bite before he has to return to buggy duty. Not an easy job in this weather."

"And why aren't you helping?"

Instead of being offended, Andrew laughed. "The novelty of my being home hasn't worn off yet. My *dat* suggested that I come to the barn and see if the children needed any supervision."

He seemed to be telling the truth, but Hannah was pretty sure he wasn't telling the whole truth. She was about to call him on it when they were mobbed by youngsters.

Amish families were large by nature. Birth control wasn't practiced, unless you counted a woman watching the calendar and being careful about when she spent extra time with her husband. That method wasn't foolproof, as the midwife had informed them all at one time or another. Children were considered a blessing—the more, the better. "No woman can be happy with less than seven to cook for" was a common proverb Hannah had heard since she was young.

She was used to seeing families with eight, nine, even ten children. Her family, with five siblings, was small by comparison. The occasional family with an only child or no children at all seemed incomplete to her. But that was a judgmental thought. God alone knew how many children it took to make a family complete.

It was easy enough to pick out Naomi's six children. They all had hair whiter than a fluffy cloud on a summer day. The older two, a boy and a girl, stood close to the younger ones, whispering to them and insisting they stay back until all the guests had chosen a dessert.

"There's enough," Hannah assured them. "I brought two plates full, and there's more in the house."

The girl's name was Lucy—it came to Hannah in a flash. Lucy seemed unconvinced. Two younger children stood on each side of the older boy, and two stood behind him. He tugged on their small hands and pulled them toward the plates Hannah still held.

Each took one treat, though Hannah had the impression they would like more.

"Lucy—it is Lucy, isn't it? I heard your *bruder* say your name earlier." Andrew's voice was pleasant and even-toned. "Hannah and I would like to speak with you for a moment. If you have time."

"I guess." She glanced down at her two little sisters.

"I'll take them over to play with the others," her brother said. The children trailed behind him like ducklings obediently following momma duck, or in this case—big brother.

"Is something wrong?" Lucy asked.

"Nein." Andrew took the large and now half-empty plates of brownies and cookies from Hannah's hands and set them down on one of the makeshift tables. "We're trying to find out what happened to your *onkel* Owen."

Hannah threw a skeptical glance at Andrew. Since when was he on their side, trying to help with this tragic mystery? What exactly had Jesse said to him?

"I don't know anything about that." Lucy took one of the sugar cookies from the plate and began to nibble around the edges.

"Could you tell us about the box your *mamm* received?" Hannah motioned toward the area to the right of them. Several wooden crates had been placed in a semicircle, no doubt put there for some game the children had been playing. When the three of them were seated, they had a measure of privacy, though the children's voices continued to echo from a few feet away as they once again resumed a game of red light–green light.

"The box the police took?" Lucy asked.

"*Ya.* Unless she's received more than one box." Andrew pulled a piece of hay from a bale someone had placed next to the crates. Examining it for a moment, he popped it into his mouth and proceeded to chew on the end.

"Only the one," Lucy muttered.

She was probably twelve years old, with a pert little nose and a nice profile. Hannah thought she would grow up to be a real beauty one day. Not that they were to focus on such things. Hannah pushed up her glasses and waited for Lucy to say more, but she didn't seem so inclined.

"Can you tell us anything about the box or about the writing in the note?" Andrew was spurting out questions as if he had been the one up all night thinking about how best to quiz Naomi's children.

"Nothing to tell. Just a box. And the way my *mamm's* name was written was nothing special."

"Print or cursive?" Hannah asked.

"A combination of both, I suppose."

"Could you tell if it was a man's hand or a woman's that wrote it?" Andrew leaned forward, elbows on his knees.

"*Nein.*"

"Could you tell if it was from someone local?" Hannah inched toward the end of her crate.

"*Nein.*"

"Did you read the note?" Andrew held out his hand in a wait gesture. "Which would have been understandable, if you did. No doubt you try to help your *mamm*, and perhaps you thought you could take care of whatever it was."

"*Nein.* I didn't read the note."

Hannah and Andrew exchanged glances. Apparently this line of questioning was a dead end. Hannah tried to think of what else she had planned to ask the girl.

"I can show it to you, if you like."

"Show us?" Hannah stared at her. Maybe she'd heard wrong.

"*Ya.*"

"Show us the note? Or the box?" Andrew dropped the straw of hay onto the ground. "I thought the police took it all."

"Surely they did. Didn't they?"

"*Ya*, the police took the note and the box. But the box was wrapped in brown paper." Lucy stood and walked over to a dozen or so bins—cubbies, actually—that were positioned next to the barn's north wall. They were filled with everything from hand tools to gloves to pieces of string and paper.

Lucy reached into a bin on the far right, third up from the bottom, and pulled out a piece of brown butcher paper. "I did unwrap it when the box came. Then after I showed *Mamm* and she began to cry, I didn't know what to do with the paper."

Hannah's heart began to race as she accepted the folded paper from Lucy.

"I didn't want to make *Mamm* sad again by asking her

whether I should throw it away. *Mamm* is sad often enough." The girl spoke in a matter-of-fact manner, and Hannah realized that much of the family's domestic chores probably fell on her, probably had for many years. "The police didn't ask for it either. I didn't even think of it until later, after they'd gone. So I folded it up and brought it out here."

Hannah opened up the paper and smoothed it out by holding it against the wall and swiping the palm of her hand across it. The sheet was approximately three feet by three feet—the right size to cover a box.

"How large was the box, Lucy?" Hannah didn't know how it could matter, but every piece of information might help.

"Oh, it was a shoe box. No doubt about that. Had 'Outlanders' stamped on the side. But . . . I don't think I was supposed to tell anybody that."

That was probably why Sergeant Avery had not mentioned the box to Amber and Tate. Any markings on the shoe box would be evidence he had not been ready to share, even with them.

"Outlanders makes hiking shoes," Andrew said. "Mostly *Englischers* wear them, but I've seen a few Amish who prefer them as well."

Lucy's bottom lip began to quiver. "We thought . . . we all thought, when *Onkel* Owen came home, that things might be different." She crossed her arms, effectively hugging herself, and stared down at the floor.

"Lucy?" Andrew waited for her to glance up. "We're going to find out who did this. It won't bring your *onkel* back, but you don't need to be afraid."

The young girl nodded once, and Andrew returned his attention to the piece of butcher paper. After a few moments, agonizing moments during which Hannah couldn't see a single clue on the object of their inspection, he reached into his pocket and pulled out a white sheet of paper.

It was lined and folded.

He didn't unfold it, but he did place it on the wall beside the butcher paper.

On the butcher paper someone had written "Naomi Graber."

On Andrew's paper someone had written "Mary Weaver."

Only four of the letters were the same, but there was no doubt about the handwriting. It was identical. Hannah turned to Andrew, and he whispered, "We have a match."

"The same person who sent Naomi the box sent Mary a note?"

"It would seem so. We don't need a handwriting specialist to tell us the two match. Look at the *a*'s. They all have a tail that goes up and breaks before the next letter."

"And the first letters are all printed, but the rest is cursive." Hannah had trouble swallowing. "These must be from the killer. He was trying to compensate for Naomi's loss, but why the note to Mary? What does it say?"

Andrew folded the butcher paper and was about to answer— at least it seemed to her he was. Lucy stood behind them, shuffling from one foot to the other. And the children continued to play.

Suddenly the familiar sounds of the afternoon were broken. Over the pattering of rain, Hannah heard the chirp of a siren. They hurried to the door in time to see two cars from the Middlebury police department pull up the lane. Several officers, including Sergeant Avery, exited the vehicles. Avery looked around and then walked up the steps of Naomi's home.

Twenty-Nine

*A*mber had plowed through a ton of paperwork after returning to her office. She had successfully cleaned out her e-mail and was taking a few minutes to do more research on survivalist groups when Elizabeth stuck her head into the office.

"You have company."

"Someone I want to see?"

"I doubt it." Elizabeth was about to elaborate when Roland Shaw stepped out from behind her.

"I'm sure Mrs. Bowman will be happy to see me." He didn't wait to be invited into the office. "Otherwise she might be obstructing justice."

Amber took the time to click the Sleep button with her mouse. It was none of Roland Shaw's business what she was doing on her computer. For some reason she couldn't pinpoint, she'd rather he didn't know.

"Would you like me to stay?" Elizabeth asked, not even attempting to hide her distrust of the man.

"We're fine." Amber waved her away. "I'm sure Mr. Shaw can't spare much time to visit with me. After all, he is in the middle of a murder investigation."

Elizabeth threw him a rather unfriendly glance, then held

up her thumb and pinky in the gesture of picking up the phone. "If you need me," she mouthed silently before marching out of the room.

Shaw walked around her office, surveying the Amish quilt on the wall, her framed business degree, and finally the view from her window.

"What can I do for you, Mr.—"

"Call me Roland." He turned toward her and offered his megawatt smile.

The guy made her skin itch, as if something creepy were crawling up her arms. What was it about him that irritated her so much? One part of her mind realized he was merely doing his job, but it was the way he did it that caused her to distrust him. His arrogant attitude set her teeth on edge. And those clothes—always the black pants and black tie. Always a plaid shirt. She'd like to suggest he try a pair of jeans or a solid-white shirt. She'd like to wipe that smirk off his face. Instead, she focused on moving him out of her office as quickly as possible.

"Mr. Shaw, what can I do for you?"

"Mainly I wanted to chat. Update you on our investigation."

"And why would you do that? I find it hard to believe that courtesy is your motivation."

Instead of being offended, Shaw laughed, sat down across from her desk, and cocked his head. "You tend to speak your mind."

"Yes, I do, and honestly, I can't think of any reason for you to be here. If there's something I need to know about the investigation, Sergeant Avery will tell me."

"Locals." Shaw dismissed them with a grunt. "Although the murder investigation appears to be coming to a close—"

"To a close?"

"I felt obliged to inform you that my investigation of area groups will remain open."

"Area groups?"

"Survivalist groups, Amber. You know about them. Right?"

"Know about them?" Amber realized she was echoing Shaw's words, but her mind was spinning. Had he said the investigation was nearly closed? And if so, how? When? Who?

"Yes. For example, I know you've been in contact with the Rhodeses."

Amber's heart began to race. She had actually called Tom and Sue to set up a meeting for that afternoon. Pam had agreed to go with her. But how could Shaw know that?

"It's not illegal to teach folks emergency preparedness, and it's certainly not against the law to learn it."

"Call it what you want." Shaw leaned forward. "These people are all the same—they're anarchists. They want the economy to fail or the government to fall."

"Why would anyone want that?"

Shaw shrugged. "Lots of reasons. Maybe they're adrenaline junkies. Maybe they're paranoid. Or maybe . . ." His gaze took on an intensity that puzzled Amber, but then she realized his words were not meant solely for her. He actually believed what he was saying. "Maybe they have a vested interest."

"How could anyone have a vested interest in the fall of the US economy or the US government? That's insane."

Shaw let out a laugh. "Now you're being purposely naive. Some people do invest in the collapse of our government. They buy up stocks in gold and silver, then blog and post and tweet about the collapse of the US Treasury. Sometimes they go so far as to push the balance a bit by spreading rumors about impending disasters."

"I don't know who you've been meeting with, but the Rhodeses are not like that."

"Surely you don't think they dedicate their time, monies, and energy out of a sense of altruism."

"Do you know what I think?" Amber stood and pushed the button on her phone to beckon Elizabeth. "I think this meeting is over."

"Fine. But the deeper you decide to go with these groups, the more you'll be watched. Can you stand up to that degree of scrutiny? Are you willing to trade your privacy to satisfy your blooming curiosity?"

Elizabeth appeared at the door.

"Would you see Mr. Shaw out, please?"

"I'd be glad to." Elizabeth ducked her chin and peered over the top of her glasses at Shaw. She might be eight inches shorter, maybe more, but she could still convey a don't-mess-with-me message with one look. Amber didn't think he would be foolish enough to make a scene.

He was at the door when she remembered what he'd said earlier, and although she'd rather not ask this man anything, her curiosity won.

"You said the investigation of Owen Esch's death was nearly closed. Why do you think that?"

"I don't think it. I know it." Shaw glanced at his watch. "By now they have the suspect in custody."

And without another word, he turned and left her office.

Jesse had fetched the Waglers' buggy. It was unusual for a family to leave before the luncheon was finished, but then, Uri and

Olivia Wagler had never been concerned about social conventions. Like several of the families in their district, they followed the *Ordnung* but held themselves a bit apart from the other members.

They weren't the only odd members in their district. Manasses Hochstetler was as friendly as could be, but he tended to talk your ear off about the why and how of camels, never realizing he was boring you into a good afternoon snooze. Strange fellow.

Naomi and Jonas Graber were another fine example. Their poverty might have embarrassed them, Jonas's illness could have changed the way they interacted with others, or possibly they pulled away because of the problems caused when Owen had chosen to leave the community. Whatever the reason, they'd never appeared at ease when the community gathered together. It was more as if they were enduring the moments until they could be alone again.

Then there was the odd behavior of the Yoder family. They appeared to be fairly outgoing. The oldest boy, Henry, also worked at the Village. He was as friendly as could be. But the family was nearly always the first to leave, which could have been due to the fact that they had twelve children to watch over during gatherings.

Jesse was thinking on these things and the strangeness of their little community. All groups were probably that way. They might look normal on the outside, boring even, but on the inside they were made up of individual people, families, and still-smaller groups. On the inside were secrets, many of which he'd rather not know.

Jesse wondered if Hannah had managed to talk with Naomi's children. He was walking back toward the main house, leading the Waglers' buggy, when the blip of a siren split the quietness of the afternoon. Two police cruisers trundled down the lane, spewing mud and splattering rainwater. Their lights were spinning, and they chirped their sirens once more—as if he wouldn't see them and get out of the way. They didn't even slow down when they passed him in their haste to reach the Graber home.

Once there, four officers exited the two vehicles, seemingly oblivious to the rain. All four glanced around. At a nod from one of them, they turned toward the porch steps and climbed them. Gordon Avery—Jesse could make the man out now that he was closer—hesitated and spoke to two of the officers, a man and a woman. In fact, it was the same woman he'd seen at the Dairy Queen the night before. Name like a fruit—Cherry. When Avery spoke to them, they walked back down the steps and stood there as water poured onto their raincoats, surveying the property.

Jesse didn't know what they were doing, but it wasn't good. It couldn't be good. His pulse began to thump louder in his veins, and sweat pooled at the small of his back.

If they'd come to deliver bad news, they wouldn't have brought two vehicles.

And they wouldn't be watching, standing at attention, as if they expected someone to make a run for it.

Avery knocked on the front door.

By now, Jesse had led the Waglers' buggy nearly to the front porch. The mare didn't mind the wet weather, but she must have sensed Jesse's anxiety, as she began to throw her head and resist the pull of the reins.

He hadn't meant to take her right up to the house, but his legs had carried him there. He'd needed to hear what Sergeant Avery said to Naomi. But he couldn't. The rain and wind carried Avery's words in a different direction. Jesse did see Naomi step out onto the porch, glance his direction once, and then point toward the barn.

They were looking for someone, but who could it be?

Who was in the barn besides the *kinner*?

That was when he turned and saw Hannah, Andrew, and Lucy Graber standing outside the large double barn doors. The roof overhang protected them partially from the rain, but as the water hit the puddles, it splashed up on them, staining the bottom of Andrew's pants and the girls' dresses. They made no attempt to stand back against the wall of the barn. Their attention was completely focused on the scene playing out in the Grabers' yard. One of them must have heard the sirens as he had, and they'd come outside to see what the ruckus was about.

Lucy pressed her fingers to her lips and backed up to the barn door when Avery made his way over to them.

Hannah raised a hand to sweep the strings of her prayer *kapp* behind her shoulders.

Andrew didn't move, except to reach over and briefly squeeze Hannah's other hand.

Adults were spilling out of Naomi's house, crowding the porch and overflowing into the yard. No one seemed to mind that the rain was falling as fast and hard as ever. No one seemed to notice that their clothes were quickly becoming soaked completely through.

Jesse dropped the reins to the horse he had been leading and ran across the space that separated the home from the barn. Cherry put out a hand to keep him back at the same time Avery slapped the cuffs on his brother.

"Andrew Miller, you are under arrest for the murder of Owen Esch."

Jesse shook his head, sure he had misheard. His brother could not do such a thing, and the fact that anyone would even consider him a suspect, as Amber had considered him for her Suspects list, nearly brought Jesse to his knees.

But there was no mistaking the cuffs on his brother's wrists, and Jesse had no trouble hearing the officer over the splattering of the rain. It seemed as if the entire world would be able to hear.

"He didn't do it." The cry came from Jesse's heart. He barely recognized the voice as his own as he attempted to step forward and stand beside Andrew. His hands began to shake and the thumping of his heart echoed in his ears. He had to fix this. He had to reach his brother.

Cherry moved in front of him to block his path. Jesse was suddenly aware of the uniform, the hard look in her eyes, and the gun on her hip.

Craning his neck, he made eye contact with Andrew, who shook his head once—a quick, jerky, sideward motion.

"You have the right to remain silent." Avery began to walk him through the large puddles of water and toward the cruiser. "Anything you say can and will be used against you in a court of law."

Jesse's parents had pushed through the crowd and were standing beside him, watching Avery escort Andrew to one of the police vehicles. Their faces had gone as pale as the *kapp* covering his mother's head.

"You have a right to an attorney. If you cannot afford an attorney, one will be appointed for you." Avery had stopped long enough to allow one of the other male officers to pat down Andrew's arms, back, waist, and legs.

Did they honestly think he might have a weapon?

When they reached the cruiser, Avery placed one hand on

the top of Andrew's head and guided him into the backseat, then firmly shut the door. That was when Jesse's mother began to weep. The sound caused a pain deep inside of Jesse, like the time he stepped on a nail that pierced through his shoe and deep into his foot. That pain was nothing compared to this. His heart ached for the agony he saw etched on his mother's face.

She clutched Jesse's arm and stared after her other son, her oldest child, as tears mixed with rain cascaded down her face.

Jesse's father finally stepped forward. Bishop Joseph was beside him in a flash, providing support, holding him steady.

"I'm Ivan Miller, Andrew's father. May I go with him?"

"No, Mr. Miller, but you may meet us at the police station." Avery sloshed through the water until he stood directly in front of the man. "We'll be holding Andrew here in Middlebury until the initial hearing. I have an officer who can go over all of this with you at the station. But you can't actually see your son until tomorrow morning."

Ivan nodded once and turned to go, but at the last second he pivoted back toward the cruiser and met Avery's gaze. "He didn't do this—this thing you are accusing my son of. He didn't. He couldn't."

"That will be for a jury to decide, sir."

The bishop said something in a low voice, just loud enough for his father to hear over the sound of the rain, and Ivan nodded. Joseph's eyes found Jesse, moved over him, and rested on Seth, who had also been helping with the horses. "I'll need my buggy. Quickly, please."

As the cruisers left, the bishop raised his hand and waited for silence. He didn't seem to notice that his Sunday dress clothes were now thoroughly soaked and clinging to his skin. He didn't bother to move out of the rain, though he raised his voice to be heard over the storm. "Let us pray for this one, that God will guide his path. Pray for Naomi and her family as they continue to walk through the valley. And pray for yourself, that you might know how to help each of these and that you will possess the resolve to do so."

The silence that followed seemed to stretch interminably into the future. Jesse wanted to pray, but his mind was a kaleidoscope of words, questions, and images. When he heard the bishop's amen, he turned to his mother.

"Are you going to be okay?"

"*Ya. Ya*, I am." She swiped at her cheeks though her tears continued to fall. "I'll be strong, for Andrew."

His father was still talking to the bishop, but Jesse couldn't wait any longer.

"Where are you going, Jesse?"

"I need to check on something, *Mamm*. It's about Andrew. It might help him."

"He's your *bruder*, Jesse. You know he isn't guilty of this."

"I know, *Mamm*."

"Do what you can, then." His mother pulled herself up to her full height as Jesse's four sisters ran to her, forming a circle of arms and love around her. "You do what you can, Jesse. You bring your *bruder* home."

Thirty

He stood on the porch with the other men and watched the police cruisers until they'd disappeared down the muddy lane.

The Miller boy didn't deserve to be sitting in the back of the squad car. He certainly didn't deserve to spend a night in jail.

But then again, a night in jail usually didn't hurt anyone. When he was seventeen, he'd been on his *rumspringa*. One night in the middle of the summer, he'd had a bit too much to drink. He hadn't done anything as foolish as try to drive a horse and buggy. Truth be told, he couldn't remember where he'd left either. So he'd started home on foot, and that was when the local police had found him. For some reason he'd decided to walk down the middle of the road. Perhaps he'd thought the yellow line would lead him home.

That evening had happened long before he'd married.

Before tragedy had visited their home.

He'd been young, stupid, and sure of one thing—he didn't want his *dat* to know what he'd done. He had refused to give his name or address to the arresting officer. The police had allowed him to sleep it off in a cell, and his parents had never received details about how he'd passed his time that evening. The night spent as a guest of the Middlebury police hadn't hurt him one bit. In fact, it had straightened him up. He learned only to drink at home, and not to be too obvious about that.

No, the Miller kid would be fine.

There couldn't be any evidence to tie Andrew Miller to Owen's killing, no matter what it was the police thought they had found to warrant an arrest. Of that he was certain. Within a day, possibly two, they'd release him.

Then the trail would grow cold, something else would happen to divert their attention, and he would be safe.

Thirty-One

Hannah stood frozen in place, feeling like one of the children playing red light–green light. Except this wasn't a game. This was Andrew's life.

She stared down at the muddy hem of her dress as the adults in the yard and on the porch all began to speak at once.

Why had Andrew slipped the note into her hand? What was she supposed to do with it? Was it evidence? Should she turn it into the police?

And most important, why had Andrew given it to *her*, not to someone else?

Jesse appeared at her side. "Come with me, Hannah."

"But the *kinner*, they might be frightened about—"

"They'll be okay." It was the first time Lucy had spoken since they'd stepped out into the rainy day. "Emily is inside. She'll help me. We'll be fine."

Lucy disappeared without another word.

"Where are we going?"

Jesse was pulling her around the corner of the barn. He leaned his head forward, out into the rain, and looked left, then right. They were alone, and the overhang of the roof provided some protection from the storm, which had increased in intensity. He tugged her toward the center of the wall, where they'd have the most privacy.

"What was Andrew doing in the barn with you?"

"Speaking with Naomi's daughter, Lucy."

"About the box?"

"*Ya.*"

"Did either of you learn anything?"

Hannah put her hand on Jesse's chest. "Are you okay? You're so wet and you're beginning to shiver."

"I'm fine. Tell me about what happened in the barn."

So she did. When she reached the part about being with Andrew in the barn, Jesse stopped her. "Why would you be out here with Andrew?"

She explained about carrying the treats to the children and Andrew's appearance with the umbrella.

"He must have been watching me, Jesse. Waiting for a moment to speak with me. Or maybe he merely had the same idea I did— the idea that one of Naomi's children might know something." She described the butcher paper Lucy had given them, what the shoe box had been wrapped in, and how the handwriting had matched that on Mary's note.

"If only we had—"

"Andrew handed it to me when the police arrived. What do you suppose we should do with it?" Hannah pulled the note from her pocket.

"The first thing we're going to do is read it."

They huddled together, Hannah with her back against the wall of the barn, Jesse in front of her attempting to block the falling rain.

Carefully he unfolded the note. The words *Mary Weaver*

were clearly written on the outside. They both bent closer to read the message the sheet held.

Mary,

I know you were Owen's freind. I know he confided in you.

It might be best if you left Middlebury for a time, but not until after the funeral.

It might be safer.

If you decide to stay, we'll have to deal with this another way.

"That's all?" Hannah flipped the note over and then back again. "I was expecting . . . more."

Jesse folded the note and handed it to Hannah. "Better that it stays with you than with me. You have a chance of keeping it dry."

Hannah nodded and stuck it deep into her pocket.

"We know the box Naomi received was from the killer." Jesse combed his fingers through his hair, releasing a stream of water.

"Who else would send her money?"

"And we know the two handwritings match. You still have the butcher paper?"

"*Ya.* It's in the barn. I can fetch it for you."

"When we're done talking, do that. Keep them both in a safe place until I ask for them."

"But what does the note mean?"

"Sounds like a threat—he's telling her to leave town."

"But why? How is Mary caught up in this? She doesn't know who the killer is."

"Are you sure?"

"Of course."

"You said yourself she's been acting strangely."

"More frightened than strange, and I assumed that was because of all that has happened."

"Or it could be because she has identified the killer and is unsure what to do next."

"Oh, Jesse . . ." Hannah didn't think she could feel any worse, but the idea of Mary being too afraid to share such a terrible thing caused her stomach to roll and twist. "That would be awful. I can't imagine living with the knowledge of who had killed your *freind*."

"Especially if you knew but didn't have any proof."

Hannah shook her head, unable to follow his train of thought, unwilling to believe her friend might be deeply involved in the incidents surrounding this murder.

"Mary didn't have the proof," Jesse continued. "We do. There are two notes now, but Mary only had the one. And now we have the paper the box was wrapped in too."

"Why was she showing her note to Andrew when I saw them together yesterday?"

"I don't know."

"Maybe she thought Andrew could figure out who sent the note or protect her somehow. Or maybe she does know who the killer is. Maybe she recognized the handwriting or thought she did. She could have put it together with whatever Owen had already told her. The more convinced she became of this person's identity, the more afraid she became and decided to tell Andrew. Then he could have left to try to confront the killer."

"*Nein*. I can't believe Andrew would have tried to handle this alone. He would have gone to the police."

"The point is that we have two pieces of evidence now. With Mary's testimony, we'll be ready to go to the police."

Hannah chewed on her bottom lip. What Jesse said made

sense. "Could this free Andrew? Why did they arrest him for such a thing? How could they possibly think him guilty of murdering someone?"

"I don't know the answers to any of those questions, but with this note . . . we're one step closer to finding the killer."

"What should we do?"

"Go and fetch the butcher paper. Put it and the note in something that will keep them dry. I'll go inside and look for Mary."

"She's not there."

"What?"

"She came to the funeral but not the luncheon. Said she wasn't feeling well." Hannah stared into Jesse's eyes, and she knew what he was going to say next.

"I'll go and get one of my parents' buggies. We brought both today."

"And I'll tell your parents and mine that we have to go, but that we'll be back by evening."

"*Ya*. If we're not back by then, we'll have more to worry about than my *bruder* and Mary Weaver."

Thirty-Two

*A*mber had made one phone call and then spent the rest of the morning attempting to work, but she'd accomplished absolutely nothing. Her mind kept replaying Shaw's words, "*The murder investigation appears to be coming to a close.*"

How was that possible? Had they identified and arrested the murderer?

That thought should have helped her relax. If the police had found the guilty person, then her friends were safe.

But she suspected the solution wasn't so simple.

For one thing, Shaw had smirked when he'd delivered the line, as if he knew something she didn't. As if he knew something that would further disrupt her world.

What was that man's problem?

She clicked off her computer, stood, and proceeded to pace back and forth between her desk and the window.

Lunch had been out of the question. She couldn't imagine eating a single bite until she had answers.

Grabbing her purse and her tablet, she decided to take her worries outside. At least it had finally stopped raining, and waiting in her office was making her crazy. She'd explained to Elizabeth where she was going and was halfway down the stairs when Pam stepped into view.

"Going somewhere?"

Today Pam wore black slacks, a white blouse, and a scarf that looked to be handwoven. It consisted of fall colors—orange and brown and red—and even from where she stood Amber could see elephants tripping up and down the cloth. Elephants! The woman had a real knack for fun clothes and accessories—even down to the precautionary umbrella she had in her hand.

"Amber? Are you all right?"

"Yes, yes. I was distracted by your scarf."

"This?" Pam's eyes twinkled. "I'll give it to you if you like it that much, but I thought I was supposed to meet you here. Why are you leaving?"

"I decided to pace outside. I was wearing out the floor in my office." As they made their way to the parking area, Amber filled her in on the morning's events, ending with, "That Roland Shaw makes me want to shake something good and hard. Who does he think he is?"

"He thinks because he's a federal investigator he can tramp all over our little town and make bogus accusations."

"Well, he can't! Or he shouldn't."

"And how does he know that you've been in contact with Mr. and Mrs. Rhodes? Surely he hasn't tapped your phone."

Amber unlocked her car, but they stood staring at each other over its roof, not wanting to believe things had reached such disturbing levels.

"Maybe he made a lucky guess." Amber opened her door, got in, and buckled her seat belt.

Pam did the same. "I suppose that's possible. He could have seen it written on your calendar—"

"I use my tablet for that."

"Or on Elizabeth's calendar, while she warned you he was in the office."

"That might have happened. She did leave him alone in the reception area for a moment." Amber ran her hand over the top of the steering wheel. "But if that's the case, if he found out after he arrived that I was meeting with the Rhodeses, then why did he come to see me in the first place?"

"He's digging, Amber. My grammy used to say that if you poked at a thing long enough, you'd stir up something . . . but you might not like what you find."

"Your grammy sounds like a wise woman."

"Roland Shaw is digging and poking and stirring. I don't like that man."

They drove out of the parking lot through all the rain puddles, and Amber made a left onto US-20.

"Are you sure it's okay for both of us to be away from the Village?" Pam asked.

"I already spoke with Preston. He's going to stay on the property until we return."

"Preston's a good man."

"He is indeed."

"And he can handle anything that comes his way, even Mr. Shaw. In fact, I wouldn't mind seeing those two tussle it up. I have a pretty good idea who would win."

"Pam Coleman, I know you are not encouraging violence."

"Oh no. I wouldn't do anything like that. Violence rarely solves things." Pam worried her thumbnail. "I do wish there was an easy and quick way to convince Shaw to leave us alone."

"I think the best way to do that is to find the killer. Like I told you, Gordon hasn't returned my call, and when I called the nonemergency number for the police department, Walter Hopkins answered. He wouldn't even listen to my questions. This is driving me crazy."

"And you still think it's important to meet with Tom and Sue?"

"If Shaw didn't want us to, then yes, that's enough to convince me it's something we should do."

Ten minutes later they were walking up to the front doors of the megachurch where Tom and Sue attended services.

"I knew it was large, but I didn't realize it was this large." Amber tilted her head back and stared up at the thirty-foot stained-glass window depicting Christ as he ascended to heaven.

"We have big churches like this in Texas."

"Don't you get lost in the crowd?"

"Not necessarily. You plug into a small group within the church. And the worship services? They are something else. All those voices raised in praise to God. I have chill bumps just remembering."

Amber suppressed a laugh as they opened the door to the building and made their way past a bookstore/library and a coffee bar—both of which were closed at the moment.

"What's so funny?"

"You'll have to attend an Amish service with me."

"You've been to one?"

"I have—once. Hannah invited me. Hard benches, several sermons, and lots of singing."

"Sounds like the old brush arbor meeting my grammy talks about. She says we all need some old-style religion to help us along, and that more importantly we need an up-close-and-personal meeting with God's Holy Spirit."

Amber didn't know what to say to that, but she found herself agreeing with the sentiment.

They walked into the church office, and the woman at the desk said they could have a seat.

Tom Rhodes was expecting them.

Three minutes later her phone beeped. She answered it and then stood and walked around her desk. She was approximately Elizabeth's age, but much rounder, with a quick smile. "I'll take you back to Tom's office."

Tom stood when they walked into the small, well-decorated room. The walls were painted a warm tan and had a few items on them—Tom's college diplomas, including a master's in education, a picture of him and Sue standing near Niagara Falls, and a quote from Saint Francis of Assisi.

Amber stepped closer and read the words embedded over a pastoral setting. *Where there is charity and wisdom, there is neither fear nor ignorance.*

"It's good to see you both again. Sue is going to join us in a few minutes."

"I didn't realize you work for the church." Amber sat in the chair he indicated across from his desk.

Tom smiled and ran his hand over his close-cropped hair. "I'm in charge of curriculum and education."

"So you teach other classes in addition to Prep to Bless?"

"I do. Mainly my job is to put the right person in charge of each class and make sure they have what they need to ensure the class is a successful experience for participants. But Prep to Bless I teach myself. You could say it's my baby."

"I like that name—Prep to Bless." Pam sat in the chair next to Amber and placed her handbag on the floor. "Makes me think of a blessing that is coming our way, headed our direction, even as we speak."

"That's the idea, but we also want to educate folks on how to prepare to bless others."

"Prep to Bless sounds like it does what its name claims." Amber tapped her tablet. "I read through your web information."

"Excellent." Tom steepled his fingers. "We believe a little planning can make a big difference."

"At first I was skeptical, but I have to agree the program you've laid out seems very well organized and logical."

"Those were two of our three main goals."

"And the third?" Pam cocked her head and waited.

"To commit ourselves to using our resources to help others— both now and in the future. To use what God has provided to banish fear and ignorance."

"Assisi's quote."

"Exactly."

"Is that biblical, though?" Pam squirmed in her seat when Tom and Amber turned to stare at her. "Think about what Christ said . . . He told us not to worry about tomorrow."

"Sermon on the Mount, Matthew 6, verse 25. We discuss this passage in my class. Those words, 'Do not worry about your life, what you will eat or drink,' come directly after Christ's instruction to give to the needy."

"Huh." Pam glanced over at Amber, who shrugged.

"We take our guidance from those passages, but also from the Old Testament." Tom tapped the well-worn Bible on his desk. "Remember when Joseph entered the service of King Pharaoh? Those were abundant years, good years for the people of Egypt. However, trouble was on the horizon. Joseph understood that tough times lay ahead, and he stored up food for the coming years of famine."

"And that's what you're doing?" Amber asked.

"Something like that, yes."

There was a light tap on the door and Sue stepped into the room. "Did I miss much?"

Today she was wearing what looked like nurse's scrubs, a lovely lavender color that accentuated her curly red hair. She shook hands with Pam and Amber, gave her husband a quick kiss on the cheek, and then sat in the third chair next to Pam. "I had a late-morning CPR class to teach at the medical center. Sorry I'm late."

"You don't have to apologize," Amber said. "We're interrupting both of your work schedules, but we do appreciate your taking the time to meet with us."

"I'm glad you're interested, Amber." Tom leaned back and crossed his hands behind his head. "What in particular would you like to know?"

"Actually, I'm fumbling around in the dark here."

"Something we do fairly often," Pam admitted good-naturedly.

Amber summarized what they knew about Owen's death, giving the general sense rather than the minute details. She ended with Mary's confession that Owen had been attempting to attend the local ISG meeting.

Tom's right eyebrow rose slightly. "The meetings are open to anyone who wants to attend. You would be more than welcome, and so would he."

Amber opened her tablet and pulled up her notes. "But our information made it sound like you have to be invited."

"No. Like our classes here at the church, they're open to all."

"Maybe Owen was confused." Pam peered over at Amber's

notes. "Sometimes the Amish, they don't understand how *Englisch* groups work. You taught me that when I first came here, that I had to be explicit and detailed in my instructions."

"Let me see if I have this right." Sue held up her right hand and counted the points off on her fingers. "A young Amish man, Owen, was murdered. An employee of yours had been in contact with Owen. She stated that Owen might have recently attended an ISG meeting." She held three fingers in the air.

"I know it sounds like we don't have much."

"What do the police say?" Tom's expression had turned grave.

"They're working it from all angles, but their response was very dramatic when they heard the name ISG. I was in the station when that happened. Sergeant Avery froze when Mary—that's my employee—said ISG, then he left the room, and a few moments after that he released her."

"Police are required to report directly to their federal counterparts when any criminal activity in their district might be related to survivalist groups. I'm sure Sergeant Avery had no option but to involve the feds."

"Roland Shaw." Pam's eyes squinted when she said the name.

Tom and Sue exchanged a knowing look.

"What?" Amber demanded.

"Apparently Mr. Shaw has been a very busy man. He came by here yesterday."

"Why? What do you have to do with ISG? You're a church!"

"And so we told him. However, Shaw is a big-picture sort of guy. At least that was my impression. He wasn't very interested in the details—"

"Or facts!" Amber felt her face flush. "He is so irritating. The man has his own agenda, and he won't listen to anyone."

"I'll agree that he has his own agenda, or goals, but we try to treat any government employee with respect to the fullest extent possible."

"So you told him about your program?"

"He already knew about that. No, he came here yesterday to ask to see it, and to ask me about you."

Thirty-Three

*A*mber squeaked, "Me?" and at the same time Pam sat up straighter and asked, "Her?"

Sue reached across Pam and patted Amber's arm. "I wouldn't worry. He struck me as the sort of man who will leave no stone unturned and then waltz back to his headquarters, wherever that is."

"I have trouble picturing Roland Shaw waltzing," Pam muttered.

"Mr. Shaw asked if I knew you, and I told him yes—that we had met by chance a few days ago. When he pressed, I told him that we had a meeting scheduled for today."

"I'm surprised he hasn't busted in, pistols drawn." Amber closed her eyes and took in a deep breath.

"In a way this is good news," Pam pointed out. "At least he hasn't bugged your phone like we feared."

"So you showed him your . . . facility?"

"We did. Would you like to see it?"

Pam glanced left and then right. "I thought we were in it."

"The Prep to Bless area of our campus is underground."

Pointing to the ground, Pam looked first at Amber, then Sue, and finally Tom. "Tell me we're not going to be crawling through a tunnel, because I didn't dress for that."

Five minutes later they had taken an elevator down and were standing in the midst of a giant storage room.

"This area can also be accessed by stairs, of course, in case we have a power loss."

Amber had never been good with figuring size as far as feet and yards. She had no idea how large the room actually was, but she could have put the Village Inn Restaurant inside of it—easily. Regardless of the actual square footage, it was enormous. Her gaze scanned over the rows of shelves that contained canned goods, bottles of water, medical supplies, flashlights, blankets . . . she was having trouble taking it all in.

"This is a lot of food." Amber walked to the closest shelf, her shoes tapping against the concrete floor, echoing throughout the cavernous room. The shelf she was staring at was filled with a variety of canned meats. Every section, every row, was neatly labeled with the item name and a bar code. "How long do you expect to be down here?"

"We don't expect to be down here at all, but should we need to be due to severe weather events, political unrest, or a biological attack, we have enough supplies to feed several thousand for six weeks."

"Members keep additional supplies at their homes," Sue added. "This is for sharing with the community."

"Shouldn't it be used to feed the community now? I know there are folks who could use these supplies—homeless, unemployed, underemployed." Pam's eyes were wide as she walked slowly around the room, finally returning to where Amber waited beside Tom and Sue.

"That's an excellent point," Tom conceded. "It's one the

committee of advisors for PTB has taken into account. We rotate the food out every month."

Amber tried to visualize how much organization such a system would take. "How do you know—"

"The bar code system helps, but also we train our volunteers. Items recently bought are bar coded into the system and put on the left and back side of each shelf. Before that happens items on the right are taken off and bar coded again to record their removal. This keeps what we have down here fresh and allows us to provide assistance—with still-viable supplies, of course—to the local food pantry for timely use."

Amber was stunned. She'd expected to see a room full of supplies, yes. But this was more like a private wholesale store. This was way beyond anything she had imagined.

"Let me ask you a question." Tom crossed his arms and smiled. "Based on what is in your pantry at this moment, how much food would you have if the grocery stores and banks were to close tomorrow? How long could you last?"

"Oh, I don't know." Amber pressed her index finger to her lip as she tried to envision their pantry. "We have a few items. Mostly things I don't like to eat."

Sue laughed. "Now you sound like me. Before we started this program, if I bought something and later decided I didn't like it, then it went to the back of the pantry shelf."

"I understand your point, but what's in my pantry is still food. It's edible. It has some nutritional value even if I don't particularly like it."

"If the 'sell by' date hasn't long ago expired."

"Not a problem for me," Pam said. "I'm storing off-season clothes in my pantry. I couldn't find an apartment with a big enough bedroom closet."

Realizing they were all staring at her, she added, "In the cabinet space I probably have a box of crackers and maybe two cans of soup."

When no one spoke, she added, "I eat out a lot."

"Many families do," Tom said. "They might have demanding work schedules or a lot of activities with the kids, both of which make it hard to find the time to cook. Then, for some, eating out is a taste preference, a habit, or even part of their social activities."

"We go over all these things in the class." Sue straightened her nurse's smock. "Plus, we offer some basic, emergency first-aid instruction."

"I can see you take this very seriously, and from what I can tell you've done an excellent job." Amber hesitated, then pulled in a deep breath. "But why? Do you think the grocery stores could close? They haven't, so what makes you think they might?"

"Of course they have, though perhaps not here." Tom looked as if she'd finally asked the question he was dying to answer. "What about during Hurricane Katrina? Or the power blackout in the northeast in 2003?"

"I lived in the South when Katrina hit. Texas cities took refugees from Louisiana. And the northeast blackout? I remember reading about that." Pam ran her finger over the bar code for a shelf filled with canned corn.

"The power outage lasted less than two days." Tom's demeanor grew markedly more serious and his smile fled. "It affected ten million folks in Canada and forty-five million in the US, and it contributed to eleven deaths."

"Folks starved to death in two days?" Amber wanted to snatch the words back as soon as they'd left her lips.

Tom wasn't offended, though. He smiled and shook his head. "No, there were a variety of reasons—car wrecks, carbon monoxide poisoning, fires due to unsafe use of candles, even falls from folks trying to break into stores."

"Which is why we try to teach a well-rounded approach to preparing for emergencies." Sue glanced around the room. It was apparent from her expression that she loved what she did. And who wouldn't? Preparing people for disaster had to be rewarding. Even if it was never used, it made them feel safe. "If we can convince people to think through how they would react to an emergency, then we can prevent many such needless accidents."

"Every blackout we've experienced so far has been for a fairly short amount of time. In the Northeast, where there's power disruption due to winter weather, folks tend to have generators. They prepare. And still there are easily preventable deaths. Imagine if we have a blackout that lasts for a week or longer."

"You've given us a lot to think about."

"And you've convinced me I need to go grocery shopping." Pam grimaced. "I wouldn't want to eat stale crackers and outdated soup for a week."

They took the elevator back up to the ground floor. Tom and Sue walked them toward the main entrance of the church.

"Please let me know if you have any other questions," Tom said.

"And you're welcome to attend our classes anytime you like." Sue beamed at them. "Dates and times are listed on the web page."

"I do have one other question. Roland Shaw characterized all survivalists—"

"A word we shy away from."

"He called them anarchists. Shaw said they were . . . what was it? Adrenaline junkies or paranoid or invested in the fall of the US monetary system. He obviously thought some of them could even be violent."

Tom nodded in understanding, as if he had heard it before.

"Tom, do we have any folks like that here? In Middlebury? And would they be deranged enough to kill for what they believe in?"

"I personally have not met anyone like you're describing, though I've found that in every group you have some folks who are hanging around the fringes with only a single toe dipped into the activities. You have others who are quite intense about the possibilities."

"Even in your group?"

"Even in our group. We pray with them, try to guide them in what our mission is—preparing and blessing others. It does not include fear or aggression in any shape or form."

"What about in the ISG?" Pam asked.

Again Tom and Sue shared a knowing look. "There are a few guys who have struck me as a bit odd, but remember, every group attracts folks who are on the fringes. That doesn't mean the group is bad."

"I don't suppose you could give me any names."

"Couldn't if I wanted to. I've only been to an ISG meeting a couple of times myself, and I didn't learn everyone's name."

"All right." Amber turned to Pam, who shrugged. "I guess we'll be going then. Thanks again for your time."

Tom called out when they'd covered half the distance to their car. When he caught up with them, Sue had apparently gone inside, and he stepped close and lowered his voice. "Remember, anyone is welcome to attend ISG meetings."

"Anyone?" Pam asked. "Even us?"

Tom nodded. "And their next meeting is at seven o'clock tonight. I know because Mr. Shaw mentioned it when he was here."

Thirty-Four

*J*esse wanted to pull his hair out from frustration—
or scream, which probably would serve to frighten
Hannah more than she already was.

"We'll find her." Hannah placed her hand on his arm.

They'd stopped at a roadside park because he couldn't decide
where to look next. Finally he turned to her and said, "What if
we don't? What if Mary's the only one who can free Andrew and
she's gone?"

"Stop thinking that way, Jesse. *Gotte* won't allow Andrew to
remain in that jail. He won't allow it."

"Then why is he there in the first place?" The cry from his
heart sounded more desperate, more miserable, than he intended.
But if he couldn't be himself in front of Hannah, the one person
he knew was on his side, then their relationship would be built
on shaky ground indeed. "I'm sorry, Hannah. There was no
need for me to snap at you."

"It's all right. I know you're worried."

"*Ya.*" He ran a hand over his face and decided to come clean.
"But it's more than that."

To her credit, Hannah didn't rush him. She sat there, waiting patiently until he had the courage to share the burdens on his
heart.

"I've resented Andrew every time he's come home. Actually, it started the first time he left, I suppose, or before. It could have started before."

"And now?"

He turned to her and was surprised to see a smile tugging at the corners of her lips.

"Now I want my *bruder* home. I love him, and I'll do anything I can—"

"Don't you see, Jesse?" Hannah reached for his hand, entwining her fingers with his. "You've changed. Already *Gotte* has used all that has happened for *gut*."

"*Ya*, but I shouldn't have needed changing."

"None of us is born perfect." Hannah ran her thumb over the back of his hand, and the knot in Jesse's stomach began to ease.

"I think Andrew knows you care about him and that you'll do anything to help him. That's why he gave me the note. He knew I'd take it straight to you."

Possibly she was right. Probably. And if she was, then it was all the more important that he not disappoint his brother.

"Let's go over it again." Jesse cornered himself in the buggy and studied her. "Where else could Mary be?"

"We went to her house."

"No one there. Her parents weren't even back from the funeral yet."

"Went to the Village." Hannah twirled the strings of her prayer *kapp* as she stared out the buggy window. "We spoke with Mary's stand-in."

"What was the girl's name?" Jesse took off his hat and scratched the top of his head. "Helen."

"Right—dark hair and bright fingernails. We even left her the number for the phone shack."

"That's it!" Jesse leaned over and kissed her on the lips—a quick, sincere, thank-you kiss. When Hannah reddened, he nearly laughed. Together they could solve this. They could set things right. "Hannah Bell, you are a genius. Time to head back to the phone shack."

"We've already been there once."

"Yes, but it could be that Helen has heard from Mary or that Amber has left us a message."

They rode along in an easy, more relaxed silence. Jesse realized Hannah had been right. His brother had trusted him, and that meant there was a way to prove Andrew's innocence. But if there was a way, why hadn't Andrew done it? Why hadn't he given the note and butcher paper to the police instead of letting them arrest him?

Jesse pulled into a gravel area adjacent to the phone shack nearest their homes. He brought his mare to a stop under the shade of a maple tree, set the break, and secured the reins. Together he and Hannah walked toward the tiny shed. Many of the local Amish teens and young adults had cell phones, and at the moment, Jesse wished he was one of them. What if they'd missed an important call? What if Mary had been here but had already left?

The two of them barely fit into the tiny wooden structure. He supposed that was because it usually took only one person to make a phone call. There was a counter running along one side of the room, probably three feet long, maybe a few inches more. On it was a telephone, a pad of paper and a pen, and a message recorder. The recorder was battery operated, and in the corner he spied a basket with extra sets of batteries. The other two things on the counter were a small box for leaving money for calls and a gas lantern.

But Jesse spent little time looking at these things. His eyes were locked on the recorder, the bright, flashing red light indicating there were messages, and the number two.

Hannah clutched the edge of the counter as Jesse pushed the Play button.

"This message is for Hannah Troyer or Jesse Miller. Hannah . . ." Amber's voice on the recorder paused. Hannah could picture her worrying her thumbnail, trying to think of how to say what she needed to say. "Hannah or Jesse, this is Amber. Please call me. I had a visit from Shaw this morning . . . Roland Shaw, and I'm worried. Call me on my cell as I'll be out of the office this afternoon."

She left her cell number, though Hannah didn't need to look at what Jesse had jotted down on the pad of paper. She'd memorized Amber's number long ago.

The second message caused her to reach out and grasp Jesse's arm.

"Mary? Mary Weaver? We need to talk. You weren't supposed to leave until after the funeral." There was a pause, and then the caller hung up.

Hannah felt the ground shift under her feet. For a moment she saw two phone recorders. She gripped Jesse's arm more tightly, attempting to steady her world.

The message was from *him*.

It was from the person who had written the notes.

It was from the murderer.

She stared at Jesse, who shook his head to her unasked question.

"Play it again, Jesse. I don't recognize his voice either, but maybe we can hear something in the background, anything that will help us figure out who the . . . the . . ."

"I think the word you're looking for is *killer*, and this tape proves Andrew is innocent." He slammed his fist against the counter, causing the recorder to bounce on the countertop. "How dare he call here? How can he be so bold?"

"He killed Owen with a bow and arrow on a public trail in broad daylight. I'd say *bold* describes him fairly well."

Jesse was reaching under the counter, unplugging the recorder from where it was connected to the phone.

"Where are we taking it?"

"To the police. They need to hear this. They need to know they have the wrong man."

"Maybe we should call Amber and ask her to meet us there."

"*Ya, gut* idea."

"And leave a note, in case anyone wonders where the recorder has gone." She wanted to glance over her shoulder to see if *he* was watching them, but of course that was impossible. They were alone in a phone shack. Still, she would be glad when they left, when they were in public with lots of people, lots of witnesses.

Amber answered her cell phone on the first ring. Hannah explained about Andrew's arrest, the note and butcher paper with identical handwriting, and the recording.

"Drive straight to the police station. Bring the recorder and the note and paper with you. We'll meet you there. We're in downtown Middlebury now."

"Who's with you?"

"Pam Coleman. We'll wait for you outside the station, and, Hannah . . . be careful. Watch and make sure you're not followed."

"What if we are?"

"Pull into the closest home or establishment, ask to use their phone, and dial 9-1-1. Whoever this is seems to be growing desperate. There's no guessing what he'll do next." She paused and then added, "I'm tired of following the trail of this creep. It's time we go on the offensive. How fast do you think you can—"

"Twenty minutes." Jesse had pressed his head close to Hannah's and was listening. Now he spoke into the mouthpiece of the phone as Hannah turned it toward him. "We'll be there in twenty minutes."

"All right. Good." Amber sighed and then added, "I love you two. Be careful."

Jesse's eyebrow arched as he placed the receiver back on the phone. "She loves us?"

Hannah waved her hand. *"Englischers* . . . they often have a need to tell you how they're feeling."

"Do I need to tell you how I'm feeling, Hannah?"

Her heart skittered, more than it had when she'd first heard the recording. "Scared?"

"Ya."

"Excited?" Her hands began to sweat as he pressed his forehead to hers.

"Ya." They stood frozen for a moment, and then Jesse pulled away a few inches.

"Perhaps this is nearly over." He traced a line with his forefinger from her temple to her chin. "I am scared and excited, but I'm also grateful . . . that you are with me through this."

As they hurried to the buggy, Hannah tried to envision what life had been like before Owen Esch had been killed.

Normal.

That's what she was missing.

Plain old boring normal.

If she ever had that again, she would thank *Gotte* for it each and every day—just as she had after the last murder she'd helped investigate.

Thirty-Five

*A*mber and Pam rushed over to Jesse's buggy before he'd even tied the horse's reins to the post.

"Are you okay?" Amber reached out and grasped Hannah by the shoulders, stared deep into her eyes, and tried to read her thoughts, her emotions. It struck her that Hannah was more than her employee and friend—she was also like a daughter or a little sister.

"*Ya*, we're fine."

"You weren't followed?" Pam's dark face was scrunched in a scowl. "Maybe I hope he did follow you. I wouldn't mind a look at this guy. Southerners don't run. We fight. Give me a whack at this guy. He's worse than crazy. He's dangerous crazy. He's psycho, deranged—"

"No argument here." Jesse held up the phone recorder. "Now if the police will listen to our proof."

"Oh, they will listen." Amber had been tempted to call ahead and tell Gordon what they had, what evidence they were bringing. She'd decided against it because she realized whoever was operating the phones probably wouldn't put her through.

She was sure they made quite the image—a middle-aged white woman, a young black woman, and a twentysomething

Amish couple, hurrying to the front door of the police station as if they were being chased.

But perhaps they were.

She'd felt a hand against her back, pushing her toward this inevitable moment, since the day Gordon appeared in her office telling her about Owen's death.

The four of them stopped a foot inside the door.

Walter Hopkins was the first one to glance up. The wrinkles around his blue eyes crinkled into a smile even as he shook his head no. "If you're here to see Sergeant Avery—he's busy."

"He's not too busy to see this." Amber pointed to the recorder Jesse was holding.

"And that's not all we have." Pam crossed her arms. "He's going to want to make time to see us."

Jasmine, the newest recruit to the Middlebury police department, sat a few desks away, working on a computer. She was young and extremely beautiful—someone Amber would expect to find in a modeling office, not a police station. Her black hair was cut in an attractive, sassy, long shag, and her ebony complexion was flawless. Jasmine was extremely talented with anything web related. She'd proven herself a real asset, helping them find some of the clues to unravel Ethan Gray's murder, but Amber hadn't had the opportunity to speak with her since. Jasmine didn't pause in her typing, but she did look up at them, obviously listening to the conversation.

Cherry stood and made her way over to where they waited. "You can leave whatever you have with me. I'll make sure that Sergeant—"

"No, Cherry. We won't leave it with you. We won't leave it with anyone until we speak directly with Gordon, until he hears what we have to say."

"Why is it that you think you're so special?" Cherry stepped closer, narrowing her green eyes to mere slits, displaying an attitude that had thankfully been missing the night before at Dairy Queen. Fortunately, there was still the counter between them. Amber did not need to get into a catfight. She'd promised Tate she would behave while he was gone, not to mention that fighting wasn't exactly the Christian response to dealing with unpleasant people.

Cherry pointed her finger at Amber. "We don't need you on this one, Miss Marple. You can run along home."

Pam squealed, "What? You did not just call her Miss Marple. Amber has much better hair and clothes than that woman from an old television show. You should—"

"You should all calm down." Gordon approached the group looking tired and markedly older.

Amber hadn't heard him walk into the large outer office, but he must have been somewhere close, close enough to hear the hollering.

"Gordon, we need to talk to you." Amber gestured toward Jesse, Hannah, and Pam. "We all do."

Instead of arguing, he nodded once. "Give me a few minutes."

"You heard the boss." Walter's eyebrows arched once again, his face a road map of soft lines that reminded Amber of a worn and wrinkled ivory sheet. She liked Walter, though he always seemed to be standing guard between her and Gordon. His voice remained pleasant. "I believe you know where the waiting room is."

The waiting room was five feet from where Walter sat, manning the phones. The room looked exactly the same as it had when she'd come in with Mary. Same black leather seats, same long table stacked with the same new magazines. The television in the corner of the waiting room was once again tuned to a twenty-four-hour news channel with the volume muted. Had she been here less than a week ago? This thing that had taken over their lives wasn't even seven days old. Nothing had changed, but everything felt different.

They stared at each other as the clock on the wall ticked off the minutes and they waited.

Finally Jasmine stepped into the waiting area. "Sergeant Avery is ready to see you now."

When they all stood, she said, "No. He asked specifically for Mrs. Bowman and no one else."

Five minutes after she walked into his office, Gordon picked up his phone and called Jasmine. "Bring the rest in."

They barely fit.

Jasmine had to bring in extra chairs, which were lined up across from Gordon's desk like eggs in a carton. Amber near the door, then Pam, and finally Hannah and Jesse. When they were all settled, Gordon gestured to Amber to close the door.

"All right. Amber has explained the basics." He leaned back in his chair and studied them.

Something told Amber he wasn't completely surprised by what she'd told him. Why was that? If he thought Andrew was guilty—and Gordon wouldn't have arrested the young man if he wasn't convinced—then why wasn't he surprised to hear someone else might be responsible?

"Jesse, first I want to tell you that anything you bring to us is going to be viewed with a degree of skepticism, since you are the brother of the accused."

Jesse didn't look particularly offended or react to Gordon's words in any way. Quietly and firmly he said, "Andrew is innocent. You need to listen to this recording."

He pressed the Play button.

Amber's voice came out of the box first, asking Hannah and Jesse to call her. There was a beep, and the recorder's programmed words, "Message two." When the message had reached its end, Gordon made a play-it-again gesture. Even sitting in the police station, the second message sent spiders tripping down Amber's spine. The man's voice was dark and sinister. She realized, with a start, that she was listening to a message from a killer.

Gordon hadn't commented as he listened to the recording both times, his expression giving away nothing. Finally he sat up straight and reached for the box. "Do you mind if I keep this?"

"*Nein*. It's why we brought it to you. Can my *bruder* go home now?"

"No, it doesn't work that way. The voice on this recording could be anyone's. It could be yours."

"Jesse was with me all day. He didn't have a chance to leave a recording, or I would have heard and seen him do it." Hannah pushed up her glasses, then crossed her arms.

"And you're willing to swear to that in a court of law?"

"I'll testify. Yes."

Gordon placed his elbows on his desk and interlaced his fingers. "Even so, this is weak at best. It could have been anyone on that recording, and it isn't necessarily the person who killed Owen. As I explained to your father, Jesse, we wouldn't have arrested Andrew without evidence."

"What evidence?"

"I can't share that with you. The prosecuting attorney felt what we had was sufficient to file a probable cause affidavit, and Judge Anderson signed off on the arrest warrant. Andrew is being held until his initial hearing, which will be Thursday, the day after tomorrow. At that point your brother will be given a copy of the charging information—"

"Charging information. Those are the reasons for his arrest?" Jesse had taken off his hat and was turning it in his hands.

"Correct. He's already been advised of his rights, and he'll be appointed a public defender if he cannot afford to hire one."

"A lawyer?" Hannah asked.

"Yes. A lawyer."

"But you haven't listened to everything we've brought." Pam wriggled to the front of her seat. "You haven't even seen the note and the butcher paper."

Her eyes squinted together and her nose crinkled, as if she were preparing for something that smelled bad, rancid even. She turned to Hannah and Jesse. "Show him. Show them to the sergeant. Then he'll understand."

They spread the note to Mary out on the desk and put the wrapping from Naomi's box next to it.

Amber knew Gordon well enough to understand that he wasn't pleased, but he was interested.

"Why didn't Naomi give me this paper when I picked up the box?"

"I don't know." Amber held up her hands, palms out.

"Actually her daughter, Lucy, had the paper." When Gordon remained silent, Hannah added, "She'd unwrapped it and given the box to her mother but not the paper. After you came and left, she didn't want to upset her mother by asking her what to do with it. So she took it to the barn and stored the paper in a cubby."

"She's twelve," Jesse reminded Gordon.

"I suppose everyone has touched this?"

Hannah glanced at Amber, then back at Gordon. "Only me, Jesse, Andrew, and Lucy."

Gordon sighed and closed his eyes for a moment. "All right. We'll get your prints before you leave. We already have Andrew's."

He called Cherry into his office and asked her to go to the Graber home and get the prints of the little girl.

"Why do you need our prints? And Lucy's?" Jesse shifted uncomfortably in his chair, bumping his knees against the desk.

"Mainly so we can rule you out. Anything left might be from the person who wrote this note." He cleared his throat and then asked directly, "How do I know you aren't the writer, Jesse? You could have sent both the box and the note to Mary to try to cover what your brother is accused of."

Jesse's face reddened with anger, but he tapped the emotion down. "First of all, I would never do such a thing. Second, I don't have five hundred dollars lying around to give to Naomi."

When Gordon didn't look convinced, he added, "Check my file at the Village. I had to fill out an employment form. You'll see that my handwriting is completely different."

"All right. I'll do that. Amber, I assume you can have the paperwork pulled for me?"

"I'm already e-mailing Elizabeth." There were times when it did help to carry her tablet with her everywhere she went. Or she could have e-mailed from her phone. My, how she loved technology! "It will be waiting at her desk."

Gordon stood, paced behind his desk, and then turned back to the waiting group. "Let's talk about Mary."

Thirty-Six

H e had the sense that things were spiraling out of his control.

It reminded him of the time, two years before, when they'd had a problem with feral hogs. Over thirty years farming on the same piece of land, and he'd never seen such destruction, except for possibly the times bad weather had skirted their area.

The weather he could do nothing about.

The hogs were a different matter, and he'd quickly dispatched them with his crossbow.

He knew how to take care of problems that required action.

Which was probably why he'd called the phone shack when Mary Weaver had not appeared at Naomi's house after the funeral. She should have been there. It looked suspicious for her, for anyone, to be absent.

So he'd made the phone call, and perhaps that had been hasty.

To make matters worse, he'd second-guessed himself and gone to the phone shack to delete the message. That was when he'd found the recorder was gone. All that was left was a square on the counter, slightly darker than the rest, an area unbleached by the sun.

There was a note from whoever took it, but it wasn't signed. The note just said it would be returned as soon as possible.

Who had taken it?

And why?

Neither of which mattered. It wasn't as if they could trace a call placed from one phone shack to another—no way to know who was making the call. Now, if he'd used a cell phone, well . . . the expansion of government surveillance was well known. It was one reason he didn't want one of the newfangled contraptions. A man's personal business needed to remain private.

As for Mary, he would find her, and then he would do what needed to be done.

He wasn't proud of his actions, but he'd come too far to repent of them now.

Thirty-Seven

mber and Pam stood in the driveway of a large ranch house. So many people had arrived for the meeting that they'd had to park in an adjacent pasture. They should have come earlier to get a good parking place.

"I didn't expect so many cars." Pam hiked her purse strap up on her shoulder.

"And buggies too." Amber pointed to an area around the side of the house where the horses and buggies were parked.

"Are you sure we have the right address? Maybe Tom gave us the time and place for an Amway meeting, or Weight Watchers. This could be a Weight Watcher meeting. I saw a full-size woman walk inside. Plus, this place looks like it belongs to someone very rich."

"This is the right place. People who are survivalists can still be wealthy. In fact, maybe it takes a certain amount of money before you begin worrying about the destruction of society."

"Yeah, most folks are more concerned about paying this month's bills."

"Exactly. It seems, though, that every time I change my ideas about these people, I meet someone new and have to change my ideas again."

"Won't hold still to be stereotyped."

"You wouldn't know that by reading most of the news articles about them."

They were walking toward the front door. The scene before them looked so ordinary, so normal, but Amber wondered, *How many people actually worry about a biological attack or a collapse in the monetary system?* Although Tom's reasoning had been logical, the things he described had never been a concern for Amber. It had seemed to her that each day's problems were enough without imagining what else might go wrong.

And yet . . ."Their logic is starting to make sense to me," Pam confessed. "And that is frightening. Yesterday I would have told you the entire group was crazy. After visiting the church . . . I don't know what to think."

Amber glanced at her friend. The sun was close to setting, but she could see well enough to make out Pam's expression of honest confusion. "I was thinking the same thing."

They were nearly to the porch, but Pam reached out, snagged Amber's arm, and pulled her away and into the shadows.

"Explain to me again why we're here. And what are we going to do if we see him?"

"That's not likely. He won't be wearing a T-shirt that says 'I Killed Owen Esch.'"

"All right. Then what are we here to find?"

"We're fairly sure that whoever the killer is, he is a part of this group. Doesn't seem to me that he could be a part of Tom's group, and Owen specifically told Mary that he was planning to attend an ISG meeting."

"Could have been a coincidence."

"Maybe," Amber said. "But I don't trust coincidences."

"You and my grammy. She always said when two things happen at the same time and they both make the hair on the back of your neck stand up, you can be certain they're cousins to one another."

"So we agree. The person who killed Owen attends this group?"

"It makes sense to me."

"Then there's a good chance he's here tonight."

"If he's here, why isn't Gordon Avery walking up to the front door instead of us?"

Amber turned away from a couple walking toward the home and lowered her voice. "Because Gordon thinks he has the guilty person. Not to mention, if he did show up here, even in an unofficial capacity, he wouldn't learn much. Think about it. Everyone knows who he is. We're a small town. The killer would be out the back door before Gordon made it through the front. That's why I also don't think Shaw will be here just because he knew there was a meeting tonight. If anyone looks like law enforcement even without a uniform, he does."

"The killer would know Gordon, but he wouldn't know us? There's not that many black women in this town. I'm thinking he can find me if he sets his mind to it."

"He could know me too. I'm not exactly a local celebrity, but most folks have had some contact with the Village. The thing is that we can feign interest in learning survivalist tactics to explain why we're here. We can blend in."

Pam rolled her eyes and turned back toward the porch. "You should have told me we were trying to blend. I would have worn something less noticeable, something with less style."

Which made Amber smile and gave her the sense, perhaps the false sense, that things would be all right. With Pam at her side, wearing designer jeans, a black top decorated with sequins in the pattern of a peacock, and a matching turquoise scarf around her neck, they might be able to pull off the image of two gals on a fact-finding mission.

Except their real mission was to find a killer.

The room looked like most living rooms, only larger. A large fireplace dominated the center of the far wall. Windows on each side looked out over fields that had been harvested and plowed clean. Through the windows, Amber could make out a barn, rising high above the home, set back on the property and painted red. Inside the living room, folding chairs had been placed here and there to allow seating for the large crowd of people that had arrived.

"More people than I expected," Pam muttered as a man and woman walked up, welcomed them, and shook hands.

Their names went in and out of Amber's mind faster than water through a cupped hand. She smiled politely, accepted the copy of the agenda, and stepped away.

"Amish men at two o'clock."

"It's seven." Pam checked her watch.

"Near the front of the room, on the right."

"Oh. Yeah, they're pretty easy to pick out in their black jackets and black hats."

At that moment one of the men turned and scanned the room, passing over them and then backing up again. He stared for a moment, then spoke to the men on either side of him. Abruptly all three turned and faced the front, effectively cutting off any chance Amber might have had to figure out their identities.

"That was rude." Pam sat in the closest chair.

"And a little odd. The Amish men I know are a little quiet, but most are polite. I'm used to a nod or a little wave."

Any further discussion was cut off by the man who had introduced himself to them at the door—Steven . . . Steiner . . . Stewart! That was it—his name was Stewart. He wasn't the owner of the house. Amber knew that because he turned and thanked Harold for hosting the meeting. While Harold was on the short side, heavy, and balding, this man was taller. He was also trim and fit for a man who had to be approaching senior status. His gray hair was longer, touching the collar of his khaki-colored shirt.

Stewart was explaining that they were meeting for the second time that month because the last meeting had been more of a social event and no real work had been accomplished.

Laughter rippled through the room until someone called out, "We managed to eat plenty of the harvest, though."

"That we did," Stewart agreed. "And combined we were able to put back more goods than we had projected."

Then it was time for business. Amber quickly grew restless and bored.

"You're not this fidgety when you call a meeting," Pam whispered.

"My meetings interest me."

She had thought she would be curious about what was being said, but basically they were going over a treasury report, an activities report, and a reminder of the next meeting's time and place.

Mary said Owen had been trying to get in with this group. Possibly—no, probably—he'd attended one of the meetings, which meant that someone in this room might have met with Owen the night before he died. But who? Everyone looked so . . . ordinary. Owen had also told Mary that he'd been invited to attend the next meeting—this meeting. That thought hit her like a punch in the stomach. If he'd lived, Owen Esch would be sitting in this room with them at this very moment.

Various members droned on, giving their reports and fielding questions. Amber was thinking about sneaking into the kitchen. Maybe she could corner someone and ply them with questions.

Then Harold stood and opened the meeting up to general questions and discussion. Things got real interesting real quick. He hitched up his pants and cleared his throat. "Now to new business. Dereck, you had something to report."

"Some of us are concerned about the possible use of drones in the area and what we can do about it. I sent an anonymous query to the local police from a computer at the library." There were several snickers at the last part, but the tall, gangly man just tucked his hands in his back jeans pockets and went on. "Apparently it's against the law for us to shoot down a drone, even when the thing flies over our private property."

Now the snickers became murmurs. Some shook their heads in disbelief. Others leaned in and spoke to the person next to them, and about a quarter became tight-lipped and said nothing. Amber couldn't tell if they didn't approve of the topic or if they were stoic over the existence of drones.

"We have drones?" Pam asked.

The man behind them leaned forward. "The FAA has come up with a universal policy to clear the use of domestic drones. Some cities are openly admitting to using them to fight crime, or so they say. In essence it gives the government the right to spy on anyone they choose."

"Spy?" Pam stared at him in disbelief.

"They can see through your curtains and your walls. Caught a teacher in Indianapolis on what they termed an inappropriate dating site, and she lost her job because of it. The police turned the information over to the school district, and the school district canned her for violating their morals policy."

Pam looked at Amber in disbelief.

"We have that here?" Amber asked.

"Not yet. At least, I'd be surprised to see any here in Middlebury."

At the front of the room, Harold had deferred to Stewart, who crossed his arms and waited for the talking to die down. Although Harold seemed to be running most of the meeting, it seemed to Amber that Stewart was the main spokesman or president or some other weighty position.

"We've filed a petition with our state representatives. At this point there have been no spottings of drones in our area, but if and when there are, we'll consult our legal counsel and decide how best to proceed."

"They have legal counsel?" Pam's eyes had rounded to the size of quarters. "Why do they need that?"

Amber shook her head. She'd gone from being bored to having a dozen questions.

"Anything else?" Stewart asked.

There was something else. Amber could tell by the way the murmuring increased, and this time it wasn't about drones that might or might not be peeking through their walls. She couldn't make out any complete conversation, but she heard snippets. "Bow . . . Pumpkinvine Trail . . . shame . . . funeral."

However, no one spoke up about those things. Finally an older woman seated near the front of the room stood and began to speak. She was apparently in charge of a co-op, where members exchanged produce for canning.

"Just like the Amish," Amber whispered.

But this woman wasn't Amish. She wore baggy black pants and an oversize men's flannel shirt.

"She could use some help with her style." Pam craned her neck for a better look as the woman spoke about dairy needs and fall vegetable gardens.

When the woman finally wound down, Harold again asked if there were any other new items of business.

There were, much to Amber's chagrin. None of the items interested her, and she wanted to mingle. She also wanted to find someone who could answer her questions.

"If that's all, this meeting is adjourned." Harold sat down and Stewart stood and reminded them all of the November meeting's time and place.

As everyone stood and began to form small groups, Amber looked over toward where the three Amish men had been sitting. They'd remained there throughout the drone discussion, but now they were gone.

She was torn between the urge to look for them and to have a talk with Stewart. Fortunately, she didn't have to choose, because the group's leader was making his way toward her and Pam.

Thirty-Eight

esse had taken Hannah home after their visit with the police sergeant. Actually, they'd stopped to eat at the sandwich shop—since it was past the dinner hour and both were starving. He wondered how he could have an appetite with all that was happening, but he devoured the club sandwich as if he hadn't eaten in days. By the time they climbed into the buggy to return home, the sun had set and evening surrounded them. Neither spoke much, but he was learning that Hannah was a calming presence. Having her by his side did an awful lot to calm his fears, and the fact that they didn't have to talk emphasized how much their relationship had grown.

She squeezed his hand after he helped her out of the buggy. "I'll pray for Andrew. *Gotte* hasn't forgotten him, Jesse. *Gotte* hasn't forgotten any of us." Then she'd stood on her tiptoes and planted a quick kiss on his lips before turning and hurrying across the yard, up the steps, and into her home.

That kiss had warmed him half the way home. Then he'd begun replaying the scene at the police station, and his confidence had melted away like a late snow on a spring day. What was he to do now? How could he help his brother? And how would he face his parents?

The latter turned out to be much easier than he'd expected.

While it was true that his parents had struggled with Andrew's absence, they were also very strong people—strong physically, emotionally, and spiritually.

His youngest sister, Teresa, had only recently turned nine years old. She was all legs, reminding him of a colt, and she pranced around like a foal set free in a pasture. Her legs were usually scratched up from her time in the barn or from chasing some critter or fishing down at the pond. Her blond hair spilled from her *kapp*, determined to resist any confinement. Tonight she was already in her nightgown, and someone had attempted to braid her unruly hair, which fell in a cloud down her back.

"We're writing down our prayers for Andrew. See?" She held up a sheet of paper that contained various handwritings. "Mine is this one."

She pulled the paper closer to her nose.

Did she need glasses? Should he alert his parents to that before the school year progressed too far and she fell behind in her studies?

But then she kissed the sheet of paper and thrust it into his hands. "You can write yours at the bottom. I left you some space."

She was gone as quickly as she had appeared, running up the stairs and laughing at something Susan said. Knowing that Susan would take care of putting the young ones to bed, he trudged into the kitchen, dreading the meeting with his parents.

His dad sat at the table, the *Budget* spread out in front of him. He glanced up, met Jesse's eyes, and when Jesse shook his head, he stared back down at the paper.

His mother wasn't so easily satisfied. She asked if he had eaten. When he told her he had, she thrust a plate of peanut butter cookies and a glass of milk in front of him. "Tell us. Tell us what you found out, Jesse. When is Andrew coming home?"

So he explained to them what he had learned at the police station, why he had gone there, about the meeting with the judge in two days, and that no one would be allowed to see Andrew until the next morning.

"Will you go back? Will you go and see him?" His mother pushed the plate of cookies closer to him, as if the sugar and flour and eggs combined into delicious tidbits could possibly make this recent turn of events easier to swallow. "Tell him we are praying, and we know he'll be home soon."

"Of course I will, *Mamm*." This wasn't much of a concession. Jesse had already decided he'd go back the next morning, back to ask Andrew what he knew about Mary's involvement.

"The police were here, son." His father spoke in a low, even tone.

"Here?"

"*Ya*. They were here when we returned after the funeral luncheon, after Andrew was arrested. They explained that even if I went to the station like the sergeant said I could, I wouldn't be able to see Andrew, nor learn anything more than they were willing to tell me."

"What did they want?"

"Went through the house and the barn. Took the crossbows and the hunting rifle."

"Why the hunting rifle? Owen was killed with a bow."

"Their warrant allowed them to take any weapons. They also carried off his pack that was hidden in the barn."

Jesse's stomach became even more unsettled at this recent news. The thought of strangers in their house, going through their things . . . it made him feel violated.

He drank the glass of milk since it was already poured but passed on the cookies. Standing, he wondered how this had happened to his family. Why had it happened to his family? Why couldn't it be someone else caught up in this mess?

His father glanced up from the *Budget*. He hadn't turned a page since Jesse had entered the room. "You're a *gut* son, Jesse. You've taken on the bulk of Andrew's work, more than you should have—"

"*Dat*, don't."

"I need to say it. Don't you see that I need to say it?" He ran a hand across his eyes and continued, "Each of you children is special to me and your *mamm*. We may not say it often. It's not our way."

His hand—sun-spotted, wrinkled, and a bit arthritic— brushed that thought away. "Now, though, is a time when you need to know. I'm proud of you, and I know you'll do your best to help Andrew."

"We all will," Jesse said.

"*Ya*. Your *mamm* and I, we'll support him in any way we can. If it takes money to find a path out of this mess, well, we have a little saved." He folded his hands on the table, on top of the *Budget*. "But you understand Andrew better than any of us. If there's someone in this house who can help him, then it's you."

Jesse wanted to scream that he didn't understand his brother at all.

He didn't scream, though.

He didn't say anything.

Instead, he nodded to his father, kissed his mother on the cheek, and made his way slowly up the stairs to his room. Raising the shade, he looked out into the night. He could see over to their neighbor's house. No doubt Linda Rainey was sitting beside her window, watching the world outside. Though it was dark and there was little to see, he understood that it was her connection with the rest of them. It was her way of "*watching the world, studying all of God's creation.*" Those had been Linda's words when he'd last visited her.

She'd said something else when he'd gone to see her with his mother's baking. What had it been? Something about Andrew and the day he'd come home, but suddenly Jesse was too tired to remember. He'd think about it in the morning. He barely managed to shuck his clothes before dropping onto the bed and falling into a deep sleep. One that was occasionally punctuated by nightmares of Andrew in the jail and a man, a faceless man, reaching through the bars and trying to attack him.

⁂

Amber and Pam had been cornered by Stewart. He spoke with them about ISG and everything they believed for a good twenty minutes, then insisted on taking them to meet other members of the group.

By the time they walked out to their car, the area was shrouded in complete darkness. Amber was exhausted, and she imagined Pam was, too, as they made their way via the flashlight app on Amber's phone.

"It was almost like Stewart was trying to keep us from wandering about," Pam said. "Do you think he could be involved?"

"It's possible, I guess. He certainly never left our side."

"Did you see anyone who looked like the killer?" Pam asked.

"How would I know?" Amber shrugged, but she was thinking of Ethan Gray's killer. That person's identity had come as a total surprise. No, she didn't think a killer was someone you recognized right away, but there was something—something off in his or her behavior or gaze. Perhaps she was making that up, though. Perhaps she was too tired to think.

"I'm so glad Tate will be home tomorrow. It feels as if he's been gone for weeks upon weeks."

"Now, see, you're talking like an old married woman already."

Amber was reaching for the door handle of her car when something whizzed past her head. She screamed and Pam dropped to the ground.

"Are you hurt? Pam?" Through the grass and pebbles she crawled around the back of the car, afraid to stand up. Her purse was still slung over her shoulder, and she'd managed not to drop her phone.

Pam was silent on the other side.

Amber envisioned the worst as she proceeded to Pam's side of the car, heedless to the fact that she was scratching up the palms of her hands and probably ruining the knees of her dress slacks.

She reached Pam the same time Roland Shaw did.

"Is she okay?"

"Where did you come from?"

"Is she okay?"

"I don't know." Amber shone the light from her phone directly into Pam's eyes. The woman looked dazed and more than a little angry.

She was sitting with her back against the car, a trickle of blood pooling on her forehead. "What happened?"

"I think you were hit by something."

"Probably a rock from a slingshot," Shaw offered, and then he disappeared into the darkness.

"I ducked," Amber said. "I must have heard him snap the rubber."

"It's because I'm taller than you. Whoever threw that rock was aiming high."

"Maybe. Could be they wanted to get our attention, not actually hurt us." Amber pulled a whole package of tissues from her purse and pressed them against Pam's forehead, where the blood had begun to make a trail close to her right eye. She had a nice-size goose egg, which would probably turn purple after the swelling subsided.

"I'm black, you know. Maybe they didn't see me. It's hard to see a black woman in the dark." She touched Amber's hand, the one holding the tissues to her forehead. "Am I going to need stitches? I don't think I'll look so good with a seam on my forehead."

"No. Looks like it grazed you, but it's going to be sore."

"Why would—"

Roland Shaw reappeared at that moment. "There's a note wrapped around the rock."

"Why are you here?" Amber ignored the sheet of paper he was attempting to read by the light of her phone. She hadn't seen him at the meeting. He'd suddenly popped out of the darkness when they were accosted by some maniac with a slingshot.

"I'm here because—"

"He was following us," Pam explained.

"What?"

A small smile tugged the corners of Shaw's lips. It looked strange on him. Amber had only seen him scowl, and now he was smiling? When Pam was thumped with a rock? That made him smile?

"How'd you figure it out?" Shaw lifted the tissues and studied the cut on Pam's head.

"Your little black car and ours seem to be the only ones left. I saw that black car twice in the side mirror while we were driving out here."

Amber stood, her hands on her hips. "Why didn't you tell me?"

"Tell you what? It's a small town. You see lots of the same folks multiple times in a day."

Amber noticed how quiet it was as Pam fell silent. No one else had noticed what was going on, but then, by the time they'd escaped Stewart, all the folks out where they had parked were gone. "Why would you be following us? What is your problem?"

"If you'll remember, I told you I'd be watching these groups."

"Which doesn't answer why you were following us."

"Because he was certain you'd come if you knew about the meeting, and he was hoping Tom Rhodes would mention it to us when Tom told him we were coming to see the church." Pam struggled to her feet. "He was using us as bait, to try to draw out the killer."

"Is that true?" Blood pulsed at Amber's temples. She wanted to scream. She wanted to kick Roland Shaw in the shins. Instead, she poked him in the chest with her index finger. "Did you know the killer was here?" Each word was punctuated by a jab.

Shaw batted her hand away and shook the note at her. "I suspected that he'd be here."

"Then why is Andrew in jail?" Pam asked.

"We think more than one person was involved, and this note seems to prove it."

Amber's anger dissolved as they all huddled over the note.

Warning—Stay out of my business.

"That's it?" Pam humphed. "This person needs to learn to explain himself better, and we know it's a warning because he delivered it with a rock."

"It's from the same person who wrote the two notes," Amber said.

Pam stepped closer. "How do you know it's from the killer? Could be anyone."

"Handwriting is the same. That *W*—he made it the same way on the word *Weaver*." Amber shook her head. "I can't believe you used us as bait."

"And I might have been able to go after him if I hadn't needed to make sure you were okay."

"Why didn't you come into the meeting? Then you could have identified and arrested him."

"First of all, we still don't know who *he* is. Second, as soon as I stepped into the meeting, one-third of the folks would have fled. Trust me, I've done this before."

"So you used us to draw him out."

"It occurred to me that he might try to warn you off." Shaw slipped the rock and the note into an evidence bag he pulled from his pocket. "And although we don't know who it is, we are one step closer. The person we're looking for was here tonight, which means he's probably a member of ISG."

"There were a lot of members in there, if you didn't notice from where you hid in the bushes." Amber stomped around to her side of the car. She wanted to go home, take a hot bath, and call Tate. "Good luck interviewing all of them."

"I don't need to interview them all." Shaw held the door open as she got in, and Pam settled into the passenger seat. "I only need to interview the Amish who were here."

When Amber glanced up at him, she was confused by what she saw. The man she'd come to loathe, the one who had been harassing all of them for the last week, had a look of concern on his face. Maybe he wasn't the monster she'd made him out to be, or maybe she was tired and imagining things.

"Didn't you hear the buggy clatter away after the rock flew

into your friend's head? Our culprit is Amish. I'd bet my pension on it."

"Why didn't he use a bow then, like before?"

"You can't deliver a note with a bow, and besides . . . maybe it's not the killer. Maybe it's someone helping the killer."

"Why would anyone do that?"

"I don't know, but this proves someone is helping Andrew Miller, and I'm about to catch him."

As they drove away, after looking in the passenger-side makeup mirror, Pam insisted she didn't need stitches and that she would be fine once she applied an ice pack to her cut.

Amber thought back over the evening. Finally she turned to look at Pam. "We can't be sure the person is Amish. Anyone can drive a buggy, shoot an arrow, even use a slingshot. All we know is the person wants to appear Amish."

"And those three things are good ways to send the likes of Roland Shaw scurrying in the Amish direction."

They drove on in silence. Once they reached Pam's home, a two-bedroom duplex that had been newly remodeled, Pam looked at Amber and said, "Why do you have that look on your face? I've seen it before, and it usually indicates trouble is brewing."

"I still don't believe Andrew had a thing to do with Owen's murder, and I'm going to find a way to prove it."

Thirty-Nine

annah was surprised to look up and see Pam Coleman walk into A Simple Blend. The early crowd had left and the lunch crowd hadn't arrived yet. She wondered why Pam was there. Hannah knew she didn't drink coffee, preferring a Diet Coke for her caffeine needs.

"What happened to your head?"

Pam fingered the bandage across her forehead. "That's what I came to talk to you about. Amber and I had an interesting evening last night."

Seth hadn't arrived yet to cover the counter, but there weren't any customers in the shop at the moment. Hannah plopped onto her stool. "Tell me! I've been waiting to hear from Jesse. He's going to see Andrew this morning. I need something to take my mind off worrying."

"Not sure this will help with that."

Pam was in the middle of relaying the night's events when Bradley walked into the shop. Hannah's mind flashed back to the morning, almost a week ago, when she'd dodged him outside Mary's yarn shop.

"How can I help you, Bradley?"

Pam moved to a table at the far side of the room and waited, pretending to focus on her cell phone, but Hannah could tell from the way she cocked her head and glanced up in their direction occasionally that she was listening.

Bradley probably wasn't aware of that since he was facing Hannah and his back was to Pam.

"I was hoping to see you today, Hannah." His red hair desperately needed cutting, in Hannah's opinion. It fell into his eyes when he spoke. He didn't attempt to move it, staring at her through the greasy strands instead.

"This is a *gut* place to find me. Can I get you something to drink?"

"I guess. I'll take a . . . uh . . . coffee?"

"That's what we specialize in." Hannah forced back a laugh when she saw Pam roll her eyes. "Do you know what flavor you'd like?"

She pointed up to the menu that hung above the counter, but Bradley wasn't interested in coffee. "Whatever you think is good."

While she poured the coffee, a pecan blend that had a slightly sweet taste to it, Bradley shuffled from foot to foot. "I was wondering if, that is, I wanted to ask . . ." He stared at the floor, apparently searching for the right words, which came out in a mumble. "Maybe we could go to a movie sometime."

Though she'd been expecting this, heat crept up her neck. "Thank you, Bradley, but I'm seeing someone right now."

Not to mention she didn't date *Englisch* boys, and she didn't go to movies, but that was probably more information than he needed.

Bradley flinched, as if he had been hit, but he didn't back down. "Yeah, I know about Jesse. I was thinking, though, that maybe it wasn't too serious yet and maybe—"

"I'm sorry, but that wouldn't be appropriate for me to do."

"You'd have a good time." Now he became more animated, waving his arms and speaking more quickly. "We could go to the movies in Goshen, and then I found this computer *café* where they allow you to play games for as long as you want. I thought I'd show you—"

"She said no." Pam was still sitting at her table, but apparently she'd heard enough.

"I know she did, but—"

"She said no," Pam repeated. This time she stood and walked over to the counter. "Hannah has a boyfriend, and she doesn't want to two-time him. Now, don't you have work to do somewhere?"

Bradley's eyes darted from Hannah to Pam and back again. He nodded once and snatched his coffee from the counter. After rooting through his pockets, he came up with a dollar bill and dropped it on the counter.

"That's our special today. You only owe me—"

"Keep it," he muttered, and then he fled the shop.

"That was awkward." Hannah grabbed a dishcloth and swiped it across the counter. "I've sort of been avoiding him. I was afraid that might happen."

"What do you mean avoiding him? Has he been following you around or something?"

"*Nein*. It's only that we seem to run into each other a lot. The Village isn't a large place. I didn't want to have that conversation, so I've been trying to stay out of his way."

"When did this start?"

Hannah sat back down on the stool. "Last week, maybe a few days before. I remember ducking into the back alley the morning Owen was killed, except I didn't know then that Owen *was* killed."

"Odd coincidence."

"Oh, I wasn't suggesting he had anything to do with the killing. I only meant that's when I remember—"

"Still an odd coincidence."

"How? How could Bradley have anything to do with Owen?"

"Maybe he resents the Amish boys around town. You saw how he reacted when you said Jesse's name."

"But no one killed Jesse." Hannah's stomach lurched at the thought.

"True. But maybe he had a beef with Owen. Something we don't know about." Pam touched the bandage on her forehead. "Someone tried to scare us off last night, and I'm going to find out who."

❧

Amber hadn't even made it to her midmorning break when she looked up and saw Tate standing at her door. She practically flew into his embrace as he walked into her office.

"You're early!"

Tate wrapped his arms around her and kissed the top of her head. "Our sunrise tee time was rained out. I decided to come on home and check on my beautiful bride."

She pulled back and placed her hands on both sides of his face. "You didn't come home early because of me, did you? Because of what happened last night?"

"No. I didn't, but I am concerned."

They walked over to the two chairs facing Amber's desk. "I was anxious to see for myself that you're okay. You've had a busy few days."

If anything, he was more tanned than when he left. She supposed a few days of golf could do that to a person. He looked better to her than a piece of shoofly pie, and that was saying a lot.

"Tell me about your trip first. How is Alan?"

"He's doing well, and his golfing skills have surpassed those of his old man." He studied her a moment. "We had lots of time to talk. He's visited his brother several times, and he was able to shed some light on Collin's attitude."

"You mean why he doesn't like me." Amber felt the unease of the familiar stone of worry in her stomach.

"Actually, he does like you. The problem is he feels he's being unfaithful to his mother, and yes"—Tate held up his hand to stop her protests—"he realizes you're not trying to replace her. Alan suggested we give him more time, not push things."

"Do you think that will work?"

"I do. I know my son, and he'll come around. We need to be patient."

Amber sighed. It wasn't the answer she'd hoped for, but she could live with it.

"Now let's go over what's happened around here."

Elizabeth appeared with two mugs of coffee. "I tried to keep an eye on her. It's a difficult job, and I'm glad you're back to take over."

Amber couldn't stop the laughter that bubbled up out of her. She was still worried about many things, and having Tate home wouldn't change what had happened or might happen, but it did change her heart. She was whole again.

They discussed Tom's group at the church, the ISG, and what had happened the night before.

"Did Shaw take the note to Gordon? To see if the handwriting matched the other two?"

"Yes. He turned in the note wrapped around the rock last night. Actually, there are three other handwriting samples—the note to Mary, the wrapping on Naomi's box, and then Naomi's note, which Gordon took from her the day she received it. I called Gordon first thing this morning. He admitted they all match."

"And they're still not releasing Andrew?"

Amber shook her head. She had tried to argue with Gordon, but he'd hung up on her.

Tate took a sip of his coffee, placed the mug on her desk, and leaned forward with his arms propped on his knees. "Then they have compelling evidence."

"It doesn't mean he's guilty."

"No, but it does mean that his lawyer is going to face a difficult job. Let's hope he gets someone who is up to the challenge."

"I was hoping he wouldn't need a lawyer, that he'd be sent home this morning."

Tate stood, and when she did too, he wrapped his arms around her and sighed when she snuggled into his embrace. "We can pray for that, but we're also going to keep our eyes and ears open. Maybe we'll see or hear something that will weaken their case."

Forty

esse scowled at the yellowed Formica tabletop as he waited for his brother to be brought into the visitors' room. The Middlebury police station was small. There was one room for visiting and one table in the room. Two metal chairs with black seats that were not leather finished out the furniture. Three walls in the room were painted a light gray, which served to render the place more depressing. The last wall, the one with the door, was solid windows. The entire room couldn't have been bigger than ten feet by ten feet.

He supposed Andrew might be the only prisoner that day, which would explain why he didn't have to wait long to see him.

What did the cells look like?

And how did his brother cope with being locked inside?

Before he could add more questions to his list, Andrew walked into the room, head held high though his hands were cuffed in front of him.

The officer sat him at the table, then retreated to wait outside the room. Jesse had already been searched, so there was no chance that he'd sneak anything to his brother, not that he'd know what to sneak someone in jail. To him, that would be the height of foolishness, as if this situation could get any worse.

"Glad you came to visit me."

Jesse stared at him, temporarily unable to speak. He'd never seen his brother in an orange jumpsuit before. He'd seen him in *Englisch* clothes, the one time he'd visited him in Chicago. This was much worse. The orange material cast a yellow tint to Andrew's skin, and the fact that it was overalls he was wearing, something an Amish person would never purchase or wear, served to highlight the seriousness of this situation.

"How are *Mamm* and *Dat*?"

"They're doing as well as can be expected. They thought it best for me to be the one to come see you. But I didn't come to talk about *Mamm* and *Dat*. I came to tell you about Mary."

"Mary?"

Suddenly Jesse felt angry again. He wanted answers, and he had a feeling Andrew still wasn't ready to give them.

"Mary Weaver? Maybe you remember her. Nice lady, never married, works at The Cat's Meow at the Village. You gave the note she received to Hannah. You know that she was friends with Owen, and now she's missing!"

"Slow down, *bruder*. You're telling me that Mary is—"

"She's gone. No one knows where. Amber talked to her parents, but they say she probably went visiting family. As if Mary would ignore her responsibilities and leave town without telling anyone."

"No. Mary would never do that."

"How do you know what Mary would or wouldn't do? Tell me, how is she involved in this?"

Instead of answering his questions, Andrew sat back and studied the ceiling for a minute. When he finally met Jesse's gaze again, he said, "Maybe it's for the better that she's gone. She'll probably be safer out of town."

"What do you mean? What do you know that you're not telling me?"

Andrew raised his hands, still cuffed, and made a keep-your-voice-down gesture. The arrogant teenage look fell away, and in its place Jesse found himself looking into the worried eyes of a man, looking into the eyes of someone he didn't know.

"I want you to listen to me. I have a lawyer coming—"

"A lawyer? How are you going to afford that?"

"Listen and stop asking questions."

"Who is it?"

Andrew sighed and closed his eyes for a moment. When he opened them, the confident boy Jesse knew so well was back. "Adalyn Landt, a woman whose office is in Shipshe. She's represented Amish folks before."

"I've never heard of her."

"You've never needed her."

"And you do now?"

"*Ya*. Tomorrow will be the initial hearing. Adalyn will help me through that."

"And how will you pay her?"

"My job will pay her, if I'm found innocent."

The clock on the wall ticked, filling the silence between them. Finally Jesse asked, "What job?"

"That's not important right now. You go home and tell *Mamm* and *Dat* that I'm doing fine and I'll be home soon."

"I won't lie to them—"

"It's not a lie. Have faith, Jesse." Andrew stood, attracting the attention of the officer who waited outside the door. Cherry Brookstone walked into the room to escort Andrew back to his cell.

"Come back tomorrow morning. Eight o'clock."

"I have to be at work for the early shift."

"Then ask off. Be here at eight, and I'll explain everything to you and Adalyn."

If Cherry had a reaction to those words, she hid it well. Andrew didn't look back as she ushered him out.

The door clicked shut behind them. Jesse was left staring at the Formica. He probably should have left right away, but instead he sat there with his head in his hands, trying to make sense of what Andrew had said.

Why wouldn't he tell him what was going on now?

He knew his brother wasn't guilty of murder, but he was involved in something. What? And was it dangerous?

Regardless, he knew he would be back the next morning. First he needed to ask for the shift off. Maybe he could trade with someone. Then he needed to go and speak to Hannah.

❧

"Mary's gone."

Amber sank into a chair next to the front window in A Simple Blend and accepted the drink Hannah handed her—espresso with whipped cream. A perfect blend, though it did little to soothe her worried heart. She was glad Hannah had stayed at the shop later in the afternoon than she usually did so she could see her there.

"Gone?"

"Gone."

"You're positive?"

"She didn't show for work today. Not even a phone call explaining why, so I went to her house after Tate stopped by my office. Did I tell you Tate's home?"

"*Nein.*"

"He is. He came home early." Amber sipped the hot drink, hoping it would jump-start her brain. "After he left this morning, I drove out and spoke to her parents. She left the funeral early yesterday, telling her parents she wasn't feeling well."

"She told me she wasn't feeling well too. So she's still not home? She wasn't there when we stopped by in the afternoon. Her parents weren't even home from the funeral yet."

"No, she's not. Last night she didn't come down for dinner. Her mom went upstairs to check on her and found her room empty."

"Empty?" Hannah's voice rose a notch, causing Seth to look up from the counter where he was restocking sugar, cream, and napkins. "How empty?"

"Her two extra dresses were gone. She also took her Bible and her knitting bag." Amber sipped the coffee, but it wasn't clearing the cobwebs from her head fast enough.

"Mary carries that bag with her everywhere." Hannah looked as miserable as Amber felt.

"I'm not actually surprised. The note warned her to leave." Amber tapped a nail against the side of her coffee cup. Surely there was a way they could locate Mary. A way to be sure she was all right.

"But it's worrisome. What if she's hurt or lost or confused? What if she's been . . ." Hannah stumbled over the next word and settled on, "injured, like Owen?"

Amber wanted to promise her that such a thing couldn't happen, not again. But her own anxiety was making her jumpy. She'd feel like a fake reassuring Hannah when her own doubts were so strong.

"Did her parents call the police?"

"No. They said she'd probably gone to visit a relative. They know she's been very upset since Owen died. Somehow they didn't think it so odd she would leave without telling them— maybe she's more independent than I would have thought—but they assumed she'd informed someone here at the Village. I mentioned Mary hadn't asked for any time off. When I told her parents that, her mother said maybe she'd forgotten she was scheduled to work."

"Doesn't sound like Mary. And she's a manager! She cares about her shop. I can't imagine her just abandoning the place."

"I called the police station, but it's not a criminal matter at this point. She hasn't been missing long enough, and there's no sign of foul play. You'd think her getting a warning note like she did, though . . ."

Hannah stared out the window, and Amber gave her a moment to digest all the new information.

While she waited, she sipped her coffee and studied Hannah. The girl had endured a lot of stress recently. First Owen's murder, then worries about Mary, and finally Andrew's arrest—to say nothing about her natural concern for Jesse. Now Mary seemed to be in real trouble, something bad enough to cause her to leave town.

"So at the funeral was the last time you saw her?"

"Yes. Like I said, she told me she wasn't feeling well and that she was going home. But of course I also saw her the day before, at the viewing. That was when she and Andrew were reading over the note." Hannah pulled on her *kapp* strings, worrying them between her fingers.

Silence enveloped them as they stared at each other. The quiet was broken by Seth, blending something behind the counter. When he finally finished, the lack of noise was a blessed balm.

"Here. Drink this." Seth set a fruit drink in front of Hannah. "Lots of vitamins. It'll help you think."

Hannah whispered, *"Danki,"* but didn't even attempt a smile.

Amber leaned forward and claimed the girl's hands in her own. "We still have hope. God gives us that, right? He tells us to hope in him and that we can trust things will work out as they should."

Tears began to fall down Hannah's face. Seth fidgeted from left foot to right foot, then apparently decided she needed napkins to wipe her face. He brought her a stack several inches tall.

"I don't have enough tears left in me to use all of these, Seth." Her voice wobbled, but she did manage a tiny smile.

"Ya, but best to be prepared. That's an important thing I've learned from you. When we're prepared, we're better able to handle what happens. Like when Mary stopped by here yesterday afternoon."

Amber's heart forgot to beat while she processed what Seth had said. She stared at Hannah. The girl's expression must have mirrored her own—uncertainty, shock, and beneath that a small measure of hope.

Hannah had been holding the fruit drink, but she set it down gently on the table and turned her attention to Seth. "Did you say she came by here?"

"Ya."

"Yesterday afternoon?"

"Ya."

"And you didn't think to tell me before now?"

Seth stared down at the floor, fidgeting with his suspenders as he tried to think how best to answer. Finally he said, "Didn't seem important until now."

Amber patted the vacant chair next to her. "Sit down, Seth."

"Am I in trouble?"

"Of course you're not in trouble. Relax."

"All right." He didn't look relaxed. His shoulders were tight, his eyes moved from right to left, and he couldn't seem to find a place to put his hands.

"Start from the beginning, Seth."

"You mean the first day I worked here?"

Hannah closed her eyes, and Amber knew she was counting to ten.

Amber picked up her coffee and sipped it, trying to appear casual. "No, let's start with the last time you saw Mary. This was yesterday afternoon?"

"*Ya.* It was nearly time to close. I'd mopped the floor and was about to put the chairs back down because it had dried."

"Why did she come to the Village? She already had someone covering for her at The Cat's Meow because she was going to be at the funeral. Was she looking for Hannah?"

Hannah placed both palms flat against the table and stared directly into Seth's eyes. "What did she say, exactly?"

Seth rubbed his forehead as if that would help him to remember. "First, she did ask if you were here. I thought that was odd because she should have known you were at the funeral."

"Did she look afraid? Or worried? Or—"

"She looked like Mary. No different from any other day."

Amber smiled at Seth. "You're doing great. This could be very helpful, Seth. Now, after she asked you if you were alone, what else did she say?"

"She wanted to know if I'd seen Uri Wagler anywhere around."

"Uri Wagler?" Hannah frowned. "He never comes by the Village. Why would she ask about him?"

"I don't know, but she seemed relieved when I said no."

"Anything else?" Amber was already gathering her keys, coffee, and purse.

"*Nein*. She might have wanted to say more, but a customer walked in and she left. Oh. I did notice she had two small bags with her. That's why I said she looked prepared."

"Bags?" Heather stared at him in disbelief. "You didn't think that odd?"

"*Nein*. Why would I? Women carry all sorts of bags. One had her knitting things—I could tell that because some needles were sticking out the top. The other was a plain canvas bag with handles. Like you would use for an overnight case."

"Big enough to hold two dresses and a Bible?" Amber asked.

"*Ya*. I suppose so."

"Thank you, Seth." Amber stood and tugged on Hannah's arm. "You're scheduled to cover the shop for the rest of the day?"

When he nodded in the affirmative, she said, "We'll be going now, but if you see Mary again, you call me right away. Understand?"

"Sure. I'll call the office."

"Call my cell phone, Seth. Here's a copy of the number if you don't have it." She pulled a card from her purse. "You call me if you see Mary or hear anything from her or about her."

Hannah allowed herself to be pulled out into the afternoon sunlight. The weather seemed in direct opposition to their moods. It should be cloudy and storming, with lightning striking in a haphazard fashion. Instead, the sun shone with a special brilliance, and the flowers the grounds crew had planted bobbed their colors in the light breeze.

They followed the path that circled the pond. Amber didn't stop until they'd reached a bench halfway around the circle. She wanted to give Hannah some distance from the shop. She wanted the fresh air to clear her head. It must have been a shock to learn that Mary had been looking for her moments before she left town.

"Tell me who Uri is."

"He's no one." When Amber gave her a tell-me-more stare, she added, "He's a guy in our church. I don't see how Mary asking about him could be related."

"But she did ask about him right before she left. It's related. Do you know Uri?"

"Not well."

"But you know him."

"*Ya.* Our church is not large. Everyone knows everyone else."

"And you know Uri."

"Him and his wife, Olivia. No kids, though." Hannah made a face and stared at the ground.

"What? What does that look mean?"

"Nothing. It's nothing important."

"Spill. It could be the one thing that turns us in the right direction. We need to crack this case!"

"But the police are working the case. You said so."

"True. They're working Owen's case, but they don't seem all that concerned about Mary and the note threatening her. She's the person I'm worried about right now. Her involvement has bothered me since the beginning. Since Owen's phone was found beside his dead body."

"With her number on the screen."

"Yes. He called her, apparently seconds before he was shot. Now tell me about Uri and Olivia."

Hannah waited to speak until two girls who worked in the restaurant passed by. "Uri and Olivia are not the most pleasant couple in our church."

"Go on."

"There was some talk of Uri leaving a few years ago, leaving the church and Olivia."

"Divorce? I thought that wasn't allowed among the Amish."

"It's not, but of course the bishop can't stop someone from leaving the Amish church and seeking a divorce in an *Englisch* court. The one who is left behind, though, they are considered still married."

Amber tried to comprehend that, but before she could fully wrap her mind around it, Hannah continued.

"Which isn't important in any way, because Uri came back and everything's been fine, or if not fine, at least back to normal."

"And Mary knows them?"

"I don't think she knows them well. Uri and Olivia keep to themselves."

Amber checked her watch. A few minutes after three. They had time.

"Do you know where they live?"

"*Ya.*"

"I want you to take me to them."

Forty-One

annah chewed on her thumbnail as they neared the Wagler farm. She didn't think this would do any good. She didn't think either Uri or Olivia knew where Mary was. All she was sure of was that her friend was missing, Andrew was still in jail, and Jesse was brokenhearted over the events of the past week. Not to mention Owen was still dead. How much worse could things get?

"Place looks different from the Amish homes I've seen." Amber drove up a lane toward the tidy one-story home set on a fair-sized acreage. A large barn sat to the south of the house, and a smaller, older barn perched beside it. "Why does it look different?"

Hannah shrugged. It looked like every other Amish home to her. No power lines. Cattle in the field and two buggy horses in the adjacent pasture.

Amber released one hand from the steering wheel and snapped her fingers. "No kids, you said. That's what it is. No bicycles, no tire swing."

"*Ya*. Olivia, she can't have children. I remember the funeral for the one child she lost. I was probably ten. There haven't been any other pregnancies since."

Hannah hadn't thought about Olivia's troubles a lot, other

than to feel bad during the baby's funeral so many years ago. She remembered struggling with the concept of *Gotte's wille*, even at that age. Now it was somewhat easier. She did honestly believe that God could be trusted, but there were still times when she had trouble reconciling God's love with her aching heart.

Amber parked the car near a hitching post and pushed the button that turned off the engine.

"Ready?"

"*Ya.*" Hannah didn't feel prepared at all, but she couldn't let Amber go up there alone. More than likely, Olivia wouldn't even answer the door if Amber had arrived by herself on her porch.

They stood together, side by side and close enough that their shoulders touched. They waited after Amber knocked. Amber motioned toward the boxes of jars stacked near the front door. Hannah shrugged, but now that she was studying them, she thought something was amiss. What was it?

Her thoughts were interrupted by the sound of footsteps, and then Olivia opened the door.

Perhaps it was the afternoon light, or maybe it was because she was seeing her without the noise and color of the other Amish women around, but weariness seemed to roll off Olivia. She was thin to the point of unhealthiness, and there was no color in her face. Even her brown eyes were lighter than Hannah remembered—almost a beige, as if the many tears she had cried had drained them of their color. Olivia Wagler looked like a waif Hannah had read about in a book at school.

"Hannah."

"Hello, Olivia. This is Amber, she's—"

"I know who she is." Olivia didn't smile, she didn't speak directly to Amber, and she didn't invite them in.

"Nice to meet you, Mrs. Wagler." Amber cinched her purse

up on her shoulder. "We would like to ask you a few questions about Mary."

When Olivia didn't say anything, she added, "Mary Weaver."

"I can't tell you anything about Mary." Olivia made a move to close the door, but Amber stepped forward and put her hand against the screen that separated them.

"She's disappeared." The words whirled, then settled around the three women. The full weight of what might have happened to Mary seemed to hang between them.

Finally Olivia shrugged and pushed open the screen door. "Can't help you, and I'm in the middle of carrying my canning to the shelter. You're free to follow me if it will put your mind at ease."

"Thank you."

"*Danki.*"

Hannah glanced toward Amber, who beamed. If she thought visiting with Olivia was going to gain her any answers, she was in for a rude awakening. Hannah had seen her boss in this mood before, when they were searching for Ethan's killer. She could be more focused than a dog gnawing on a bone. There was no stopping her until she found the answers to her questions, even when that put her in danger.

Not that they would be in any danger here.

The worst that could happen would be that Olivia wouldn't offer them tea or a snack. Hospitality wasn't high on Olivia's list of social skills.

Olivia had always seemed more than a tad peculiar to Hannah, though she hadn't said that exactly to Amber. It seemed rude. It seemed as if she were betraying a confidence. But everyone within the community knew it. Olivia didn't fit in, had never even tried to fit in. Yes, there was the fact that she was childless, but that alone shouldn't have caused the chasm that existed between this family and the community.

No, something else was wrong.

She'd asked her mother about it once, and Eunice had reminded her, "We each learn to live with grief in our own way."

Olivia bent to pick up a box of the canning jars. There were so many. Hannah knew all about canning. She'd asked for a day off next week to help her mother do theirs. But even with their large family, they didn't have this many jars. How had Olivia canned so much? *Why* had she canned so much?

"We'll help you carry these over." Amber bent and picked up one of the boxes, practically staggering under the weight.

Olivia shrugged and proceeded down the porch and across the yard.

"Grab a box," Amber muttered. "If we help, maybe she'll soften up."

"Doubtful." But Hannah did pick up a box. Hers looked like it was half filled with pickled okra and half filled with stewed tomatoes.

They hurried to catch up with Olivia, who wasn't acknowledging their presence in any way. Hannah was surprised when they stopped in front of the old barn. Most folks kept their canned goods closer to the house, in a basement usually. Olivia paused in front of the barn and set her box on the ground. She fished in her apron pocket for a key, unlocked the door, and then picked up the box and carried it into the barn.

Who locked their storage area? No one Hannah knew.

Amber darted a look toward Hannah, her eyes scrunched together and her nose wrinkled. Apparently she wasn't sure about entering the barn, so Hannah stepped in front of her. They both stopped as soon as they walked a few feet into the room, as soon as their eyes adjusted to the near darkness. Small slivers of light shone in from a few unblocked windows high up in the lofts. Olivia stopped and turned on a battery-operated lantern, which illuminated the room.

The scene in front of her was unlike anything Hannah had ever seen in a barn before. It reminded her of the time she'd gone with her old boss, Carol, to the wholesale dry-goods store outside of Shipshewana. There was so much stuff—more than Hannah could imagine ever needing. Shelves lined all four walls, floor to ceiling. Many of the items on the shelves she recognized, but a few she didn't.

"Vegetables to the left. Fruits to the right." Olivia carried her box to the right.

"What do I have?" Amber whispered.

"Chowchow." Hannah nodded to the left, to the area where her box went.

"This year's canning goes on the left end of each shelf. I choose from the right to cook so I use the oldest goods first."

"Do you sell some of this?" Amber placed her jars on the shelf Hannah indicated and then turned in a complete circle, taking in the large room and the vast store of supplies.

"Sell it? *Nein.* The purpose of storing these goods is so we'll have what we need."

"I'd say you have enough to last several years."

"That's the idea." Uri Wagler's voice was flat and low and meant to put an end to any discussion.

Hannah jumped in spite of her intention to remain calm. She nearly dropped her box, which she'd been holding as she struggled to make space for it.

Either Amber didn't pick up on Uri's tone or she chose to ignore it. "You must be Mr. Wagler. Pleased to meet you."

She didn't offer her hand, which was smart in Hannah's opinion, but she also kept talking, which probably wasn't so smart. "You have a lovely home and . . . storage area."

"Why are you here?"

Uri probably looked like a typical Amish man to an *Englischer*. He wore dark-colored pants, suspenders, and a blue shirt with the sleeves rolled up. The hat on his head was straw, to block out the sun. And of course he had the traditional beard. He wasn't tall, but he was stocky. The expression on his face reminded Hannah of a window with a shade pulled down tightly.

Hannah noticed, in that split second, all that was off about Uri. Things she hadn't taken the time to see at church meetings. Or maybe she was becoming overly suspicious.

His unfriendly tone.

His nearly angry expression.

The way he clenched his hands into fists at his sides.

"I'm the manager of the Village, and one of my employees is missing. I believe you know her. Mary Weaver? She runs the yarn shop at the Village."

Uri didn't offer any opinion about that, and Olivia was busying herself, moving more canned goods to the right, no doubt so she would have room to store all that was on her porch.

Was she worried the next year's crops wouldn't be sufficient? Did she fear drought or fire or something else?

Or was she merely preparing against the day when she might be left alone again?

Given the combination of canned goods and hunting items, plainly this room had been planned by both of them. There were also items covered with a tarp—large, bulky things that she couldn't begin to guess the nature of.

"We thought you or your wife might have seen her."

"No reason for Mary to come here."

"Does that mean you haven't seen her?"

Instead of answering her, Uri turned to leave. On his way outside, he paused to straighten a crossbow hung near the door and then turned back toward them. "My *fraa* has much work to do today. You should both go."

He walked out of the barn, which didn't fool Hannah for a moment. Hannah knew he would wait somewhere nearby and be sure they'd gone. It was plain that they weren't welcome.

Instead of following him out, Amber turned to Olivia.

"Have you seen her? Has Mary been here?"

"My husband's right. I've no time for visiting, with Mary or anyone else." She stared at Amber, her lips forming a tight line and her hands frozen on top of the jars in front of her. Finally she added, "You can find your own way back to your car."

Amber moved toward Hannah then, and Hannah motioned toward the door with her head. She had been ready to leave ten minutes ago.

The first step into the fall afternoon caused her to feel like a bird freed from a cage. Hannah breathed in deeply of the crisp air, finally daring to relax a little. Then Amber grabbed her arm, and she shrieked as if a snake had bitten her.

"Don't look around. He's watching us."

"Uri?"

"Yes. He's standing in the shadow of the large barn."

Hannah naturally turned that direction.

"Don't look!" Amber's fingers dug into Hannah's arm as she pulled her toward the little red car. They were in the vehicle and moving down the lane before Hannah dared to look back. The windows were tinted—surely it was safe to do so. She saw him then, standing near the barn in the shadows, assuring himself that they were leaving.

"Explain to me what happened back there." Amber clutched the wheel as she pulled out onto the county road.

"We went somewhere we weren't welcome. That's what happened."

"I've never met Amish folk that unfriendly."

"But you've met *Englischers* that unfriendly?"

Amber laughed, a nervous, forced sound. "Maybe. I seem to remember some rude folks in the city. Back in the day I was volunteering with a charity group in college. We'd go door-to-door asking for donations. Most people were friendly, even if they didn't donate, but a few would slam the door in your face."

"Olivia didn't slam the door."

"I think she probably wanted to."

"Indeed."

The sound of road noise wasn't as calming as Hannah's mare clomping down the road, but it did help to settle her nerves a bit, or maybe it was the distance they were putting between them and the Waglers' home.

"Okay. From the top of your head, tell me what you noticed that was off back at that house. Sixty seconds. Go."

"This is not a game, Amber."

"Fifty seconds."

"Too many jars of food on the porch, way too many in the barn. The lock on the door was odd. I've never seen anyone store rifles and crossbows and arrows with their canned goods, and there was something off about Uri."

"Uri? Not Olivia?"

"*Ya.* Olivia was behaving as she always does—rude and

indifferent. Notice she didn't mind us seeing the barn. She didn't care if we were there or not. We were like a pesky fly to her. But Uri—"

"Thirty extra seconds because you're making good points. Tell me about Uri Wagler."

Amber's enthusiasm was contagious, and it was a relief to be doing something, to be trying to figure out where Mary was, which could lead them to Owen's killer, which could free Andrew and help Jesse.

"No tan line. He had his shirtsleeves rolled up, which is common, but his arms weren't tan at all."

"He might lease his land."

"Yet every Amish man spends a certain amount of time outdoors. There's always a tan line on their arms, usually halfway up the lower arm because they roll up their sleeves. Not so with Uri. Also, when he reached to straighten the crossbow, something that didn't need straightening, I had a good look at his hands. Perfectly clean nails and no calluses."

"Maybe he's fastidious about his appearance."

"Which would be odd for an Amish man."

"Do you think he knows where Mary is?"

"*Nein*. But he was surprised that we asked. He flinched slightly."

Then she told Amber all the details she knew about Uri and Olivia—about the child who had died in infancy, about Uri and Olivia's estrangement, and about Olivia's oddities. By the time she was finished, Amber had parked the car in front of Hannah's home.

"It might be hard for her to be around families." Something softened Amber's expression. "Maybe it reminds her of what she can't have."

"And then there's the fact that her husband is away so much. That would cause some people to grow closer to other women, but in her case it appears to have done the reverse. She seems more comfortable when she is by herself."

"Why is Uri away so much?" Amber angled in the car and studied her in the fading light.

"Something to do with his work. I can't remember exactly what he does, but he hires a driver every week, and he's gone for three to four days at a time."

Amber cocked her head. "I didn't realize Amish men ever do that—work away from home, I mean."

"It's becoming more common as some are employed by factories. I've heard that several will rent a home together and live near a factory during the week, then come home on weekends. It's not a *wunderbaar* solution, but sometimes it's the best one available to younger men." Hannah hesitated before adding, "Jesse's fortunate that he will have his *dat's* land to work. If we . . . well, if we marry, we'll be able to live there, and his hours working at the Village combined with what he'll make farming should be enough."

Hannah wasn't sure Amber even realized she had just revealed she was thinking about marriage to Jesse.

"But you said Uri is usually gone only a few days a week. What type of job would require that?"

"I don't know. I've never asked."

Amber reached across the car and enfolded her in a hug. "Thank you for going with me. I wouldn't have wanted to endure that scene alone."

"You looked ready to run when you said he was watching us."

"I was ready to run! I could envision him with a bow and arrow pointed at my back."

"I don't think Uri would do that, Amber. He might be odd, but I don't see him being violent. It's not our way."

"Neither is stockpiling several years' worth of food, but he's done that."

"It is strange. He might know something that he doesn't want to tell, but information on Owen's murder? *Nein*. I don't see how it's possible. He barely knew Owen, or Mary for that matter. He had no—"

"Motive? There's always a motive," Amber agreed. "Figure out the motive, and we'll be one step closer to locating the murderer." Before pulling away, she added, "And, Hannah, I hope you and Jesse do get married. You're one of the sweetest couples I know, and I think you would be good for one another."

Before Hannah could respond to that, Amber had put the little car in gear and sped off down the lane.

Forty-Two

*A*mber found Tate in the west field. He was wearing old jeans, work boots, a T-shirt, and over that a flannel shirt. The day was growing colder as evening approached, but she loved these moments they spent outside together after her workday was finished. Tate was doing maintenance on an interior fence, and he had an audience of two.

"I don't spend enough time with Trixie and Velvet."

"I spend too much with them. Those two follow me all over this place, and I don't doubt for a minute that they are the reason this fence needs fixing." Tate was wearing work gloves, but that didn't stop him from shaking a finger at the two donkeys.

Trixie had a white patch between her ears, a place she loved for Amber to scratch.

The second donkey Amber had named Velvet because of his glossy reddish-brown hide.

"They've bonded to you," she explained. "It's why they follow you around and watch you work. Now you have two friends for life."

"Do I get a say in this?"

"You did when you bought them."

"Not my finest decision."

Amber rubbed Trixie between the ears, on the white patch that in her mind resembled a clover. Trixie could be their lucky donkey. It was possible. Perhaps God had sent them this animal to encourage them. Hadn't their preacher spoken of Balaam's donkey last week? Maybe their donkey was special too.

"When you think about it, these two are sort of responsible for our being together."

"How's that?" Tate didn't look up as he spoke. He'd pulled a metal post straight and was tightening the wire attached to it.

"Remember the first night I came over? During the rain and after the . . . the incident on the trail behind your property."

"Our property now."

"I would have headed straight home if it hadn't been for Trixie and Velvet." She moved to the donkey whose coat had a reddish tint and gave Velvet an affectionate pat. "You'd have never convinced them to follow you into the barn that night."

"I convince them to do very little."

"It was probably there that I first started to fall in love with you."

Now Tate did pause in his work and glance up, a smile sneaking onto his face.

It lasted less than five seconds. The next thing Amber knew, he'd dropped his tools and was shouting, "Get down!"

He threw himself on top of her, and she heard a sound like the wind in the trees at night. It was followed immediately by a *plink*—something hitting Tate's ATV.

"Are you all right?"

"I think so."

He held her face between his hands. "Are you all right?"

"Yes. I am, but what—"

Tate frowned over at his all-terrain vehicle. "That's a new John Deere. Wait until I get my hands on whoever is shooting at us."

"Shooting?"

Trixie and Velvet were braying at the top of their donkey lungs. Had Tate said someone was shooting at them?

All Amber could hear was "hee-haw, hee-haw" as the donkeys fled to the far side of the pasture, that and the beating of Tate's heart. His body still covered hers, protected hers.

He raised his head enough to glance around.

"Stay down," he whispered. "Stay flat."

His four-wheeler was a few feet to the north of where Amber lay on the ground. It had an area on the back to store his tools, water, and whatever else he might need. Tate crawled to it, reached up, and pulled out his rifle.

"You keep your rifle—"

But he had two fingers on his lips, shushing her.

Still crouching, he kept his body next to the ATV. He raised the rifle, peering through the scope to the north, away from the house and toward his property line.

With a disgusted shake of his head, he stood up.

Holding the rifle in his left hand and pointing the barrel toward the ground, he strode over to her and helped her up.

"Did I hurt you?"

"No, but what happened?"

"I don't know. I was looking at you, and then I noticed movement, noticed someone to the north. I saw them raise a crossbow."

"A what?"

"Fortunately, they were too far out for an accurate shot."

"Did you say crossbow?"

"I want to look around. Are you sure you're all right?"

"I'm fine." Her heart was still beating faster than a wood-pecker determined to attract a mate.

"Help me search the area."

"What are we looking for?"

"An arrow."

"What?" Amber felt all the blood drain from her face as the reality of what had happened, of what Tate was suggesting, sank into her addled brain. The world took on a decidedly fuzzy cast as she reached out and placed her hand on Tate's shoulder to steady herself.

"Hang on there, sweetheart. Are you going to faint on me?"

"No. Why would I do that?" Amber was not the fainting type. At least that was what she wanted to argue as Tate guided her to the ATV. "Is it safe here? Are they still—"

"They're gone. Whoever it was is a coward. Probably the shot was a warning or they would have come closer and one of us would be dead."

"Dead?" Amber's mind still refused to process what had happened. She couldn't wrap her mind around it, and the sudden humming in her ears was a distraction. She put her head between her knees and took several deep breaths.

"Either that or the man's an idiot to think he could make a shot from that distance. Wait here." Tate left her to search the surrounding area.

By the time he returned, her head had cleared. She felt fool-ish, behaving like a little girl, caving at the first sign of danger. But then she remembered all she'd endured the previous spring, and she decided a little shock was probably normal.

Tate wore a victorious grin. In his right hand he carried his rifle, and in his left he held an arrow. He'd taken off his flannel shirt and wrapped it around the shaft. "Found it!"

"What are you going to do with it?"

"Give it to Gordon. He can see if it matches the one that killed Owen. Maybe he can even get a print off it."

❧

Twenty minutes later Gordon was standing with them in the middle of the field. Cherry had been scouring the area and found an additional arrow to the south of where they stood.

"That must have been the one I heard whir over my head." Amber had moved past shock and marched straight into angry. "Who does this creep think he is?"

Tate ran his hand over the top of his head. "If he'd wanted us dead, we'd be dead. He could have gotten closer without attracting attention. I was focused on the fence—"

"And I was focused on the donkeys."

"I still think it was probably a scare tactic."

"Why? Why would anyone want to scare us?"

"Are you still digging into my homicide?" Gordon frowned at the two arrows Cherry had slipped into large, clear evidence bags.

Amber's silence gave her away.

"Tell him, honey. It's best he knows what you've found."

So she told him Mary was missing and about her visit to the Wagler place.

"Why didn't you call me about Mary?"

"I called the station. They told me a missing person's report couldn't be filed so soon and then assured me she probably wasn't even missing."

"Who told you that?"

Amber cocked a thumb toward Cherry, who was walking north in search of footprints.

Gordon sighed. "Technically she's right, but in this instance I would have liked to know that she had left the area. And going to the Waglers' house was not your responsibility."

"Mary is my responsibility. She's my employee, and I'm worried about her." Amber's temper nearly peeked through, but she pushed it down. "What about Uri's place? Doesn't it sound strange to you? Something is definitely out of whack there."

"It's not illegal to be eccentric."

"I'm telling you, there's more going on at that farm. He practically threatened us. I could feel his stare searing into my back."

"I think you have an overactive imagination."

Amber started to argue, but Tate placed an arm around her waist to dissuade her. "You are imaginative, dear. Remember last week? You were talking to the donkeys and insisted they were talking back."

"I said they *seemed* to be talking back."

"Overactive imagination." Gordon shook his head as if she were his worst nightmare.

"I didn't imagine those two arrows!"

Tate stared out over his field and then shrugged as if he were agreeing with her. "In this case, maybe you should check Wagler out."

"I can't search his place without a reason, without a warrant. But I can definitely stop by and let him know that he's on our radar."

"If he was the person shooting—"

"We don't know that." Gordon sighed and cinched up his belt.

"We know it wasn't Andrew, since you put him in jail."

"This doesn't mean Andrew is innocent, Amber. Do you think it makes me happy to place that young man in a cell?" Gordon lowered the volume on the radio on his belt. Someone was reporting a minor accident on Main Street. "It's possible that the person who did this was working with Andrew. It's my job to protect these people, all of them. At this point, Andrew might be safer in jail—and no, before you ask, I am not dropping charges. The evidence we have still points to his guilt."

Forty-Three

*H*annah stared at the notebook in Jesse's hands, afraid to touch it. What if it made things worse? What if it proved Andrew's guilt?

They were sitting at Sandwich Bites in downtown Middlebury. Outside the window the sun shone the last of its light on a perfect fall day, but nothing felt perfect to Hannah. She was beginning to wonder if she'd ever experience a normal day again.

When Jesse had shown up at the *kaffi* shop asking her to go with him, when he'd asked her to wait after her shift until he was off, she'd known it was important. So she'd sent a message to her parents that she wouldn't be home for dinner. Now she and Jesse sat next to each other in a rear booth, the remains of one large sandwich they'd split pushed to the other side of the table and night beginning to fall over the streets of their town.

"The police searched the house when they arrested Andrew. They also searched the barn."

"So where was it?"

"Down by the creek. There's an old deer blind there. When we were boys, we'd spend hours in that blind, watching wild turkey and deer. We even saw a fox a time or two."

"What made you think to look there? What made you think to look at all?"

"Our neighbor, Linda Rainey, had seen Andrew walking toward the creek a few hours after he arrived. With everything going on, it took until today for me to remember what she said. I decided I'd better go down there and take a look. Today, after I saw him at the jail, I was so disappointed, disappointed and"— Jesse ducked his head as if he had trouble looking directly at her—"feeling guilty that I've spent years being angry with him. Angry when he left, angry when he came back, and more recently angry that he'd come back and become messed up in this situation with Owen."

"We've talked of that, Jesse. Don't worry over it anymore. You were concerned for your parents and your *schweschdern*."

"*Ya*. I can't say my attitude is completely adjusted, but I've been praying about it. I know *Gotte* has forgiven me for my bad behavior and harsh feelings. Andrew is my *bruder*, no matter what he's mixed up in. I should love and pray for him."

"And you do."

"Sure. Some days, though, some days it's still hard, like when I went to see him this morning."

Jesse looked up at her then, and Hannah could see the struggle he was still enduring. She loved him all the more for it.

"I do believe *Gotte* is in control, even though I can't see how this will end well."

"We don't have to see the solutions. We are called to be faithful."

"*Ya*. Hard to remember when someone like Roland Shaw is breathing down your *bruder's* neck."

Hannah started to argue with him but stopped herself. God would change Jesse's heart and ease his worries. Instead, she touched his arm and asked, "So you remembered to go and look by the creek, and you found the journal in the deer stand?"

"*Ya.* We would sometimes hide things there when we were boys. You know, stuff we didn't want our *schweschdern* to see—like car magazines and such."

"So what is in the journal?"

He held the spiral notebook in his hands. It was smaller than any tablet they'd used in school, something that might have fit in a coat pocket, though it probably would have stuck out. The cover was black, and the edges of the pages were frayed. Jesse opened it, and they both stared down at the messy, cramped writing.

"Did he write this badly on purpose, to try to confuse anyone who might find the book?"

"I don't think so. Andrew never was *gut* with his penmanship."

"I'll say. What is this word?"

"I'm not sure. Could be *dead* or *deed* or even *dat.*"

"It would help if he'd consistently cross his *t*'s."

They paged slowly through the book, stopping occasionally to try to read specific portions. A cloud of confusion settled over the table as they realized that the notebook was quickly raising more questions instead of answering any of the ones they had.

"Two things we know, Hannah Bell." Jesse sat back and pushed the book toward her. "This book was meant for Andrew's eyes only. No one else could have read it."

"And the second thing?"

"He was worried enough about what might happen, about who might read these pages, to hide it."

"The dates stretch back over a year."

"*Ya.* I noticed that too."

"So this isn't a description of something he stumbled on recently. I don't see how it can be related to Owen's death."

"Perhaps the beginning of the notebook isn't, but I'm guessing the second half is, at least in some way. Maybe he does know the person who did it, or at least who Owen was involved with. I recognize several names here." Jesse thumbed back through the pages and showed her different spots with names of people in their community. "Mary, Owen, the bishop. And this looks like Uri's name."

"Hard to tell. Maybe we're seeing what we want to see."

"The other thing I'm noticing is that the initials *ISG* appear in multiple places."

Hannah picked up her cup of soda and took a drink. The ice had long since melted, and it tasted like badly flavored water. "Do you think Andrew was involved with the group?"

"I don't know, but that would be a solid connection between him and Owen. The first one we've found."

"Why would he write all this down? Why even risk it? If he's involved in something—something he shouldn't be—then he wouldn't want to take a chance that someone might find it. And if it's something honest he's involved in, well, I can't imagine what it would be."

"I don't know either. I want to take it with me tomorrow when I go to meet Andrew and his lawyer."

"Should you take it into the police building?"

"Maybe not. I think they search visitors each time, and they might confiscate it."

Hannah reached for his hand and gave it a squeeze. "We should ask someone who understands the *Englisch* system better than we do."

"Amber?"

"*Ya*. I'll call her from the phone booth over there and see if it's okay for us to stop by."

Amber answered the door before Jesse or Hannah had a chance to knock. She'd been watching for them. She'd been pacing back and forth across the living room floor since their call, pausing every few minutes to stare out the front window.

"Come in. Let me take your wraps."

Jesse shrugged out of his coat, and Hannah handed over her poncho-like shawl. The dark-blue yarn was tightly knitted, and Amber wanted to ask if she'd made it. The sight of the knitting reminded her of Mary, though, and she bit back her question. They needed to stay focused and find some answers. Amber had the strangest feeling that a clock was ticking somewhere, one that would count down to another disaster if they weren't careful.

Tate walked into the room with a tray containing a teapot full of hot water, various instant drinks, and four mugs. His expression remained grave as Amber explained what had happened in the field that afternoon—both the apparent attack and the fact that Gordon had filed a report.

Hannah's face paled as she listened. "*Ach!* That's terrible, Amber. You shouldn't be in the middle of this."

"It involves one of my employees, and whoever this creep is needs to answer for what he's doing. He can't go around scaring people by shooting arrows at them. This isn't the days of Robin Hood."

"Who?" Jesse squinted at them over his mug of hot chocolate.

"Never mind. Tell me what you've found."

Hannah reached out and stopped Jesse, who was about to hand over the small notebook. "Did Roland Shaw come out this afternoon when you called the police?"

"No, and I'm glad he didn't."

"Shaw's probably a good investigator." Tate sat back and

crossed his right foot over his left knee. "Somewhat overzealous, but on the right side of this."

"I'm not so sure." Hannah accepted the notebook from Jesse and flipped the pages in search of something, turning forward, then back again. Finally she found the section she was looking for. "Doesn't this look like *Roland* to you?"

"Maybe. It's hard to tell. The handwriting is terrible!"

"*Ya.* Makes it difficult to read," Jesse agreed. "And his notes are very cryptic anyway."

"Tell me again what this notebook is and where you found it." Amber had been restless all evening, convinced there was something they should be doing. It felt good to have Hannah and Jesse in their home. It felt right to be working on this together.

So Jesse explained about meeting with his brother at the police station and his frustration with his brother's talk of a job. "It always seemed to me that he bummed around. I never imagined him having a job."

"He would have needed a way to pay for the place he lived in when he was in Chicago." Amber sat back and sipped her hot tea.

"*Ya,* but when I visited, he was living with a few other Amish guys, so maybe they let him stay for free. Or maybe he found odd jobs to do, enough to earn a little money. Regardless, Andrew always talked big, but I never saw him actually go to work."

"Maybe it was something he thought you wouldn't approve of." Hannah stared down into her mug of apple cider. "Perhaps he didn't tell you because he knew you would try to talk him out of what he was doing."

Tate cleared his throat. "We could talk maybes from now until sunrise. Better stay focused on what we know. Or at least on what we suspect."

Amber pulled her tablet from her work bag. "Point well

taken. I'll make another list, this one of what we suspect, what we know, and what questions we have."

"My first question is, why is Roland Shaw's name in this book?" Hannah frowned at the page she still held open.

Jesse's brow wrinkled as he studied the notebook. "Is Shaw even who he says he is? Are we sure he works for the government?"

"And why was your brother keeping the notebook?" Tate added.

"What type of job did Andrew have?" Hannah set the notebook on the coffee table.

"Does my *bruder* know who killed Owen?" Jesse's last question settled over the room like a wet cloak, muffling all sound.

Tate broke the silence when he added three more questions. "Who shot at us today, why, and how is ISG involved?"

Amber typed as fast as she could and then ran her finger down the list of questions. They had a lot to learn, but this was a good start. "Two things we left out. Is Uri Wagler involved, and where is Mary?"

It took no time at all to list what they knew, since they knew, for certain, practically nothing. Owen was dead, pierced by someone's arrow. The same person may have slung a rock at Amber and Pam. And someone had tried to scare her and Tate, though why she couldn't imagine.

That was it, and Amber wasn't confident that the police knew any more than they did—except for whatever it was that made them think Andrew was guilty. Gordon was usually pretty forthcoming with everything he was allowed to tell, but when he'd met them in the pasture earlier that day, he'd seemed frustrated.

As for what they suspected, it could have filled a book.

Tate stopped them after twenty minutes. "I suggest you hand

Andrew's notebook over to Adalyn Landt tomorrow. She'll know what to do with it."

"Won't she already be inside when I get there? If the police find it on me—"

"It could be we want the police to have it, especially if what's written in there can help them to find the real killer. Also, you don't want to be guilty of withholding evidence. Adalyn will know what to do with it. Arrive at the station early. That way you can intercept Adalyn before she enters the building."

"How will I know who she is?"

"She's *Englisch* and dresses conservatively. Her gray hair is usually pulled back, and she always carries a Louis Vuitton leather bag."

Amber stared at Tate, her mouth slightly ajar. She pressed her lips together, realizing how foolish she must look, but then she noticed Hannah and Jesse were also staring at her dear, sweet husband.

"What? I read the paper, and she's been in there often enough with the murders in Shipshe."

"It sounds as if you know her." Amber crossed her arms and gave Tate the look. "She carries a Louis Vuitton bag? How do you even know what that is?"

"There was a feature piece in the paper on her. Seems she's a bit eccentric, especially in her choice of handbags." He pulled Amber into his arms as they stood. "I don't know her, but I know *of* her and she's a good lawyer—something that's hard to find when you need it."

Jesse and Hannah were nearly to the door when the house phone rang. Amber was standing closest to it, so she reached over, picked up the receiver, and said hello.

The voice that responded was male, low and sinister. For

a moment he breathed heavily into the receiver, and then he spoke. He only uttered five words, but they were enough to rock Amber's world once again.

"Next time I won't miss."

Forty-Four

He lay in his bed in South Bend, Fern curled at his side. She'd fallen asleep over an hour ago. Running his fingers through her hair, he thought again of how precious this life was to him.

Why should they take it away from him?

He wouldn't allow it. He'd defend what was his, and that included Fern, their tiny home, and the family they might one day have.

The feeling of desperation closed in on him once more. He'd thought when they arrested the kid, Andrew, that the police would back off. But that wasn't happening. Instead, the hunt seemed to have grown more intense.

Slipping out of their bed, he walked into the living room. From the front window he could see up and down the tidy street. The streetlights cast halos on the cars parked beside each home.

Perhaps he should stay here. Why keep returning to Middlebury? Why take the risk?

Stay here. Lay low. Allow things to cool off for a while.

It wasn't how he'd planned it, but then, what had been?

His life had spun out of control when Owen Esch had stopped into the sandwich shop in South Bend. That the lad had recognized him—had actually stopped to talk—sealed his own fate.

At least he hadn't asked about Fern, hadn't raised her suspicions, though Owen had looked at her curiously enough.

He had known, in that moment, what he'd have to do.

The same certainty came over him again as he stood in the predawn studying the scene outside his home.

He'd stay away—not forever, but for a time.

But he would return. He wouldn't allow them to take what was his.

Forty-Five

Hannah thought she wouldn't rest well that night, but she did. She enjoyed a deep, dreamless sleep. She woke the next morning refreshed and confident everything would work out for the better, and soon.

When her family prayed over their breakfast meal, she remembered God's promise that in all things He works for the good of those who love Him.

In that moment, it was something she could easily believe.

Mattie was full of sunshine and giggles.

Her brothers left for school on time and without any argument.

She had walked to work along the Pumpkinvine Trail, praying as she enjoyed the fall morning that smelled of falling leaves and fresh-cut hay. Hannah prayed for Jesse and Amber and Andrew. She prayed God would protect them all and grant them wisdom, mercy, and grace.

And she made it to the *kaffi* shop a few minutes early, which always made opening easier.

Everything was going well, better than it had since Owen's death, when Roland Shaw walked into the shop.

She stared at him as if he might pull out his badge and arrest her on the spot.

"Good morning." Shaw had both hands in his pants pockets.

He wore the same thing he'd worn every time she'd seen him—black pants, plaid shirt, and black tie. His black hair was precisely cut above his ears and along the neckline. He looked like an *Englischer* arriving for an interview with Amber, but of course he was not in search of a job. He had one. Unfortunately, it involved harassing people.

Was Amber even at the Village this morning? They'd decided last night that she would go, first thing that morning, to the police station and report the threatening phone call. Not that there was any need to call Amber. It wasn't as if Shaw had come by to threaten her.

She also realized that Roland Shaw wasn't standing in her shop because he had happened by on his morning commute. That much she knew for certain.

Hannah blushed, realizing she hadn't answered the man. Perhaps he wished to purchase a drink.

"*Gudemariye.*" She pointed toward the menu board, which included their special for the day. "Would you like a drink?"

"I would love one. How about a double espresso in your darkest blend, no room for cream necessary. I like it strong and black."

Hannah didn't respond to that, but she did turn to pull the shots of espresso.

"Your little coffee shop is a bright spot here. Not quite what I'm used to in the city, but not bad."

Had he been in before? Wouldn't Seth have told her?

"Say, Hannah—I can call you Hannah, right? That's not breaking any Amish rules or anything?" His tone was pleasant enough, but now he stood with his hands behind his back, the way a child did when he or she was hiding something. And the look on his face would have been comical on anyone else. He'd scrunched up his nose as if he smelled something that offended him slightly. Hannah knew that her shop smelled nice.

She became conscious that she was standing mute. She hadn't answered his questions, so she nodded her head yes and then shook it no. Then she handed him his order and told him how much he owed. Hopefully he would leave with his highly caffeinated drink. She didn't want him in her shop.

"I imagine you see and hear a lot of what's going on in your community." Shaw paid her, accepted his change, and dropped it into the tip jar. Then he removed the lid from his coffee and blew on it. "Have you seen anything strange lately? Anything that might worry or frighten you? Anything at all since Owen's brutal murder?"

Hannah's palms began to sweat, but she resisted wiping them on her apron. She would not allow this man to see how much he rattled her.

"You know, Hannah, not everyone is who they appear to be. For instance, you're looking at me like I'm a relative of the Big Bad Wolf, but I'm actually a nice guy." He sipped the coffee and smiled. "I'm trying to do my job."

When she still didn't respond, he added, "You can't blame me for being suspicious of folks who live like you do."

The cat that had held her tongue walked away, and suddenly Hannah couldn't have stopped herself if she'd tried, and she did not want to try. "Like *we* do?"

"Sure. Your dress—nice color, by the way, but it's quite old-fashioned."

She stared down at her dark-green dress.

"The way you keep to yourselves. It's rather suspicious. You've barely spoken to me since I walked in . . . other than greeting me in that strange language—"

"It's Pennsylvania Dutch."

"—and taking my order."

She was beginning to wish she could rethink that decision.

"Then there's the way you people contradict yourself. You don't have cars, but you hire drivers. You don't have electricity, but I've seen plenty of kids with cell phones and even iPods. I'd heard of telephone shacks, but someone told me there's a television shack around here. Is that true?"

Hannah didn't answer, though she was certain her face was turning as red as the beets they'd grown in their garden. She forced herself to remember the rules of their *Ordnung*, how they were to be kind and compassionate yet live a life set apart. How could she ever explain those things to a man like Roland Shaw?

He added, "It's all a little bizarre."

"It is not bizarre. We live the way we always have, the way most people in this country lived two generations ago."

"That's my point. Why haven't you changed? What are you all trying to hide?"

"Maybe you should leave." Hannah's eyes flicked toward the door.

Instead of being offended, Shaw laughed and leaned against the counter, causing her to take a step back.

"Now see, when you get flustered like that, I think there's something you're not telling me. What about that boyfriend of yours? Do you think he knew what his brother was doing? And are all of you survivalists?"

Hannah had been raised to be polite. She couldn't believe she'd found the courage to suggest he leave, but his final questions were too much. She had never met anyone so arrogant and so closed minded and so misinformed in all her life.

Closing her eyes, she prayed for help. She petitioned God for some sort of intervention and for grace to handle this situation.

Then the door to the shop opened and Preston Johnstone walked in.

"Hello, Hannah."

She smiled at him nervously, relief flooding through her heart that she was no longer alone with Shaw.

"Thought I'd stop in and pick up a cup of coffee."

"Espresso?"

"Nah. Plain coffee is fine for me." Preston turned and fixed his gaze on Shaw. He didn't say a word to the man, but it seemed he didn't have to.

Shaw nodded to them both, turned, and walked out the door.

Hannah handed Preston his coffee and plopped down on the stool she kept behind the counter. "I'm so glad you came in when you did. That man makes me *naerfich*."

Preston had stopped by often enough when something needed to be done, but he never bought coffee. Employees were given free coffee in the break room. Unless they wanted something special, there was no reason to purchase it from her shop.

"Why is he so unpleasant?" She worried the strings of her prayer *kapp* and pecked around Preston, assuring herself Shaw had left and wasn't lurking around outside.

"His goal is to make you nervous, maybe even make you angry. With some people that works. They become upset and tell him what he needs to know."

"I don't know what he needs to know!"

"Something he was slow to realize."

"How did you happen to come in?" Hannah reached into the pastry case and pulled out an apple Danish. "This is on the house, and you'll hurt my feelings if you don't take it."

"Thank you, Hannah." Preston took a bite. The contentment that covered his face was all the thanks Hannah needed. "I was working outside on the drainage system that feeds into the pond. In fact, I was almost directly across from you. I saw him walk in. I didn't see him walk out, so I thought I should come and check with you. Was he giving you a hard time?"

"*Ya*. He was asking me questions."

"About the murder?"

"About . . . things. Like how we live and why we live the way we do."

"He can read that in a book."

"I wish he would! His comments were ignorant and offensive. Why can't he go back to whatever city he came from?"

"This case will be solved soon and he'll leave. Don't let him upset you.

"Solved? You don't think Andrew—"

"No. I do not." Preston finished the Danish, swiped at his mouth with the napkin, then threw it away. "I've known folks who kill, each for different reasons."

"In the military?"

"Yes." A quiet sorrow flooded Preston's eyes. "Some did so because they had to, because they were protecting others. But some killed because they enjoyed it. Andrew doesn't strike me as either type."

It was good to hear that someone believed in Andrew besides Amber and Tate, someone else outside of their community.

Preston finished his coffee and deposited the cup into the trash can. He stared out the door for a moment and then turned back to Hannah. "You should tell Amber about Shaw. I think she would want to know."

"She's here?"

"Yeah. There was a plumbing problem on the second floor of the inn, and she wanted to help move the guests to another room."

"She's supposed to be at the police station."

"I know. She told me about last night's call, and we agree that the caller is probably the same person who shot at her and Tate. He might even be the same person who killed Owen."

"It's a little frightening."

"You don't have to be afraid. This person is a coward, and he's trying to run her off his trail. I had the impression she was going to the police station on her lunch break."

Hannah sighed and refused the money Preston tried to give her for the coffee. "It's on the house too. I'm relieved you did come by. I was afraid Shaw would never leave."

"Next time you call me. Do you have my number?"

When she shook her head no, he borrowed a pen and wrote it on a napkin.

"Don't call the switchboard. Call this number and I'll get here faster. It's my cell, which I keep on me." He hesitated and then added, "Shaw reminds me of people I worked with in the military. Sometimes they're bad and sometimes they're merely overeager to bring resolution to a situation. Then there are the times when it's hard to tell the difference between the two. Regardless, it's not you Shaw is interested in. He was probably hoping you would say something that would point him to the killer."

Hannah picked up a dishcloth and began wiping the countertop, her tension finally melting away. Maybe Preston was right. If he was, Shaw probably wouldn't come back.

"You call me if you need anything."

Forty-Six

esse met Adalyn Landt outside the Middlebury police building. He had no problem recognizing her. She was exactly as Tate had described—an older woman, dressed conservatively.

Today she was in light-gray slacks, a starched white shirt, and a dark-gray jacket. She had a more medium build than most *Englisch* women he'd seen . . . not fat, but not rail thin. She looked as if she enjoyed a decent meal. Her hair was gray, not dyed as many women had, and pulled back in a practical bun. He was sure he had the right woman when he saw the dark-gray leather case she was carrying—as Amber had described, it boasted a *V* over-laid on top of an *L*, the Louis Vuitton emblem. He wondered what something like that cost. More than a rig for his work horses, that was for sure.

"I'm Jesse Miller, Andrew's *bruder*."

She had led him to a bench outside the station, and he'd shown her the journal and explained where he'd found it and what some of the contents were.

Adalyn didn't even hesitate. She stood and said, "Let's go."

"Inside?"

"Yes. That's where your brother is—"

"I know he's inside."

"And his initial hearing is at ten so we shouldn't waste any time."

"What about the journal?"

"I'll take care of it. Wait for me in one of those chairs."

So he'd sat in the waiting room, wondering what this *Englisch* woman would do and whether it would help Andrew's case.

Thirty minutes later the officer at the front desk, an older man with a name tag that read "Walter Hopkins," offered to take him back to the visiting room. He hadn't been there the day before. He had thin, white hair and bright-blue eyes. He reminded Jesse of some of the older men in their community, except for the uniform he wore.

Walter tapped on the door once, then opened it for Jesse. Adalyn was already sitting at the table with what looked like copies of the journal pages in front of her. Andrew was ushered in before Jesse could sit.

The room had seemed small before. With the three of them, it was crowded. Adalyn introduced herself to Andrew, explaining that she'd helped the Amish involved in the Shipshewana murder cases. She also assured him he was in good hands.

Andrew looked rested and not at all worried.

Adalyn didn't waste any time. "Want to tell me about this notebook? We surrendered the original because it's evidence, and we don't want to anger the judge by withholding evidence. Plus, I won't do anything that's illegal, even if I think it would help with your case."

"Glad you found it, Jesse. I didn't have time to fetch it before the funeral, before they came after me, and anyway . . . I didn't want to lose my notes."

"Notes?" Jesse's voice rose in surprise.

"*Ya.*"

"Is that what you call them—because we could barely read it."

"The important thing is what's in it and why you wrote it." Adalyn pushed the copied sheets to the middle of the table.

"We haven't talked about your fees." Andrew crossed his arms on the table and leaned forward. "I want to make sure I can afford you."

"My time is donated in cases like these, unless the employer you mentioned when you contacted me decides to pay, and then I bill at $125 per hour."

"They'll pay."

"Who is your employer?" Jesse reached out and touched the copies. "We couldn't make any sense of this. What is it? And why did you hide it?"

Andrew studied the clock on the wall and then leaned back against the metal chair. "I hid it because I didn't want to lose it. I have a story to write when this is over, and I'm going to need those notes."

"A story?"

"*Ya.* I'm a reporter and they pay me to write." He named the newspaper he worked for. Jesse had heard of it, even seen it at the newsstands in town and at the local library.

"Since when?"

"A few months after I moved north, I started there. Small things at first. Back when you came to see me in Chicago, I was working for the *Chicago Tribune* on a piece about Amish in the city. My editor liked it, and I've been doing feature pieces since."

"Is that why you were back in Indiana, here in town?" Adalyn had pulled a pad of yellow paper out of her leather bag and was taking notes with what looked to be a very expensive fountain pen. No wonder she charged so much. Jesse wondered about that, but then he remembered her saying that she would waive her fees if Andrew couldn't pay. Why would she do that?

"Yes, that's why I came home." Now Andrew crossed his arms, his eyes darting left and then right.

"What story were you working on?"

"Can anyone hear us?"

"No." Adalyn tapped her pen against her pad, then pointed to a tiny box mounted in the corner of the room. "They can and will watch everything you do via that camera. They also keep video recordings, but they're not allowed to listen in and tape any audio."

Andrew shifted in his chair.

"I understand you're uncomfortable with the cameras." When Andrew looked surprised, Adalyn added, "I've lived here in northern Indiana most of my life, and I'm well acquainted with your beliefs. I assume that's why you called me."

"*Ya.* It is."

"Try to forget the camera and tell me what story you were working on."

When he still didn't reply, she added, "In a little over an hour, the police are going to tell the judge that you were seen entering the Pumpkinvine Trail not far from where Owen Esch was murdered. You were carrying a large pack that might have contained a compound bow, and such a bow was later found at your home. Based on the proximity of the shooter, the police are going to lay forth that Owen knew his killer, and of course they have plenty of witnesses who say you two did know each other. Furthermore, you turned down a ride from an Amish person named Nathan."

Andrew gave a quick nod.

"That was fairly near the place of the murder—certainly within walking distance. The police will say you turned down the ride because you had a plan—what the court system calls intent to murder."

Sweat trickled down the back of Jesse's neck.

He was glad Adalyn was on their side. This woman didn't fool around.

"At this very moment they are dissecting every hour of your time in Chicago and everywhere else you've been in the last few months—interviewing people you lived with, people you knew, and showing them Owen's photo. Yes, they took a photo of him, a crime-scene photo. If you ever had an argument with this boy, they'll know it within a few days. They won't stop hunting until they find the evidence and motive they need to convict. It's what they do. It's their job."

Andrew flicked his gaze to Jesse. "I told you she was good." Then he cleared his throat and turned his attention to Adalyn. "*Ya*. Owen and I did argue, but it was in South Bend, not Chicago. As far as I know, Owen didn't come up to the big city."

"Was he working with you on this story?"

"*Ya. Ya*, he was."

"And what was the story?"

"We were supposed to find a way into the ISG."

"Indiana Survivalist Group."

Andrew sat forward, clasping his hands together on the tabletop. "My editor wanted a story on survivalists in the Indiana area. But he wanted it from the inside. Also, he'd read an article somewhere, comparing the survivalist lifestyle to the Amish. He wanted me to find a way into the group. He especially wanted me to see if any Amish folks were members. I was told to bring back hard facts about what type of men and what type of families these people were."

"How did Owen fit in?"

"I had traveled down to South Bend. I wanted to move into the area slowly so as not to spook anyone. I met up with Owen at a Mennonite church service . . . *ya*, we still go to church even when we're on our *rumspringas*, or like me, when we've moved away and are living a life outside the Amish community. Church is still important, or at least Owen and I thought so."

"So you met up with Owen by accident."

"Didn't even know he was in town. The bishop of the church can confirm that." Andrew gave her the bishop's name, and Adalyn added it to the notes she was taking.

"Go on."

"Owen needed work. I had a little money and offered to loan him some. Then I told him that if he'd help me out, I'd give him part of my payment for the piece. That's when we argued. He wanted to storm in and earn the money fast. I told him newspaper writing didn't work like that, at least not when it was about Amish communities. Slower is better."

"Newspaper reporters don't make that much. It wouldn't have been enough to share."

"Usually that's true. But I was on assignment. At this point I'd already turned in several good pieces . . . I'd been to Chicago, Michigan, and Madisonville."

"Why?"

"I was studying the Amish communities I visited. Different things."

"You spied on people?" It was the first thing Jesse had said in several minutes. He'd sat there listening to the questions and answers as if he were viewing a volleyball game. Except this was his brother's future, not a game.

"*Nein*. I didn't spy. I gave an accurate portrayal in the media, which the *Englisch* could use. They need to know that it's not like the reality television shows or sensational books that are so popular. And I always changed people's names and locations. I respected their privacy."

Jesse tried to act as if this weren't a surprise, as if his brother were revealing what they'd always expected, but in truth he was stunned. This wasn't the happy-go-lucky brother he'd known all his life. This was a man with a passion and a determination to see things through. He'd misjudged Andrew, and he regretted that. He sincerely hoped he'd have the opportunity to tell him as much.

Adalyn quickly checked her watch and made a tell-me-more gesture with her left hand as she wrote with her right.

"Owen agreed to come here to Middlebury first and try to attend a meeting of the local ISG, maybe even join up. I continued to do research from South Bend. He called me the night before he was killed and said he was in."

"That's it? That's all he said? Because the police have a record of a phone call to a cell phone number they say was leased to you. The call lasted for seven minutes."

"There was something else he wanted to tell me. Something he was pretty *naerfich* about. But his sister walked into the barn, and he had to hang up before he could say more."

"No hint at all?"

"He managed four words—*Amish man* and *South Bend*. I had no idea what he was talking about."

Adalyn clicked her pen twice. "So what happened the morning you arrived in town?"

"I'd caught a ride, hitchhiked. I don't know the name of the driver. It was an old Ford truck—black color. The guy let me off outside of town, and I walked the rest of the way. I was supposed to meet Owen on the trail that morning, which is why I turned down Nathan's offer of a ride. Talking to him slowed me down a few minutes too. By the time I reached the spot on the trail where we were supposed to meet, the area was swarming with police. I melted into the crowd that was growing, then I hiked back to town and called my editor. After that I walked on to my parents'."

Adalyn sat back and studied him. Finally she picked up the copied pages of the notebook. "And these are your notes for your assignment?"

"*Ya.*"

"What is your boss's name at the paper?"

He told her.

"If you've written for them before, the police should already have found that."

"*Nein.* I wrote under my initials. A. M. Miller—Andrew Mark."

Jesse had a question.

"Is that who you met with the night you snuck out? Was it your editor?"

"Yes. He told me to keep a low profile. He said we could get the story and the killer. He said if I knew anything about Owen's death I would need to tell the police, but I didn't. I still don't."

"And the men you were talking to at the viewing?"

"They were some of the elders from our community. Apparently they thought I knew something about what had happened, which I didn't. I suppose they were trying to take care of things without involving the police more than they already were. They thought since Owen and I returned to Middlebury within a few months of each other, there was a connection."

"All right." Adalyn stood and stuffed her pad back into the leather bag. "This doesn't clear you, but it puts you a long way toward reasonable doubt. Maybe the judge will grant bail, and we'll go from there."

They were all standing, and Adalyn had knocked on the door to attract the attention of the officer when Jesse thought of the one question Andrew hadn't answered.

"Why was Roland Shaw's name in your notes?"

Andrew smiled, the old, confident, young-boy smile. "My editor had a tip that he was here, looking into survivalist groups and trying to find reasons to break them up if possible. He gave me specific instructions to stay clear of him, and up until Owen was murdered, I did that pretty well."

Jesse had never believed his brother was capable of killing someone, but as they walked out of the interview room, he realized that a huge weight had been lifted off his shoulders. It was one thing to believe in someone because he was kin, to trust him on faith. It was another thing entirely to be given a glimpse into his secret life. Although he was stunned by all Andrew had revealed, he was also hopeful the information Adalyn had written down would be enough to grant Andrew's freedom.

Which still left the question, if Andrew didn't kill Owen, then who did?

Forty-Seven

*A*mber had planned to go straight to the police department. She wanted to report the threatening call from the previous evening in person, not via telephone. And though Tate had offered to do it for her, she was the one who had answered the phone call, the one who had heard the creep's voice. She should be the one to report it.

As she finished up her notes on the plumbing mishap, she stopped and stared out her office window. How had they managed to get involved in another murder? Marriage to Tate was supposed to mark the beginning of a new phase in her life. This all felt achingly familiar. Once again, she, Tate, and possibly even Hannah were in danger.

And what of Mary? Where was the young woman?

Worry constricted her heart, and her mood grew as dark as the clouds on the horizon outside. She steeled herself against the knock at her door, prepared to plaster on the expected smile. Then Pam's friendly face appeared from around the door, and her guard dropped.

"Honey, you look like you lost your new puppy."

"I don't have a new puppy."

"You still look like you lost one." Pam sat down in a chair across from Amber's desk. Her usually bright and cheerful expression had vanished, and in its place was a look of real concern. "Was the plumbing problem that bad?"

"No. That's all resolved." Amber pressed the fingers of her right hand over her lips, suddenly fighting tears, suddenly afraid she would unload all her problems on this woman she'd known only a few months.

"Go on. It's plain you want to talk about it."

Amber shook her head.

"My grammy always said that two can carry a burden more easily than one. I don't have to report for work for another forty-five minutes, and my boss isn't that much of a stickler for precise hours anyway."

"You're probably wishing you'd never come to work here. I'm beginning to think we're the most dangerous employer in Indiana."

Pam handed her the tissue box as the tears began to fall. "That bad?"

Amber told her about the arrows shot at her and Tate and the phone call the night before.

"There's more than what you're telling me. You don't spook easily, even when facing threats. What else?"

They talked about Mary and Hannah and how Amber felt responsible for the employees under her care, especially the Amish employees.

"That's sweet and all, but the Amish are not children, Amber. I know we tend to think of them as innocent and vulnerable as newborn kittens. Truth is, they're more like a longhorn my daddy used to keep. Thing was as gentle as a lamb, but he didn't need us to protect him. In that case his horns could do the job, giant things that stretched more than six feet." Pam held out her arms, indicating the span of the horns. "Sharp too."

"The Amish don't have horns. That's the problem. They're so defenseless."

"Honey, they have their faith. There's no stronger defense than that."

Amber wanted to argue, but Pam's words rang true in her heart. Pam reached forward and grabbed hold of both of Amber's hands. "What we need to do is pray."

And they did, right in the middle of Amber's office, before she left for the police station, and as the rain began to patter against the window. Amber had expected Pam to be from a charismatic background, but that stereotype fell away as Pam's soft words fell over her, soothing her soul, petitioning their Father on her behalf.

When they were done, Elizabeth peeked into the room.

"Did I hear a prayer circle going on in here?"

Pam and Amber smiled at each other.

"Well, next time invite me to join. For now, I'm here to tell you that Tate called, asking if you were back from the police station."

"Oops."

"When I told him you hadn't left yet, he offered to come over and escort you."

"Not necessary." Amber stood and picked up her purse, tablet, and keys.

"I told him that too. Still, I'm thinking it might be better if you're gone next time he calls. That man worries about you, and I'd say that's a good thing."

Twenty minutes later Amber stood in Gordon's office. She'd told him about the phone call, which elicited a sigh and words of reprimand for not calling him immediately, and now she was studying his whiteboard. "I've seen these on television—crime shows, that sort of thing. I didn't know you actually use them."

"We do when we need to. Since the judge released our only suspect—"

"Andrew's free?"

"He left the building ten minutes ago. Jesse picked him up. That lawyer of his, Adalyn Landt, had her stuff in order. The judge suggested he keep us informed as to his whereabouts, or better yet remain in the area in case we have further questions, but he's no longer a suspect."

"Oh, thank the Lord."

"Yes, but now it looks like we need to begin again. Since I have no clue how to restart my investigation, feel free to take a look. Figure it out and *I'll* start calling you Miss Marple."

She turned to face him. "Did you actually believe Andrew killed Owen? Did you believe he could commit murder?"

Gordon shrugged. "It would surprise you what people are capable of doing."

She turned back to the board.

In the center was the Pumpkinvine Trail. Lines stretched out in every direction, and written on the lines were the details of the case—dozens, some of which seemed awfully minor to Amber. In capital letters were the major events such as Andrew's appearance in town, Mary's disappearance, and the arrows fired at her and Tate. The board was accurate geographically, and each event was numbered and labeled with time, date, and persons involved.

She was surprised to see a line stretching off to the west in the direction of South Bend. She traced the line with her finger.

"Why South Bend?"

"Andrew and Owen spent some time there."

"I saw something in Andrew's notebook about South Bend."

Gordon leaned back in his chair, causing it to squeak. "I suppose I shouldn't be surprised that you know about the notebook."

"You can thank me later. I told Hannah and Jesse to bring it to you."

Gordon's reply was a grunt.

"You have another person's name here, or initials."

"Roland Shaw's contribution. He had a list with the names of members of the ISG who reside in northern Indiana, including South Bend. He's still running that angle, and it is tangentially related since Andrew was researching the group and Owen was attempting to become a member here. It appears to be another dead end."

"What does B.E.W. stand for?"

Gordon consulted his notes. She was a little shocked he was humoring her curiosity, but then, as he said, the investigation seemed to have stalled.

"Not sure. He's listed on his government ID as B. E. Wagler, which is a bit odd. Usually you have full names, but with the Amish you'll see unusual things like this occasionally. Since they're often born at home, backtracking their paperwork can be a bit of a challenge."

Amber had turned and was staring at him, her pulse thundering in her ears. "Did you say Wagler?"

Gordon frowned, instantly understanding her connection.

"Wagler isn't the most common Amish name, but it's not unusual either."

"So we have a B. E. Wagler and a Uri Wagler both connected to this case."

"We don't know that Uri is connected."

"But he might be, and this B. E. Wagler might be."

"No. This guy lives in South Bend, and we have no solid link between him and Andrew. The single connection was that he was a member of the Indiana Survivalist Group at some point."

"Must be a lot of members. Why did Shaw focus on him?"

"There was a legal complaint filed against him, and that probably attracted Shaw's attention."

"Complaint about what?"

"He didn't pay his last couple of months' rent, and the owner was going to have to dispose of his things in another week. The dispute was resolved when the man showed up and paid his back rent plus another month in advance. The girl living there delivered the money—cash, actually. The owner didn't have any phone number to contact the man on the lease."

"Girl?"

"Woman. He was married."

"Can't be our Uri, then."

"Nope."

Amber picked up her things to leave, but something was bothering her. Something was wrong here. She felt it as surely as she'd felt comfort and peace from Pam's prayers in her office.

"Did you ever go and see our Uri?"

"I tried. He wasn't home, and his wife, Olivia, said she didn't know when he'd be back. Apparently he travels most of the week. I have it on my calendar to check again tomorrow."

Amber sat back down and clutched her purse in front of her. "Do you have a picture of B. E. Wagler?"

"Government IDs don't include photos for the Amish."

Amber sighed. It had seemed worth a try.

Gordon was typing on his keyboard as he talked. "Fortunately, this guy may be considering leaving the Amish. Two months ago he applied for an Indiana driver's license, and we do have access to that database." He keyed more words into his computer and then turned the screen to face her.

She found herself staring at a photo of Uri Wagler.

Forty-Eight

Two weeks passed before Amber fully recovered from that meeting with Gordon. Seeing Uri's photo there, realizing he was living a double life and that he was probably the one who had killed Owen in broad daylight, caused her world to tilt and totter.

How could such violence exist in the world?

What could they do to protect themselves against it?

Two weeks and she found her equilibrium, both spiritually and emotionally. She still had the occasional nightmare where Uri Wagler abducted Mary Weaver and dragged her off to some bunker, but those terrible dreams were lessening in length and intensity. She'd met with her pastor, who had given her a list of verses to focus on—verses that proclaimed God's sovereignty, his love, and his care for his children.

Tate stepped out onto the front porch. "Ready?"

Amber nodded hard enough to cause her ponytail to flop about. In truth, the thought of walking the Pumpkinvine Trail continued to make her somewhat nervous, but she knew there was nothing to fear.

"Do not fear, for I am with you." She'd read those words earlier that morning.

"I've been looking forward to spending time with you all

day." She studied her husband and marveled that she could love him so much though they'd been married less than six months. Already he felt like her other half. When she was with him, the world was balanced, peaceful, and right.

"You could have helped me in the fields instead of giving those donkeys all your attention."

Amber had spent the morning cleaning out the donkey stalls and brushing Trixie and Velvet. She'd also checked and cleaned their hooves. Caring for the donkeys was a special kind of therapy for her.

She accepted the bottle of water Tate handed her and knelt to retie her tennis shoes. No use in risking a trip or fall. The last thing she needed was an injury. They didn't jog the trail, but they were fast walkers. The exercise never failed to lift her spirits.

"Gordon called this morning." She fought to keep her voice neutral.

"Did he want to chat or was this official business?"

"Business, I suppose. He was updating me that there are no updates." She stood and smiled up at her husband.

Tate pulled her to him, kissed her forehead, and then snagged her hand. They made their way down the porch steps. Amber turned and spotted Leo sitting on the porch rail and blinking at her in the late-afternoon sun. Suddenly she could see the way he looked before, during the other investigation, when he'd saved her life. Who knew? Perhaps God had provided Leo to take care of her then, as he now provided Tate.

The thought was comforting. She let go of Tate's hand, walked over to Leo, and scratched behind his yellow ears, causing his purr to rumble like a small engine. "We'll be back in a flash, kit."

Then she joined Tate.

Saturdays off were still a new thing for her. Before she married, she was in the habit of working Saturday mornings, but she was learning more and more that time was precious, as was family. Moments spent together were never wasted. If it meant all her paperwork wasn't filed, she could live with that.

"Gordon say anything else?"

"Forensics confirmed Uri Wagler and Ben Wagler are the same person—at least there was a lot of Uri's DNA at Ben's place in South Bend. There's a warrant out for his arrest—"

"For the murder of Owen."

"Yes. Other members from the survivalist group—"

"Individuals prepared for disaster," Tate corrected her.

"Yeah, but it's easier to say survivalists, though I realize folks around here don't appreciate that term. What made you think of it?"

"There was a feature in the paper on the local group and how they're helping folks in the Midwest who have lost everything in the recent wildfires. The group here donated an entire semitrailer full of food and supplies."

"Huh. Gordon said quite a few of the families came forward and spoke with him. They didn't know anything specific, but they could confirm Uri was a part of their group, and he was at the meeting the night Owen attended. He was also there the night Pam and I attended. He pointed us out to a couple of other Amish men and told them we were there to snoop."

"Why was Gordon telling you all this?"

Amber shrugged. "I suppose he knows I'm spooked, or rather, I was spooked. Plus, our friendship seems to have solidified since I married you."

"Wouldn't hurt Gordon Avery to find a woman and settle down."

A picture of Pam Coleman popped into Amber's mind, but

she didn't mention the possibility. She was out of the meddling business, if she'd ever been in it. "As soon as members of the group heard Uri was wanted in a murder investigation and that he had fled the area, they asked how they could help."

"Not exactly the antigovernment folks they've been portrayed as."

"Nope. Nice people, from what Gordon says. Shaw came in for the interviews and was completely disappointed by the entire lot of them. He claims they're not *real survivalists* and his work here is done."

"Well now, I suppose we could say some good has come out of the situation, then."

Amber almost laughed. Roland Shaw was one person she wouldn't miss. The man made her feel like a cat being scratched the wrong direction. Though she had to admit he certainly had a passion for his job.

They'd made their way down the lane and across the Village property to the Pumpkinvine Trail. Usually they walked to the west, but today she tugged Tate's hand and pulled him east. They would pass the spot where Owen was killed, but it was time. She was too old to live her life in fear, and she didn't want to be hesitant to approach portions of their town anymore.

It was time to put the past behind them.

"What of Uri?" Tate took a swig from his bottle of water. "Do we know any more about why he was living two lives?"

"No one knows why or even when it began, though evidently his marriage to Olivia was not happy, and I suppose they can trace back the rental records and figure out the dates. The bishop here did meet with Gordon. Gordon didn't give me all the details, but apparently Uri had a brother named Ben. He died when Uri was newly married. That might be what pushed him over the edge."

"Died of what?"

"Fell out of a fishing boat and drowned. He didn't know how to swim. That was when Uri first began preparing, taking swimming lessons, learning to shoot with a bow rather than a rifle, and so on. Soon he was stocking up on food and prepping for major disasters."

"But he had two lives."

"Yes, and Gordon doesn't know why. It's all very confusing. Gordon hasn't been able to locate Olivia yet to see if she has any clue as to Uri's whereabouts or his alternate life. The bishop is putting out inquiries in other communities, but he isn't optimistic."

"And the other girl?"

"You mean his wife in South Bend? Turns out they were married, a short civil ceremony in which he used the name Ben Wagler. She's moved home to a small town in Michigan, but she still refuses to believe that Uri deceived her in any way."

They were a good way down the trail now, the sun's light slanting through the trees. Their habit was to walk thirty minutes in one direction, then turn and return home.

Amber had looked down to study her watch when she heard Tate pull in a sharp breath. Before she had time to wonder about that, before she had time to be afraid, Uri was standing in front of them. Grasped in both of his hands and pointed directly at them was his crossbow.

❧

Jesse walked next to Andrew, who walked next to Mary.

Mary's time away, the days she had spent with an aunt in Goshen, weren't talked about. They were all glad she had returned. They were glad she was safe.

The three were making their way toward the Village.

Jesse had not had a shift at the Village that day. He'd spent it with his *dat* and his *bruder*, working in the fields, preparing their farm for winter. Though the weather was pleasant for late October, it would turn cold soon. The nighttime temperature had already dipped below freezing on several occasions. Together the three of them had weatherproofed the barn. He was actually looking forward to the months of snow, less work, and more time with Hannah.

Hannah was the reason he was walking to the Village.

She'd worked late because they were doing a remodel of the coffee shop. The actual remodel was done, but she had wanted to put everything back in place for the grand reopening the following week.

"Andrew's offered to buy the ice cream of our choice, right?" Mary had been home for nearly two weeks since Uri Wagler had disappeared. She and Andrew had been as close as two newborn kittens. Apparently they'd grown quite fond of each other during the time Andrew lived away. Mary had been his lifeline to the community, and now it seemed they were considering moving forward in their relationship. Jesse wouldn't be surprised if there were two weddings in the Miller household in the spring.

Weddings?

He hadn't even asked Hannah yet, but today he would.

Glancing around at the path covered with fall leaves and the bare limbs overhead, he knew that today was the day. He couldn't have explained why he'd waited so long. Maybe he needed to have issues resolved at home. Andrew had joined the church the week before, and it finally seemed that their lives were moving in the right direction. His brother's baptism, representing his commitment to the church, the *Ordnung*, and their faith, confirmed that he was staying. He was dedicating himself to a plain life, though he'd talked to the bishop about continuing his writing.

It seemed his brother had a knack with words.

However, he was serious about learning to do his job the plain way. The cell phone he'd kept hidden in the barn was gone. He would use the phone shacks as needed, like everyone else. And he'd continue writing in his notebooks. If he was going to turn his articles in handwritten, he'd need someone to type his pieces for him. Or hire a tutor to help him with his penmanship. There was still a chance the bishop would approve the use of a computer, especially if the internet was not connected.

The weight of responsibility on Jesse's shoulders had fallen away as the leaves strewn along their path had fallen from the trees.

His family no longer depended solely on him, though in truth he now understood they never had. They'd depended on God and their community and each other, which was the Amish way. Jesse no longer felt the need to have everything taken care of before he dared to marry.

"*Ya*, I'll pay for your ice cream. I received my payment from the newspaper."

"You'll splurge for a double dip?"

"I think I can handle that." Andrew nudged her with his shoulder as they walked along.

"Wind is changing," Jesse noted. "Coming from the north now. Maybe you should buy her a slice of warm pie and a cup of hot *kaffi* instead of ice cream."

"Good idea, *bruder*. If you can pull your girl away from her work, you two can join us."

And that was when he looked up and saw her—saw his Hannah, running toward them, pale and frightened, waving her hands as if she was terrified they wouldn't notice her. By the time she reached them, she was speaking so fast that he had to put his hands on her arms and say, "Slower. Deep breaths first, then tell us. Are you all right? What has happened? And why are you so frightened?"

Forty-Nine

annah nodded her head up and down, trying to draw in deep breaths as Jesse instructed. She wasn't used to running, and it felt as if something sharp were stuck in her side beneath her ribs. More than anything, she was seized by the fear of what might be happening to Amber and Tate. What she had seen, what might be happening as they spoke, was stealing her breath away.

She bent over, hands on her knees, and gasped, "He had them. He forced them into the woods and—"

"Who has them?" Andrew had moved closer.

"Uri."

"He's back?" Mary looked as if she might faint, or turn and run in the other direction.

"*Ya*. He's back, and he has Tate and Amber."

"Hannah, take two deep breaths and then tell us exactly what you saw." Andrew's words were calm and direct. Jesse's hand was still rubbing circles on her back.

Hannah pulled in first one breath and then the other. Her heart rate began to return to normal, but her hands were sweating and she couldn't stop the trembling up and down her arms. She straightened and looked directly at Jesse.

"I finished early. Wanted to meet you on the trail. I was a good distance back behind them."

"Tate and Amber?" Jesse asked.

"*Ya.* Neither knew I was there, but I could tell it was them. They were close to one another, walking quickly down the trail as they do when they're exercising. I thought to call out to them, but suddenly Uri jumped out of the brush. He was armed and—"

"With a bow?" Andrew moved to the left, looking down the trail past them, down back the way Hannah had come.

"*Ya.* Looked like a crossbow. I was too far away to hear what he said. Tate and Amber stopped suddenly. Uri waved the bow around and then they all left."

"Did Uri see you?" Jesse's voice resembled a growl.

"I don't . . . I don't think so. I ducked behind a tree as soon as I saw the bow. He pointed it at them and shouted something, and then they all walked off into the woods. Uri stepped off the trail last, still pointing the bow at them."

"I expect he took them back to his place, maybe even to one of the barns or outbuildings." Andrew peered down the trail, first in the direction they had come from and then in the direction Hannah had come running from. "I'm going over there."

"It's not safe." Mary shifted from foot to foot and clutched her arms around her stomach. "He's crazy. It's why he left. It's why he had two different families. Why would he come back?"

"I don't know, but I plan to find out." Andrew pulled Hannah toward Mary. "You two go to Hannah's house. It's not far. Mary, stay there until we come and get you."

"I'll run to the Village." Jesse's voice was grim, determined.

"*Nein.* Go toward town. If you pass anyone with a phone, flag them down and call 9-1-1. Tell the police what's happened. Tell them to come to Uri's farm. If they're there and he tries to leave with Tate and Amber, I'll think of a way to stall them."

"We can't let you two go alone. It's dangerous." Hannah looked from Andrew to Jesse. She realized, as if it were a fresh idea, how much she loved Jesse, and how important Andrew had become to her. Mary was like the older sister she'd never had. Since she'd returned home, they'd become fast friends.

Now this terrible tragedy was beginning again, and people she loved were in danger.

The one thought that echoed in her mind was that they were a family, the four of them. "Shouldn't we stay together?"

"Go to your house, Hannah. Do as Andrew said." Jesse squeezed her hands. "Go and wait and pray. I'll come to you as soon as I can."

She wanted to argue with him, but he'd already let go of her hands and was sprinting down the trail. Andrew leaned in and kissed Mary on the cheek, and then he was gone, running through the field, running toward Uri's.

Hannah and Mary clasped each other's hands and watched the brothers until they were out of sight; then they turned and made their way to Hannah's home.

❧

Amber stumbled through the woods. Tate walked beside her, his hand holding tightly to hers. Uri followed, close enough that he could lurch forward and strike them with his weapon, far enough that Tate couldn't wrestle him for the crossbow.

Tate's gaze brushed over Amber like a fresh breeze on a summer morning. In that quick look she saw so many promises and so much love that she found herself gasping for a deep breath.

He loved her and would protect her.

They would be all right.

God was still in control.

Hold tight to the faith and *do not fear.*

She had the surreal experience of hearing his thoughts. There was no doubt in her mind that his meaning was coming through loud and clear. Tate didn't look one bit afraid, though the wheels in his brain were turning.

He would find a way out of this.

And why was Uri after them, anyway? What had they ever done to him? She turned to look back and he snarled, "Keep moving."

They crossed first one field and then another. When they came up through the back of someone's property, and she saw that it was Uri's home, she wasn't exactly surprised.

Where else would he go?

His friends, his community, would turn him in.

His wife was gone.

Both of them, though the one in South Bend apparently would have helped him if she'd known how. Amber could almost see her—younger, full of hope, unwilling to believe the facts the police had laid out for her, clutching her dreams desperately to her breast.

Amber bumped into Tate when they reached the front of Uri's house. The place looked as if Uri and Olivia had merely stepped away from it. The garden had been harvested and the rows sat waiting for winter. The front door was shut, but the window shades were raised with the late-afternoon light shining through into the rooms. There were no longer any canned goods on the porch.

This wasn't a house that had been closed up and left. It reminded Amber of a family that had gone to town on an errand.

The house looked as if it expected them to return at any moment. But Uri and Olivia wouldn't be returning. Amber knew that as surely as she knew he meant to kill them. They were here, with him, and alone. There weren't even animals in the pasture or the barn. She knew because they were headed toward it.

"Not the house. Keep walking."

The door to the barn had been latched, but it was plain that someone had taken the livestock. She whispered a prayer of gratitude that the horses hadn't suffered.

Uri motioned toward the older barn. "That one."

Tate turned and faced him when they reached the front of the structure. "We're not going in there, Uri. You have something to say to us, you say it out here."

"You'll go where I tell you to."

Tate didn't respond, but he didn't move either, except to shift closer to Amber.

"You think you can withstand an arrow to the heart? You want to take that chance?"

"I think you should let us help you."

"And how would you do that? By turning me in to the police? From what I read in the papers, your wife already identified me. She couldn't stay out of something that was none of her business."

Amber wanted to stomp her foot. Why was Uri talking about her as if she weren't there? And why was he threatening them with a crossbow? Was it the same crossbow that had killed Owen?

"If I made a mistake, Uri, then tell Sergeant Avery. If you're innocent, stand up for yourself. Straighten him out if you didn't . . ." She stumbled to a halt as his face turned crimson, not wanting to anger him any more than she already had.

"Didn't what? Kill Owen?" He stepped out of the shadows, directly into the final rays of sunlight. It was the first good look she'd had of him since he'd been walking behind them the entire way. Amber nearly gasped at the changes in this man she barely knew. He'd lost weight, even in so short a time, but more obvious than that was the haunted look he wore. Dark circles created a rim beneath his brown eyes, and his hair was practically matted to his head. Where had he hidden for two weeks? And what had caused him to return to Middlebury now?

"Did I kill him? Is that what you want to know? If he'd stayed out of my business, I wouldn't have needed to. If he'd stayed away from home, stayed in the city where he belonged, he'd be alive right now."

"Everyone has a right to go home." The words slipped through Amber's mind. She was surprised to hear them, surprised she'd found the courage to utter them.

"And I suppose you think home is a picture-perfect place that dropped out of your *Englisch* books? A *wunderbaar* place full of love and harmony." The afternoon had cooled, but Uri reached up and wiped the sweat off his face. "Not every home is. When your wife can't bear children, when she turns her back on you and everyone else, that's not a home you would want to go to."

Tate held out a hand. "We didn't say—"

"Shut up! I don't care what you do or don't say. I did right by Olivia. I continued to support her in spite of the coldness in her soul. And that other life, the one in South Bend, the one you ripped from me . . ." He was clutching the crossbow so tightly that Amber feared he'd shoot it inadvertently. His finger was precariously close to the trigger.

"That life was the one thing I had to live for."

Looking away from his intense stare, Amber saw movement down the lane, but she didn't dare continue looking in that direction.

"So what are you going to do now?" Tate's voice was calm and cool, but Amber heard the edge of anger behind his words. "You can't stand there holding that bow all day."

Tate would make his move soon. Amber could feel him pulling himself taut, judging the distance to Uri.

"Get in the barn. I won't say it again." Uri stepped forward, and at that moment whoever was in the lane dove into the bushes.

Uri jerked around, and Tate pounced.

Amber spied a metal bucket sitting on the ground near the barn door. She grabbed it, waited until she had a clear shot, and then rammed it into Uri's skull.

She didn't hear a crack, but she imagined that she felt one. Uri's fingers released the bow, his eyes drawn down almost in surprise, and then he passed out cold.

Fifty

esse watched Hannah as she crossed the bridge that spanned the creek on the east side of the Village property. The old wooden structure was once again in tip-top shape. They'd managed to complete the painting and the roof repairs. The red covered bridge seemed to represent the Village—providing a way to cross from the present to the past.

There were some things about the past that Jesse was more than eager to put behind him, especially the events of the last few weeks. More than that, there were things about the future that he was ready to embrace.

Hannah looked as pretty as the sunset splaying across the Indiana sky. Yellows, purples, and pinks combined to cast a rainbow over this very special moment.

When she saw him, Hannah raised a hand and smiled. His heart tripped as he realized again what he was about to do. Though he'd thought about it for weeks—no, for months—now that the moment had arrived he found his palms sweating profusely. His last thought, as Hannah stepped onto his side of the creek, was that it was probably normal to be nervous.

Hannah was wearing her dark-green dress and white apron. She'd spent the day at her shop and then at the library researching drinks to offer during the winter months. He could tell by the smile on her face that she'd had a good day, and he thanked the Lord for that. Hannah had been through a lot since Owen's murder, and even before that with Ethan's death. The stress had taken a toll on all of them. It eased his worry to see the casual, relaxed way she walked toward him.

"This is my favorite spot along the creek." She dropped her flowery print lunch bag to the ground and sat beside him.

"I know it is. That's why I picked it."

"You picked it?" Her eyes crinkled into an even bigger smile.

"*Ya*, I wanted somewhere special to talk with you."

"You're worrying me, Jesse Miller. Tell me you haven't found any more notebooks. Tell me Andrew is still at home—"

He claimed her hand. "Andrew is fine. He was going with *Dat* to look for a new mare today."

"New mare?"

"*Ya*. He's going to need a buggy since he'll be doing a column on Middlebury, Goshen, and Shipshewana for his fancy newspaper."

"That's *wunderbaar* news."

"It is indeed."

Silence stretched between them as Hannah waited. She was a patient girl—woman—and he knew that would be an asset in their home since patience wasn't one of his better qualities.

If she said yes.

Looking down at their hands, hers nestled inside of his, he found the courage to pour out his heart.

"I've known for a long time that you were the girl for me, Hannah."

"You have?"

"Don't look so surprised. You stole my heart when you shared your lunch with me, right here, way back in April."

"You remember that?"

"I do. And I could have asked you that day what I want to ask you today. Because I was certain even then." He looked up and found Hannah's eyes were brimming with tears. It put an ache in his chest, to see her cry, even if it was for a good reason. "But I needed to wait. I needed to settle the problems with my family and . . . with my heart."

When she started to protest, he stopped her.

"I lived each day with anger and resentment and bitterness."

"Because of Andrew."

"*Ya*. But I see now it wasn't actually because of Andrew as much as it was because of me. I was angry that my burden had been increased, resentful too. I envisioned Andrew out living the life of leisure, enjoying all the fun he could find."

She ran her other hand gently up and down his forearm.

"And that anger and resentment made me bitter. I would not have made a *gut* husband." He looked at her—this lovely woman he believed God had provided to be his helpmate, to be his friend—and asked the question that had been circling in his mind for weeks.

"Hannah Bell, will you marry me?"

"*Ya*. Of course I will."

Though she was smiling, tears slipped down her face. He brushed them away and kissed her softly on the lips.

"Of course you will? You don't need to think about it?"

"I've been thinking about it for a very long time."

"Oh, you have?" Jesse flopped back onto the grass and looked up at the kousa dogwood tree. He was able to see the evening sky through its bare limbs. Most of its red leaves had dropped to the ground and been raked up weeks ago. They'd even collected and harvested the pinkish-red fruit so that it could be used at the bakery. He was able to see the stars as they began to make their appearance.

Then suddenly he wasn't looking at the sky; he was looking at Hannah as she leaned over and put a hand to his chest.

"I've been thinking about it since you ate my lunch . . . sitting right here back in April."

"That long?"

"At least that long."

"So you'll marry me?"

"I will."

He touched her face and realized what a special gift God had given the two of them—each other.

Epilogue

A week later Hannah and Mary made their way up the stairs and into the corporate offices of the Village. Elizabeth was on the phone, but she gestured them through to Amber's office. Though Amber knew she was coming, Hannah still paused and tapped lightly on the open door.

"Hannah, come in! And you brought Mary. This is a nice surprise."

She walked around the desk to greet them, enfolding each girl in a hug. "Sit down, and tell me about this big basket you've brought."

Hannah and Mary exchanged a smile. They all took chairs around a small coffee table. The sitting area looked out over the Village. Hannah figured she could see Jesse from there, though she didn't look for him. He'd be downstairs in another thirty minutes, ready to walk her home.

"We brought the basket for you," Mary explained.

"For me?"

"*Ya*. Remember at the police station? After Uri was arrested? You said you needed a new hobby, something more relaxing than catching killers."

"To be fair, I didn't exactly catch Uri. That credit goes to

Tate, who tackled him, and Andrew who distracted him, allowing Tate to make his move."

"And Jesse for calling the police." Mary's face was somber, but she looked more relaxed than Hannah had seen her since the arrest, and she saw her every day. They walked to work together now. And they were planning their weddings together.

"Yes, and you girls prayed." Amber wrapped her arms around her middle. "We make quite the team. We've become skilled at this sleuthing thing."

"Hopefully that's a skill we'll never need again." Hannah was terribly serious, but Amber started laughing, and then Mary began to giggle, and soon she was joining in.

"If you're having a party in there, I want to come." Elizabeth's voice from the outer office brought Hannah's attention back to the reason they'd scheduled a time to visit Amber.

"We wanted to give you this basket. Mary and I picked out each item especially for you."

Amber accepted the gift and stared down at it as if she were holding a newborn animal she might break. "Oh my. This is amazing. Let's see, we have yarn—"

"All your favorite colors," Hannah said. "We checked with Elizabeth."

"Lovely—purples, blues, and ivory. They're so soft."

"Also the best brands." Mary beamed.

"And hooks!"

"They're knitting needles and these are crochet needles." Hannah pointed at each item as she explained what was in the basket.

"This is very thoughtful, girls, but I'm afraid I don't know how to use any of it."

"Which is why we're including free lessons. Every Friday at

my shop." Mary pulled her *kapp* strings forward and worried them. "It's something new I wanted to try, and we thought you could be our first guinea pig."

"Now I am touched." Amber wiggled her eyebrows in amusement. "And here's Elizabeth with some hot tea and cookies."

The wind rattled the windows. They had their first forecast for snow, supposedly to fall the next day. Hannah realized she wouldn't be walking home anymore. Soon she would need to take the buggy or ride with Jesse. That thought warmed her all the way to her toes.

Once they'd each chosen their favorite teas from the basket and sat back with a cookie, Amber sighed. "We need this winter to heal. There's been too much tragedy these last few months. I'm looking forward to quiet time and to the holidays with my new family."

"Quiet time is *gut*," Mary said.

Hannah was astounded at the change in her friend. She seemed to have blossomed since coming back to Middlebury, as if she'd left her fears and troubles behind her. Or maybe she was looking at what love could do for a person. Mary and Andrew seemed content with each other—perhaps because they both worked in unusual jobs. Mary was the manager of a knitting shop. Most Amish women quilted, but few were managers. Andrew was still determined to write for the newspaper in some capacity. Both stepped outside of the stereotypes for plain people, and perhaps that helped to build a strong bond between them.

"Mary." Amber spoke hesitantly. "This might not be my business, but what happened to the man with the cowboy boots, the one who used to come and visit you?"

"Some of the details of that situation are private, but I can share with you that he's offered to marry the girl—"

"The one you were saving money for? That's what Pam found under your counter—the number to a doctor and money so she could get medical help. She's expecting a child, right?"

"*Ya.* The man, who is Amish, has met with her parents and our bishop. It seems he had been away from his community for some time, and perhaps that was why he looked so natural in the *Englisch* clothes. Together they will probably join a Mennonite community nearby."

"And marry?" Hannah asked.

"Yes, they have both wanted to for some time, but they were afraid her parents would forbid it."

"You're a big help to this community." Amber leaned forward and patted Mary's hand.

"It's too bad I couldn't be more help to Uri. I recognized his handwriting from the note he sent me."

"How?"

"Not so long ago he would trade with my father. He'd bring a note listing the produce he would like, and in return he'd give us feed for our animals. It was always my job to gather up what was on the list. He hadn't done that in the last year or so, but he has a distinctive handwriting."

"So you knew it was him."

"I suspected it was."

"Is that why you came to see me?" Hannah asked. "The day you left town?"

"*Nein.* I wanted you to watch my shop. I hated leaving but didn't see how I could stay."

"You can trust me to take care of your shop if you ever have to be out."

Hannah thought Amber looked amused.

"I suppose. Anyway, I suspected it was Uri, but I didn't know what to do. I didn't know that our local police could be trusted to handle things fairly. Of course, I also had trouble believing that Uri was capable of leading a double life and killing someone to maintain it."

"It is tragic, *ya*, but for Uri it might be best." Hannah set her cup down when the other two women stared at her in disbelief. "Jesse and I have talked about this several times. If Uri hadn't been found out, he would have continued trying to live two lives. He might have had children with the other woman, but he wasn't free to leave Olivia."

"You're saying a life in jail is better than coping with the double life he was living?"

"Maybe so. At least this way he'll have time to pray and draw closer to *Gotte*."

"And our church is committed to supporting him any way we can." Mary cocked her head to one side. "Andrew told me that the bishop intends to go and see him at least twice a month."

"And Olivia?" Amber asked.

"She finally contacted the bishop. He put her in touch with Sergeant Avery. While she may be called on to testify in Uri's trial, she still plans to put the place here up for sale. She'll stay in the north with her family."

"Is there a possibility that someday she'll divorce and remarry?"

"*Nein*, but perhaps she will find a measure of peace there. At least she won't be living in a home with a stranger, with someone who doesn't love her."

"In his own way, maybe Uri did love her. The tragedy is that he didn't know how to cope with their problems." Amber set her cup down and twirled the wedding ring on her finger. "All marriages do have problems, girls. You realize that, right?"

Both Mary and Hannah grinned.

"This is beginning to sound like the talk my *mamm* had with me last week." Hannah reached for a second cookie.

"*Ya*, mine too. You would think we were young girls, marrying too soon."

"Your parents care about you." Amber hesitated and then confessed, "I remember receiving the same talk myself."

"You do?" Hannah stared at her in surprise.

"Sure. My sister gave it to me before I married Tate."

That brought on more laughter, until Hannah grew serious. "But you're happy married to Tate. Right, Amber?"

"I am. God had a plan for my life, and I'm certain that plan included Tate."

As they were standing to leave and gathering their things, Amber added, "It's a shame about Owen. He stumbled into something he didn't mean to, and he paid the ultimate price."

Hannah reached forward and placed her hand on Amber's arm. "We believe when a life is ended then it is complete, even when we don't understand the why and how."

Mary folded her hands in front of her apron. "And we will all support Owen's sister and her children, in every way we can."

"You have a good, strong community." Amber studied the scene outside the window—a beautiful, bright, cool fall day. "We have a strong community, and we're strongest when we join together, Amish and *Englisch*."

"We share the same faith. Only the way we worship is different." Hannah pushed up her glasses.

"I'm glad it's a little different. I'm not too keen on sitting on hard benches."

"But you'll come to our weddings, right?" Mary looked momentarily worried.

"I'd be there even if I had to stand."

"They can be long weddings," Hannah reminded her. "We'll be sure you have a place to sit."

The teasing felt good. It felt right to Hannah. As her mother had reminded her, there was no use living in the past, and the terrible situation with Uri was behind them.

And the future?

It held all the trials and joys and love God had promised. It was a future she couldn't wait to see.

Acknowledgments

This book is dedicated to Dorsey Sparks. I first met Dorsey while teaching at a middle school in the Dallas area. I was the head of the reading department, and she was a new-hire English teacher. We soon coined the phrase "What Would Dorsey Do?" because she has such a wonderful perspective and excellent skills for teaching children. That phrase bled over to my personal life when we began hiking together. Dorsey also pre-reads all my books before I turn them in to my editor. It's been ten years since that first meeting, and I'm still learning from her.

I'd also like to thank my friends in Middlebury—both Amish and *Englisch*. You were a joy to visit, very welcoming, and an author's dream as far as offering information about your lovely town. A special thank you to Jeffrey Miller, operations manager of Das Dutchman Essenhaus. Tom and Sue Welch were incredibly kind to share their knowledge of "survivalists" with me.

Thank you to Donna and Kristy, my other pre-readers. I also appreciate the work of my agent, Mary Sue Seymour, and my editor, Becky Philpott. My husband deserves continued praise. He is loving, patient, and kind.

I enjoyed this return visit to northern Indiana. If you're in the area, I encourage you to stop by Middlebury, Goshen, Nappanee,

Elkhart, and Shipshewana. Visit the local shops—both Amish and *Englisch*. You're bound to find things you'll enjoy.

And finally, ". . . always giving thanks to God the Father for everything, in the name of our Lord Jesus Christ" (Ephesians 5:20).

Blessings,
Vannetta

Discussion Questions

1. In chapter 2, we have the reunion scene between Jesse, his parents, and his brother. Much like the story of the prodigal son found in chapter 15 of the gospel of Luke, Andrew's return is a cause for rejoicing for the parents. However, Jesse is the brother who stayed home and took care of the farm. He has conflicting feelings about Andrew's return. When have you felt like someone from this parable? Were you the parent, the child who left, or the child who stayed? What did you learn from the experience?

2. When Hannah discusses Owen's death with her mother, Eunice points out that God's will rules their lives and then adds, "I can remind you of his promise—to never leave us or forsake us." What does this reveal about her faith? What was your reaction to this scene?

3. We learn in chapter 12 that all is not perfect with Amber's new family. Tate's older son, Collin, seems to be having trouble adjusting to his dad having a new wife. Worse, he's avoiding them, so there's little chance of improving their relationship. When has a family relationship disappointed you, and what did you do to restore it?

4. During the celebration scene in chapter 15, Jesse understands that he had stepped away from their community,

from their faith, just as Andrew had. He simply hadn't stepped as far. Think of a time you rebelled against family or faith. What was the result?

5. In chapters 20 and 21, Hannah and her family visit Naomi before Owen is buried. The viewing is done in the home, and Owen's body is there for folks to see and pay their respects. Hannah's mom explains to the family that the point is to be with Naomi, Jonas, and the children during their time of grief. The point is to share the burden. How has someone helped share your burdens in the past? Or how have you helped someone else during his or her time of need?

6. What did you think of the scene that takes place in chapter 24 between the Amish kids and the *Englisch* kids at the Dairy Queen? When the Amish kids refuse to press charges, are they acting in a Christlike manner? Why or why not?

7. In chapter 29, Jesse is thinking about their group of Amish families and how odd some of the folks are. Often the Amish are portrayed as perfect, even saintly, but of course they are a group of human beings. Like any other group, they're bound to have a few odd ducks. What does the Bible say about being a community, being a family of believers?

8. We see another side of Roland Shaw in chapter 38. He's genuinely concerned about Amber and Pam. He's not the cold, calculating federal agent Amber thought he was. Think of a time when someone surprised you, showing you a different, softer side of his or her personality. What did you learn about yourself from that experience?

9. When Hannah is at her lowest point in chapter 40, Amber reaches across the table and reminds her that "God . . . tells us to hope in him and that we can trust things will work out as they should." This scripture from Romans 8:28 is often

a source of hope. What scripture do you lean on when you face desperate times?

10. In chapter 47, Pam reminds Amber that the Amish don't need protecting, that their faith is the only shield they need against the world. What do you think about that?

11. Near the end of the story, Amber is leaning on the words "Do not fear, for I am with you." The Bible reminds us not to be afraid more than three hundred times. What things frighten you? How can you claim God's promise in your life?

About the Author

*V*annetta Chapman is the author of the bestselling novel *A Simple Amish Christmas*. She has published over one hundred articles in Christian family magazines, receiving over two dozen awards from Romance Writers of America chapter groups. In 2012 she was awarded a Carol Award for *Falling to Pieces*. She discovered her love for the Amish while researching her grandfather's birthplace of Albion, Pennsylvania.

VISIT VANNETTA'S WEBSITE AT WWW.VANNETTACHAPMAN.COM
TWITTER: @VANNETTACHAPMAN
FACEBOOK: VANNETTACHAPMANBOOKS

Find more inspiring stories in these best-loved Guideposts fiction series!

Mysteries of Lancaster County

Follow the Classen sisters as they unravel clues and uncover hidden secrets in Mysteries of Lancaster County. As you get to know these women and their friends, you'll see how God brings each of them together for a fresh start in life.

Secrets of Wayfarers Inn

Retired schoolteachers find themselves owners of an old warehouse-turned-inn that is filled with hidden passages, buried secrets, and stunning surprises that will set them on a course to puzzling mysteries from the Underground Railroad.

Tearoom Mysteries Series

Mix one stately Victorian home, a charming lakeside town in Maine, and two adventurous cousins with a passion for tea and hospitality. Add a large scoop of intriguing mystery, and sprinkle generously with faith, family, and friends, and you have the recipe for *Tearoom Mysteries*.

Ordinary Women of the Bible

Richly imagined stories—based on facts from the Bible—have all the plot twists and suspense of a great mystery, while bringing you fascinating insights on what it was like to be a woman living in the ancient world.

To learn more about these books, visit Guideposts.org/Shop

Sign up for the
Guideposts Fiction Newsletter
and stay up to date on
the books you love!

You'll get sneak peeks of new releases, recommendations from other Guideposts readers, and special offers just for you . . .

and it's FREE!

Just go to Guideposts.org/Newsletters
today to sign up.

Guideposts®

Visit Guideposts.org/Shop
or call (800) 932-2145